TERMS OF ENDEARMENT

TERMS OF ENDEARMENT

*Hollywood Romantic
Comedy of the 1980s and 1990s*

Edited by
Peter William Evans and Celestino Deleyto

Edinburgh University Press

© The contributors, 1998

Edinburgh University Press
22 George Square, Edinburgh

Typeset in Palatino Light
by Pioneer Associates, Perthshire, and
printed and bound in Great Britain by
The Cromwell Press, Trowbridge, Wilts

A CIP record for this book is available from the
British Library

ISBN 0 7486 0885 0

CONTENTS

v

LIST OF ILLUSTRATIONS

LIST OF CONTRIBUTORS

Bruce Babington, University of Newcastle upon Tyne. Co-author of *Blue Skies and Silver Linings: Aspects of the Hollywood Musical* (1985), *Affairs to Remember: the Hollywood Comedy of the Sexes* (1989) and *Biblical Epics: Sacred Narrative in the Hollywood Cinema* (1993).

Steven Cohan, Syracuse University. Co-author of *Telling Stories* (1987) and *The Road Movie Book* (1997); co-editor of *Screening the Male* (1993); and author of *Masked Men: Masculinity and the Movies in the Fifties* (1997).

Chantal Cornut-Gentille, University of Zaragoza, has published widely on British and American literature, culture and film, including 'The Hidden Gender of Money in *Breakfast at Tiffany's* and *Pretty Woman*' (1995) and 'Gender Implications and Political Undertones in Peter Greenaway's *The Cook, the Thief, His Wife and Her Lover*' (1996).

Constanza del Río, University of Zaragoza, has published several articles on film and literature, including '*High Sierra*: Going Back Home' (1992).

Celestino Deleyto, University of Zaragoza. Editor of *Flashbacks: Re-reading the Classical Hollywood Cinema* (1992), has published in *Cinema Journal*, *Film Criticism*, *Forum for Modern Language Studies* and other British and Spanish journals.

Peter William Evans, Queen Mary and Westfield College, University of London. Author of *The Films of Luis Buñuel: Subjectivity and Desire* (1995) and *Women on the Verge of a Nervous Breakdown* (1996); co-author of *Blue Skies and Silver Linings: Aspects of the Hollywood Musical* (1985), *Affairs to Remember: The Hollywood Comedy of the Sexes* (1989) and *Biblical Epics: Sacred Narrative in the Hollywood Cinema* (1993).

Frank Krutnik, University of Aberdeen. Author of *In a Lonely Street: Film Noir, Genre, Masculinity* (1991) and co-author of *Popular Film and Television Comedy* (1990). Author of several articles on Hollywood comedy, and currently writing a book on Jerry Lewis.

Kathleen Rowe Karlyn, University of Oregon. Author of *The Unruly Woman: Gender and the Genres of Laughter* (1995) and 'Comedy, Melodrama and Gender: Theorizing the Genres of Laughter' (1995).

Isabel Santaolalla, University of Zaragoza, has published on postcolonial literatures and on ethnic and gender issues in British and American film and literature, including 'This Island's also Mine: New cinematic Expressions of a New Britishness' (1995) and 'East Is East and West Is West? Otherness in Capra's *Bitter Tea of General Yen*' (forthcoming).

Deborah Thomas, University of Sunderland, has written several articles on Hollywood cinema, including 'Psychoanalysis and Film Noir' (1992), 'How Hollywood Deals with the Deviant Male' (1992), on John Wayne and on the films of Max Ophuls.

ACKNOWLEDGEMENTS

―⊸―

We gratefully acknowledge assistance, support and encouragement from the following: The Ministerio de Educación y Ciencia for a grant given to Peter William Evans to stay at the University of Zaragoza for a semester in 1995–6 when the idea for this book was conceived; the BFI stills library; the University of Zaragoza and the Research Committee of the School of Modern Languages, Queen Mary and Westfield College, University of London for funding towards stills; colleagues in the Departamento de Filología Inglesa y Alemana, Universidad de Zaragoza (especially Susana Onega and Chantal Cornut-Gentille), and the Department of Hispanic Studies and Italian, Queen Mary and Westfield College, University of London; students on the Curso de doctorado at Zaragoza and on the European MA at QMW for lively discussions on Hollywood Romantic Comedy; Anita, for her much more than romantic love, and Elena and Esther, for putting up with daddy's work; and Isabel.

The still from *Annie Hall* is courtesy of Warner Bros; still from *When Harry Met Sally*, courtesy of Polygram; still from *Victor/Victoria*, courtesy of MGM; stills from *Murphy's Romance* and *Peggy Sue Got Married*, courtesy of Columbia Pictures; stills from *Alice* and *Something Wild*, courtesy of Carlton; stills from *Jungle Fever*, courtesy of Universal; still from *Working Girl*, courtesy of Orion; still from *Gas Food Lodging*, courtesy of Main Line; and Meg Ryan still, courtesy of the BFI Stills Department.

Chapter 1

INTRODUCTION: SURVIVING LOVE
Peter William Evans and Celestino Deleyto

⊃⊂

It seems that when the new self pulls itself together, it is away from the ground of full sexual dialectic. To argue this is to argue the death of romantic comedy.

(Brian Henderson 1978: 19)

What are you going to do now that you know how the other half lives . . . The other half of you?

(Lulu/Audrey to Charlie in *Something Wild*, 1986)

The very conventionality of its message suggests that it [romantic comedy] endures in part because it speaks to powerful needs to believe in the utopian possibilities condensed on the image of the couple – the wish for friendship between women and men, for moments of joy in relationships constrained by unequal social power.

(Kathleen Rowe 1995: 212)

It has become almost a commonplace of recent criticism of contemporary romantic comedy to start, or at least, at some point, to engage with Henderson's too hasty prediction of the death of the genre. Various writers such as Babington and Evans (1989), Frank Krutnik (1990), Andrew Horton (1991), Steve Neale (1992) or Kathleen Rowe (1995) have remarked on the popularity of the genre in the late 1980s and early 1990s, and they all share the belief that romantic comedy can and will survive by adapting to changing historical circumstances. The genre tends to privilege the eternal, unchanging nature of romantic love and to gloss over those aspects from the surrounding culture which threaten it, or, as Neale and Krutnik have argued, to hold cultural transformations in place (1990: 171). Yet, in spite of the resilience of the genre's basic structure, changes have taken place which have prompted Krutnik to identify and theorise the cycle of the 'nervous romances', a group of films starting with *Annie Hall* (1977), *Manhattan* (1979) and *Starting Over* (1979), which 'betrays an intense longing for the restitution of faith in the stability of the heterosexual couple as some kind of bulwark against the modern world' (1990: 63). A few years later, Neale distinguished between the 'nervous romances' and the popular romantic comedies of the late 1980s, which he labelled 'new romances' – films such as *Splash!* (1984), *Romancing the Stone* (1984), *Murphy's Romance* (19857) or *Something Wild* (1986), which represent a frank return to the old-fashioned values of traditional heterosexual romance (1992: 287).

As can be seen, both Krutnik and Neale characterise the new romantic comedies as self-consciously establishing a link with their own tradition, insisting on the validity of its conventions and suggesting an unbroken line of continuity with the filmic and literary history of the genre. The popular success of Kenneth Branagh's *Much Ado about Nothing* (1993), neither strictly a nervous nor a new romance, although sharing traits of both, attests to the apparent irrelevance of those cultural and historical changes that have affected the genre since its Renaissance beginnings. Both a faithful adaptation of Shakespeare's play and a very contemporary romantic comedy, *Much Ado*, in spite of its double British origins (a British film adapting a British play), can be taken as representative of the Hollywood genre that the different chapters of this book will deal with. This is not to argue for the universality and ahistoricity of romantic comedy but, in fact, quite the opposite. The success of Branagh's film lies, to a great extent, in choosing the right text to be reintroduced in the culture of the 1990s and producing the right emphasis on or reinterpretation of those aspects of the original that most obviously tap into contemporary men and women's sensibilities. Whereas recent critical studies of different periods of Hollywood comedy stress the specificity of the historical factors that made the genre culturally viable and appealing to audiences (see most of the essays in Karnick and Jenkins, 1995), the lesson that *Much Ado* teaches us is that, important though the historical emphasis may be, divorce and remarriage, screwball and sex comedies, nervous and new romances all belong to an artistic tradition which embodies a very specific and relatively unchanged view of love, sexuality and marriage, a view which was already being put into circulation four hundred years ago. Love, argues C. S. Lewis, is a special state of affairs, which had a beginning in eleventh-century Provence and will have an end one day (1936: 3). Likewise romantic comedy. In the last two decades the genre is characterised by a self-conscious acknowledgement of that tradition, an acknowledgement which is also a defence against social convulsions in those very institutions of love, sexuality and marriage on which the genre is based. At the same time, however, cultural variations have been incorporated into the genre in several areas that attest not only to the genre's resilience but also to its flexibility to adapt to historical change. The various ways in which these changes are addressed and negotiated in the films will constitute the object of study of this book and will be returned to in this introduction, but discussion of changes becomes impossible without an initial awareness of their cultural origins and a critical receptivity towards what has not changed or what the texts themselves wish back into existence. The concept of love itself, the ultimate *raison d'être* of the genre, has, as will be seen below, undergone important changes in our culture, but, in a certain sense, all those changes were already part of the contradictory structure of Shakespearean comedy.

   In the passage reproduced above, Henderson rightly links the fate of cultural representations of romantic love with a project of the self. This has been so since the beginnings of romantic comedy in the European Renaissance. Salingar has characterised Shakespearean comedy precisely as a process of discovery of a new identity through the vicissitudes of erotic attraction and courtship between lovers (1974). The modern perception of romantic love as the place in which identity is constructed or reconstructed relates it to Michel Foucault's views of sexuality. According to Foucault, we understand sex as the space in which we expect to find out the ultimate truth about ourselves, and we demand that it tell us our truth, what has been hidden or reshaped by a repressive society and its attendant ideology (1981: 69–70). Romantic comedy, therefore, inscribes itself within these historical discourses concerning love and sex. Henderson perceives a dissociation between contemporary examples of the genre, such as the film he singles out for analysis, *Semi-Tough* (1972), and what he calls the new self and, consequently, draws the conclusion that, without this foundational connection, romantic comedy cannot survive. The film is characteristic of what has been defined as the 'me decade' (Lasch 1991: 237). At the same time, however, a group of films was beginning to appear, particularly those directed by Woody Allen, in which an obsessive, narcissistic search for self-identity was being repositioned at the centre of the love entanglements. Some years later, *Something Wild*, a typically postmodern generic hybrid which also includes elements of *noir* and even horror films, illustrates how the link between love and self in romantic comedy is back in place and in good health. At the end of the rocky process of his romantic involvement with Lulu/Audrey (Melanie Griffith) and his rather more sombre acquaintance with her husband Ray (Ray Liotta), Charlie (Jeff Daniels), the film's male protagonist, has discovered a new world totally unknown to the new yuppy class that he represents, but, above all, he has learned about the other in himself. Lulu/Audrey herself has also found a new, rather unexpected, identity. The project of a life together for the two characters with which the film predictably finishes is based on the mutual awareness of each other's 'new' selves. If there had ever been a dissociation, romantic love and self-identity are back in their traditional partnership.

Whereas an emotion more or less identifiable with love is, according to sociologists, a universal phenomenon (Giddens 1992: 37–8), romantic love is culturally specific, a type of relationship which appears in the European Renaissance, according to some, and no earlier than the end of the eighteenth century, according to others. C. S. Lewis, as is well known, has argued for a continuity between the medieval tradition of courtly love and literary representations of love in our time. What we understand by love was created by a group of poets in southern France in the eleventh century. Yet Lewis himself admits that even Andreas Capellanus, the most prestigious medieval theorist of love, ends up advising his fictional character, Walter, that 'no man through any good deeds can please God so long as he serves in the service of Love' (Lewis 1936: 41). In other words, even in Andreas, love is still the unruly passion that is most similar to a form of madness and brings about evil consequences for those who indulge in it. Traces of this form of madness can be found everywhere in Shakespeare, as can be seen in Theseus' famous comparison of lovers and lunatics in *A Midsummer*

Night's Dream or in Olivia's experience of falling in love when she first sees Cesario: 'Even so quickly may one catch the plague' (I.v.299). However, a shift can be found taking place in this period: love is increasingly differentiated from lust as having its origin in the mind. Desire begins to be legitimated in this ideal union of minds, and it is in this period that, for the first time, love and marriage are united, and love becomes a moral and spiritual experience, the basis of a lifetime of happiness. The arbitrariness and unreliability of the passion gradually give way to a civilised, domestic feeling which is constituted as the centre of a social structure based on marriage and the family. It is in this context that romantic comedy, a literary form that celebrates love and marriage, is born (see Belsey 1985: 138–48 and Rose 1988: 12–42). But love is not now the kind of madness that it was in classical litera- ture, the devouring passion of the Middle Ages or the frivolous game of late medieval romances. It begins to be represented as a complex spiritual and emotional force which guarantees the stability of the social structure into which it has been incorporated. According to Giddens, romantic love only starts making its presence fully felt towards the end of the eighteenth century and, unlike the intense, unruly pas- sion which it culturally replaced (which he, following Stendhal, calls *amour passion*), it introduces the idea of a personal narrative in people's lives. While the phrase 'love at first sight' is often associated with romantic love, this 'first glance' is a gesture which implies the discovery of potentialities in the other for a life together, and not (or not just) the compulsive erotic desire which it seems to indicate (1992: 39–40).

Yet passionate love is, as Giddens affirms, a universal feeling that was not erased from our culture by the increasing prestige of romantic love, to the extent that, in theoretical and critical analyses of the phe- nomenon, the two have often been mixed together. It is as if romantic love has, in the course of the past four centuries, gradually absorbed into its own experience all other known love experiences. Virginia Wright Wexman, for example, in her brilliant study of love and marriage in Hollywood cinema, argues, via Niklas Luhman, that there is a basic contradiction between 'the concept of romantic love as an intense, all-consuming passion that is by its nature short-lived and its status in the modern world as the cornerstone of lifelong monogamous marriage' (1993: 8). She goes on to say that Hollywood films erase this contradiction by making the happy ending coincide with marriage as the culmination of romantic passion and freezing this passion in an eternal moment of unproblematic happiness. What happens after marriage is never known. Yet, if we look at classical Hollywood romantic comedy, from the 1930s to the 1960s, there is usually little place for Wexman's all-consuming passion, and erotic intensity is most often replaced by a sexual drive that is also a socialising force and the foundation of a project for the future. Whereas romantic melodramas often feature a form of *amour passion* which, by its very nature, dies at the moment of maximum intensity and is never fulfilled, and, therefore, not part of a joint narrative of the two lovers,[1] the idea of love put forward by 'screwball' comedies and other classical genres is closer to Giddens's description of romantic love.

Love and marriage have, therefore, been indissolubly linked in romantic comedy. It has been argued that the periods of greatest success of the genre, such as the early divorce comedies and the 'screwball' cycle, coincide with historical crises of the institution of marriage (see Charles Musser 1995 and Tina Olsin Lent 1995), and can be seen as rearguard attempts on the part of the dominant ideology to ward off the fragmenting threats of modern societies. Similarly, it has been said that the cycle of 'sex comedies' of the 1950s and early 1960s appears at a time of unprecedented open discussions of sexual matters in the USA and one in which marriage is increasingly perceived as a repressive institution (see Krutnik 1990: 58–62), but the comedies themselves, for all the tensions and aggressiveness (usually directed at 'independent' women of the Doris Day type), stick firmly to the traditional happy ending in which marriage is still perceived as the best solution. It could, then, just as easily be affirmed that the new romantic comedies of the 1980s and 1990s appear as a conservative response to one more period of profound crisis in marriage in Western societies, and their success is due, as Neale and others have argued, to a deeply felt nostalgia for a paradise of innocence, evoked by classical examples of the genre (see Neale 1992: 287, 294–9).

Yet, as such paradigmatic films as *Annie Hall* (1977), *Manhattan* (1979), *Broadcast News* (1987), *Big* (1988), *Green Card* (1990) or, more recently, *My Best Friend's Wedding* (1997) among many others show, marriage or the prospect of a wedding seem to have become less central elements of the genre and, certainly, less centrally associated with the happy ending. In other no less successful cases, such as

Something Wild, Peggy Sue Got Married (1986), *Pretty Woman* (1989) or
Housesitter (1992), the more unambiguous project of a lasting monogamous heterosexual relationship is put in inverted commas, openly
parodied, as if the films were afraid to feature a wedding between their
protagonists as the culmination of their love. Even though it may be
argued that the nominal absence of wedlock, or the films' nervous
self-consciousness about it, are just poses to adapt superficially to the
Zeitgeist, and, deep inside, the institution itself is not only not threatened but intensely supported, some things seem to have changed. It is
not that love features less centrally (it is still hard to imagine a romantic comedy without love), but perhaps what the films pit against the
everpresent dangers of fragmentation and dissolution threatening its
central tenet is not any more, or not so clearly, the concept of romantic
love, either in Wexman's or in Giddens's sense, but something slightly
but significantly different.

Steve Seidman has argued that important changes in US American
intimate conventions have taken place in the course of the twentieth
century. The dominant spiritual ideal of love of the Victorian period was
replaced, in the first decades of this century, by a concept of true love
that combined sexual fulfilment and idealised solidarity. This sexualisation of love obviously affected discourses of romantic love even in
cases such as screwball comedy, in which the sexual drive was not
represented in direct fashion but in more metaphoric or displaced ways.
More recently, however, sex has become more and more separated
from the sphere of love and romance and acquired a certain prestige as
a medium of pleasure and self-expression, even though, to a very large
extent, it still remains entangled with the emotional and moral reso-
nances of love (1991: 4–5 and *passim*). These often conflictive meanings
of sex as part of the ethos of romantic love and sex as a medium of
pleasure in itself and as carrier of individual identity, and, further, the
relation of both meanings to an institution such as marriage that has
been in crisis since the beginning of the twentieth century, have
gradually found their way, in more or less direct or displaced manners,
into the structure of contemporary romantic comedies. As Neale has
argued referring to the cycle of nervous romances at the end of the
1970s, these comedies reflect 'the dislocation of fucking from "commitment" and the (ideological) dislocation of both these things from
marriage' (1992: 286).

Four Weddings and a Funeral (1994), although, like *Much Ado about Nothing*, a British film, likewise caught the imagination of both US and European audiences and became one of the most successful romantic comedies of the early 1990s. In the film's final scene, after Charles (Hugh Grant) decides not to marry his fiancée in the last minute, because he is in love with Carrie (Andie MacDowell), he makes the following proposition to Carrie: 'Do you think, after we've dried off, after we've spent lots more time together, you might agree not to marry me? And do you think not being married to me might maybe be something you'd consider doing for the rest of your life?' To which Carrie, in a repetition of the traditional formula at weddings, replies, 'I do'. The mechanisms of representation conjured up by the film for this happy ending are no different from those used in the past; the feeling of exhilaration experienced by audiences resembles that described by Kathleen Rowe in one of the opening quotations of this introduction; and the conceit used by Charles practically amounts to a fully-fledged proposition of marriage. But, as the comedy explicitly asserts, this is a proposition that excludes marriage and one, which, in its absurd use of the negative, undercuts the long-term engagement which it apparently enunciates. Giddens suggests that romantic love does not, in our end-of-the-twentieth-century society, represent the highest aspiration of men and women any longer and it has been replaced by what he calls 'confluent love'. Confluent love is active, contingent love that excludes the 'forever' and the 'one-and-only' qualities of romantic love. In this type of love, it is 'the special relationship' and not 'the special person' that counts. It presumes equality in emotional give and take and, unlike romantic love, it is not necessarily monogamous in the sense of sexual exclusiveness. What holds the relationship together is the acceptance that each partner gains sufficient benefit from the relation to make it worth their while. The sustained increase in divorce and separation rates is not so much the cause as the consequence of this new type of love (Giddens 1992: 61–3). Clearly, *Four Weddings and a Funeral*, like other recent comedies, still abides by some of the 'precepts' of romantic love – the specialness of the chosen partner, among them – but, in its interrogation of the social convention of the wedding and its intermittent but firm endorsement of the contingency of contemporary relationships, it becomes one of many ideological instruments in the problematic but relentless evolution of the concept of love in Western societies and their attendant artistic institutions such as Hollywood cinema.

Like *Four Weddings*, *My Best Friend's Wedding* revolves around the idea of marriage as the culmination of love and the start of a narrative of the couple. Yet, in an apparently unexpected turn for a mainstream romantic comedy, the protagonist, Julianne (Julia Roberts), ends up losing the man she is in love with to her rival and has to make do with her relationship with her gay friend George (Rupert Everett), a relationship which, as he says to her, will involve no marriage, certainly no sex, but a great deal of dancing. The film ends with the two dancing together at the other couple's wedding. Like *Four Weddings*, this film uses all the conventions but with a twist that questions their validity, introducing the concept of friendship as a rival for romantic love in the genre. It is not only that, as Krutnik concludes, the happy ending, although remaining a structural necessity, is 'for as long as possible, delayed, problematized, and cast in doubt' (1990: 70), but the convention itself is being rethought from text to text in order to incorporate social attitudes to love that will continue to make sense in our culture. It is not a question either of the contemporary romantic comedies being consistently transgressive of dominant views of gender relationships. Rather, the narrative and generic norms are, given their resistance to disappear in this genre, gradually changing their meanings. Romantic love is not what it used to be and contemporary romantic comedy teaches us, as will be seen in this book, that the texts themselves are being transformed by the experience, even though the genre itself remains alive and well.

Our choice of films has sought to balance coverage of some of the most interesting examples of the genre in recent years with concentration on their mediation of key issues in contemporary American society. In keeping with our aim to theorise the development of modern romantic comedy against the background of the genre's history and the shifting social and material realities which have helped mould its newest forms, Frank Krutnik (Chapter 2) opens with a discussion of two major films, one a 'nervous romance', *Annie Hall*, and another, a 'new romance', *When Harry Met Sally* (1989). Noting the way that *Annie Hall* both disturbs the conventional order of romantic comedy and undermines the primacy of the heterosexual couple, he goes on to consider how *When Harry Met Sally* strives to recuperate the structures of heterosexual romance. Popular music and allusions to familiar romantic narratives reinforce this pattern in the later film, which in a sense rewrites the earlier one, reconstituting traditional values and reaffirming the place of the heterosexual couple even though, in what is a highly postmodern text, the idealisation of the couple is clearly figured as something rooted in fantasy and deception. In films like *When Harry Met Sally* the audience is taught not only to recognise but also to love the lie of modern romance.

In Chapter 3 Steven Cohan considers, through his discussion of *Victor/Victoria* (1982) the way in which the climate of post-Gay Liberation politics in America opened up a space in mainstream Hollywood cinema for queer romantic comedy. While reaffirming the normality of heterosexual romance, both the subsidiary gay romances in the narrative and the key relationship between Victor/Victoria (Julie Andrews) and King Marchand (James Garner) draw attention to the performativity of gender, questioning, through the complex desires aroused by the lovers and by those who surround them, fixed categories, while simultaneously stressing the provisionality of all relationships.

Challenges to inflexible categories of genre and gender are further explored (in Chapter 4) by Deborah Thomas in *Murphy's Romance*, also starring James Garner, in a role that here problematises his more patriarchal meanings in films like *Victor/Victoria*. In line with changing social attitudes, the Garner character, not Sally Field's, is willingly 'settled', the Field character, not Garner's, arrives from nowhere out of the dusty horizon. These reversals clearly invert patterns in which the male's identification with outside spaces and the female's with domesticity are the axiomatic principles of countless Hollywood films. Subversion of convention and of generic expectation are also much in evidence in *Peggy Sue Got Married* (Chapter 6), a more self-consciously 'postmodern' film which, as Bruce Babington argues, nevertheless equally sustains the 'reparative comedy's' optimistic embrace of generic traditions. Traced over with elements of melodrama, the film inevitably moves towards an ambiguous closure, its explorations of pleasure-principle affirmations of romantic love wittily filtered through the reality-principle suffused aesthetics of a destabilising nostalgia of 'time-trip' intertextual rhetoric. In this chapter, too, an opportunity is taken to consider representations of male and female subjectivity through analysis of their projection by two of Hollywood's most charismatic stars of the last decade or so, Kathleen Turner and Nicolas Cage.

Like *Peggy Sue Got Married*, *Something Wild* is a hybrid film, here traced over with thriller as well as melodramatic elements and one which, as Constanza del Río argues (Chapter 5), is characterised by tensions between the ingrained conservatism of traditional romantic comedy and a progressive agenda concerning subjectivity, the relations between the sexes, cultural, ethnic and social politics. Relying on Deleuze's theories of masochistic aesthetics, she explores the film's problematisation of masculinity – to the point where the male is forced to confront his own fears of homosexuality – but notes the extent to which its flirtation with radical gender politics, especially in its treatment of femininity, is finally subverted by ultimate obedience to the genre's classical conventions.

Working Girl (1988) is another film made in the aftermath of the liberation ideologies of the 1960s. Here, as Chantal Cornut-Gentille notes (Chapter 7), the focus is on strategies for countering the stereotyping of women in popular art. While acknowledging the genre's traditional prioritisation of women, she stresses the originality of *Working Girl*'s concentration on women's spaces and issues, decoupling the couple for long periods in the narrative, outlining the working life of a single woman. Even though it remains compromised by dominant assumptions woven into the fabric of its generic conventions and allusions, the film is inevitably marked by shifting attitudes towards gender, subjectivity and the place of women beyond the domain of domesticity.

These are issues identified perhaps above all with the figure responsible for arguably the wittiest and liveliest romantic comedies of recent years, Woody Allen, and no book on the genre would be complete without reference to his work. While Allen has often been characterised as a filmmaker largely preoccupied with the burdens of modern masculinity, Celestino Deleyto (Chapter 8) reflects on his undoubted interest in female subjectivity. On this reading women are more than just the projection of a nervous masculinity. This chapter also offers scope through concentration on *Alice* (1991) for exploration in greater detail of the sophisticated aesthetics and social realism of someone whose verbal comedy has often deflected attention away from these other crucial areas, especially in so far as they contribute towards the subversion of the genre's utopian tendencies. Like *Alice*, *Gas Food Lodging* (1992) (Chapter 10) is another film that prioritises female-related questions, here given a feminist perspective by its director, Allison Anders. In this chapter Kathleen Rowe Karlyn also studies the extent to which independent films draw on and self-consciously raid the conventions of traditional Hollywood genres. *Gas Food Lodging* reformulates classic Hollywood romantic comedy, pursuing much more freely, in addition to specifically women-related questions, issues concerning class and race.

Race is a primary component of *Jungle Fever* (1991) (Chapter 9), a film which, as Isabel Santaolalla points out, has been identified as a key moment in the Hollywood history of interracial romance. But, in her view, although it breaks taboo in the portrayal of a relationship between an Italian American female and an African American male, the film is ultimately a comedy of remarriage, relegating its interest in interracial relationships beneath concern with the restoration of the black couple's marriage, thus reaffirming simultaneously traditional values and the primacy of race. In her discussion of black masculinity and other related issues she further examines the extent to which racial questions refocus the priorities and conventions of romantic comedy.

The book concludes with a glance at one of the most characteristic of romantic comedy stars of recent times, Meg Ryan (Chapter 11). Peter Evans argues that although expected to conform to the 'new romance's' recuperation of traditional values, the Ryan persona often lets slip the mask of conventionality, revealing even here – in this safest of images of femininity – the complex realities, desires and frustrations of modern women.

The aim of this book has been to account for the rebirth of a staple Hollywood genre. Alongside brief excursions into independent cinema our choice has been determined by the desire to include a range of films which have above all mirrored and adapted their shape to changing social realities. Even though some of these films are ultimately compromised by generic history or social attitudes they are all, in our view, worthy of serious attention for the ways in which they have contributed towards the revitalisation of a genre once considered, prematurely, to be virtually extinct.

NOTE

1   See Neale and Krutnik's discussion of the differences between romantic comedy and melodrama (1990: 133–9).

WORKS CITED

Babington, Bruce and Peter William Evans 1989. *Affairs to Remember: The Hollywood Comedy of the Sexes*. Manchester: Manchester UP

Belsey, Catherine 1985. *The Subject of Tragedy: Identity and Difference in Renaissance Drama*. London and New York: Methuen

Foucault, Michel 1981 (1976). *The History of Sexuality, Vol. 1: An Introduction*. Trans. Robert Hurley. Harmondsworth: Penguin

Giddens, Anthony 1992. *The Transformation of Intimacy: Sexuality, Love and Eroticism in Modern Societies*. Cambridge: Polity Press

Henderson, Brian 1978. 'Romantic Comedy Today: Semi-Tough or Impossible?', *Film Quarterly*, 31, 4 (Summer): 11–23

Horton, Andrew S., ed. and intro., 1991. *Comedy/Cinema/Theory*. Berkeley, Los Angeles and Oxford: University of California Press

Karnick, Kristine Brunovska and Henry Jenkins, eds, 1995. *Classical Hollywood Comedy*. New York and London: Routledge

Krutnik, Frank 1990. 'The Faint Aroma of Performing Seals: The "Nervous" Romance and the Comedy of the Sexes', *The Velvet Light Trap*, no. 26 (Fall): 57–72

Lasch, Christopher 1991 (1979). *The Culture of Narcissism: American Life in an Age of Diminishing Expectations*. New York: W. W. Norton

Lent, Tina Olsin 1995. 'Romantic Love and Friendship: The Redefinition of Gender Relations in Screwball Comedy'. In Karnick and Jenkins, eds, 314–31

Lewis, C. S. 1936. *The Allegory of Love*. Oxford: Oxford UP

Musser, Charles 1995. 'Divorce, DeMille and the Comedy of Remarriage'. In Karnick and Jenkins, eds, 282–313

Neale, Steve 1992. 'The Big Romance or Something Wild?: Romantic Comedy Today', *Screen*, 33, 3 (Autumn): 284–99

Neale, Steve and Frank Krutnik, 1990. *Popular Film and Television Comedy*. London and New York: Routledge

Rose, Mary Beth 1988. *The Expense of Spirit: Love and Sexuality in English Renaissance Drama*. Ithaca and London: Cornell UP

Rowe, Kathleen 1995. *The Unruly Woman: Gender and the Genres of Laughter*. Austin: University of Texas Press

Salingar, Leo 1974. *Shakespeare and the Traditions of Comedy*. Cambridge: Cambridge UP

Seidman, Steve 1991. *Romantic Longings: Love in America, 1830–1980*. New York and London: Routledge

Shakespeare, William 1975 (1623). *Twelfth Night*. Ed. J. M. Lothian and T. W. Craik. The Arden Shakespeare. London and New York: Methuen

Wexman, Virginia Wright 1993. *Creating the Couple: Love, Marriage, and Hollywood Performance*. Princeton: Princeton UP

Chapter 2

LOVE LIES: ROMANTIC FABRICATION IN CONTEMPORARY ROMANTIC COMEDY

Frank Krutnik

Annie Hall: *The split screen anticipates the fragmentation of the couple as Allen grants more (neurotic) space to himself as Alvy than to Annie (Diane Keaton)*

On stage, on screen, in literature, romantic comedy has been around for an embarrassingly long time. Endlessly recirculating, remobilising and rearticulating a stock repertoire of narrative and representational stratagems, the genre tells the same old story of heterosexual coupling. Only, it is never quite the same old story. To succeed, romantic comedies

15

must do more than simply redress themselves in contemporary fashions: they must engage with the shifting priorities and possibilities of intimate culture and with the broader cultural, social and economic spheres that organise its forms and meanings. In the past three decades, Hollywood romantic comedy has had to deal with a series of especially intense reorientations within US intimate culture. The insurgent discourse of 'sexual revolution' promoted the acceptance of non-monogamous and non-heterosexual choices and lifestyles, and this inevitably weakened the previously forged bonds between love and marriage, eroticism and romance, pleasure and procreation. From the mid-1970s the liberationist sexual ethic was itself vigorously challenged by a counter-critique that 'highlighted the dangers and undesirable consequences of a free-wheeling, pleasure-centred desire, from depersonalisation and sexual objectification, to the destabilisation of intimate bonds and exposure to disease, exploitation and violence' (Seidman 1992: 58). Spurred on by moral panics over herpes and AIDS epidemics, opposition to the liberationist sexual ideology became a fixture of popular discourses by the mid-1980s (Seidman 1992: 82).[1] In 1984, for example, a *Time* magazine cover feature jubilantly proclaimed that 'The Revolution is Over':

> From cities, suburbs and small towns alike, there is growing evidence that the national obsession with sex is subsiding. Five-speed vibrators, masturbation workshops, freshly discovered erogenous zones and even the one-night stand all seem to be losing their allure. Veterans of the revolution, some wounded, some merely bored, are reinventing courtship and romance and discovering, often with astonishment, that they need not sleep together on the first or second date. Many individuals are even rediscovering the traditional values of fidelity, obligation and marriage . . . The buzz words these days are 'commitment', 'intimacy' and 'working at relationships'. (Leo 1984: 48)

In a 1978 article in *Film Quarterly*, Brian Henderson suggested that alongside its challenge to the traditional agenda of heterosexual relations the liberationist ideology also threatened the viability of romantic comedy as a genre. Henderson's article laments the capitulation of the heterosexual dialectic to an ethic of individual fulfilment which prizes sex not as a vehicle for the consummation of the couple but as an

When Harry Met Sally: *Harry (Billy Crystal) and Sally (Meg Ryan) begin their quest for a trouble-free paradise*

instrument of self-realisation. Romantic comedy has reached an impasse, he argued, because men and women are no longer:

> willing to meet on a common ground and to engage all their faculties and capacities in sexual dialectic . . . What we begin to see now in films is a withdrawal of men and women from this ground (or of it from them). Or we see – in effect the same thing – false presences in the sexual dialectic or divided ones (one realises at the end that one did not want to play the game at all) or commitments for trivial stakes only. It seems that when the new self pulls itself together, it is away from the ground of full sexual dialectic. To argue this is to argue the death of romantic comedy. (Henderson 1978: 19)

Henderson develops his argument through a reading of *Semi-Tough* (1977), one of several films produced in the late 1970s and early 1980s to initiate a tentative dialogue between the inherited voices and values of traditional romance and the competing utterances of contemporary intimate culture. In their exploration of the fragile state of heterosexual relations, these nervous romances frequently blamed the new social and psychic horizons that feminism had opened for women.[2] For example, *Starting Over* and *Manhattan* (both 1979) centre upon men who are cast adrift in the post-feminist emotional wilderness, their problems inspired by narcissistic wives – respectively Jessie Potter (Candice Bergen) and Jill Davis (Meryl Streep) – who desert them in order to realise self-seeking desires (to achieve success as a writer, a singer-songwriter). In each case, the beleaguered male protagonist claws back his self-respect through a relationship with a woman over whom he can maintain greater control: the neurotic teacher Marilyn (Jill Clayburgh) in *Starting Over*; the teenage girl-woman Tracy (Mariel Hemingway) in *Manhattan*.

As they catalogue the perils of loving in the modern world, the nervous romances detail the difficulties men and women face in initiating, establishing and sustaining attachments in an age that has seen the splitting of sex and self from previous guarantees of romantic and emotional fulfilment. *Starting Over* makes this point clearly in the scene where Phil Potter (Burt Reynolds) tries to surmount his desire for Jessie by sleeping with Marilyn, whom he has previously spurned:

PHIL: 'I want to have sex with you.'
MARILYN: 'I don't like the way you put that. It – it makes me feel very strange.'
PHIL: 'I know . . . it did . . . did sound a little bit like Tarzan. It's just that . . . I was trying to avoid the whole romantic thing.'
MARILYN: 'I don't like that either. I *hate* that. But can't you just personalise it a little – "I want to have sex with you, *Marilyn*?" '
PHIL: [Kneels beside her, speaks with breathy sincerity] 'I want to have sex with you . . . Marilyn.'
MARILYN: 'I want to have sex with you.'

In the post-1960s' world, heterosexual engagement is posed as a perilous voyage into unmapped territories beyond the frontiers of the old cartographies, where lovers must steer between the wrecked vessels of romantic discourse and the abysmal prospect of emotional limbo. With the security of the 'whole romantic thing' in tatters, they must make their own rules and compromises in mediating between desire and language, self and other.

While traditional romantic discourse could be oppressive and constricting, these films imply that it nonetheless provided guidelines from which individuals could wring their own variations. Like *Semi-Tough*, *Starting Over* beats a tactical retreat from the battlefield of romantic disarray to the hopeful sanctuary of romantic comedy convention, a haven more symbolic than secure. Even though it exposes the disordered state of romance and romantic comedy, the film ultimately cannot find anywhere else to go. In her *New York Times* review of *Starting Over*, Janet Maslin complained that director Alan J. Pakula and scriptwriter/co-producer James L. Brooks

> have spent the early part of the story establishing a complicated and difficult situation, [but] they devote the second half of the film to pretending it's something that can be laughed away . . . Nervous, demanding, high-strung and nevertheless charming, Marilyn is all wrong for Phil – that's what makes the affair so unexpectedly touching and gives the story so much life. So when the movie begins to insist that these two were made for each other, it gives the lie to all that has gone before. (Maslin 1979: C8)

As both Henderson and Maslin emphasise, the nervous romances betray a wistful nostalgia for the 'whole romantic thing' while acknowledging its impossibility. By contrast, the romantic comedies which have proliferated since the mid-1980s reveal a more confidently wishful embrace of idealised heterosexual union. These new romances, as Steve Neale has termed them (1992: 287), seek to banish nervousness by asserting the previously discredited values of old-fashioned romance and reclaiming the conventions of romantic comedy.[3] To make plain what is at stake in the reinvention of romance in the contemporary cycle, I will explore how the dismemberment of the conventional armature of romantic comedy in Woody Allen's 1977 nervous romance *Annie Hall* is structurally and strategically reconfigured by the influential 1989 new romance *When Harry Met Sally*.[4] As I will suggest, this Rob Reiner-Nora Ephron film bids to transform its eponymous protagonists into a couple through a direct revisioning and reorientation of the disordered intimate terrain mapped by Allen's film. Reviewers routinely noted the debt *When Harry Met Sally* owes to Woody Allen,[5] and Kathleen Rowe goes so far as to describe it as 'something of a remake' of *Annie Hall* (1995: 197). But, as I will suggest, the film is not a remake so much as an extended and self-conscious attempt to reassemble 'the whole romantic thing' from the debris left in the wake of *Annie Hall*'s dismantling of romantic comedy. Where *Semi-Tough* and *Starting Over* lurch from the landscape of heterosexual disarray into the emergency exit of romantic comedy convention, the new romances are able to embrace convention more readily by framing it as a necessary lie, a strategic fabrication.

SMOTHERED BY SINATRA?

The most formally audacious of the nervous romances, *Annie Hall* marks an ambitious departure from Allen's earlier comedian films. Presented as the self-critical confessional of Alvy Singer (Woody Allen), the film weaves together romantic comedy, comedian-comedy and melodrama to create an unsettling vision of the emotional battlefield of modern romance. The film offers many of the scenes conventionally found in a romantic comedy, but disassembles the structures that traditionally organise their meaning. Jumping back and forth across the history of the relationship between Alvy and Annie Hall (Diane Keaton), the film fractures the classical ordering of romantic comedy narrative – the clearly signalled progression from exposition, through complication, to resolution.[6] It further disorders and destabilises the presentation of the love-story through the insertion of denarrativising devices like the comic monologue, spoof documentary scenes and the sliding of characters back into scenes replayed from their past. *Annie Hall*'s flamboyant narrative derangement makes the breakdown of structures a principal issue in the film's representation of intimate affairs, implying the difficulty of sustaining attachments in a post-1960s' world in which traditional conceptions of heterosexual intimacy have lost their authority.

The film focuses upon specific problems of and with the protagonist-narrator – his obsessions with sex and death; his anhedonic inability to reconcile the claims of mind and body; his recurring difficulties with emotional commitment. The urban artist-neurotic Alvy Singer may be too idiosyncratic to operate as a representative figure, but the film nonetheless suggests that the confusion he experiences connects to a more general disintegration of confidence in the traditional scripts of heterosexual intimacy. This is most readily apparent in the persistence with which *Annie Hall* mines the disarray of conventional romantic discourse for comic effect. The problem of how to articulate and syn-chronise desire is an axiom of romantic comedy, which forces the lovers to undergo a tortuous process of learning and negotiation so they can establish a secure basis for communication. With *Annie Hall*, however, *dis*articulation is foregrounded consistently.

The early scenes of the Alvy–Annie courtship make this plain. As they struggle to express their mutual attraction through small-talk, subtitles playfully expose the gap between what they want to say and the disengaging platitudes they actually mouth. Alvy and Annie are highly self-conscious players of a scenario of romantic initiation that seems both tightly prescribed and worryingly prescriptive in its de-individualising force. A couple of scenes later, Alvy expresses his anxiety about the rituals or romance. Walking through the streets with Annie on their first proper date, he beseeches her:

> Hey, listen, listen – give me a kiss . . . Yes, why not? – because we're just gonna go home, later, right, and – and – there's just gonna be all that tension – you know, we've never kissed before, and I'll never know when to make the right move, or anything. So we'll kiss now, we'll get it over with, and then we'll go eat – okay? We'll digest our food better.

Between these two scenes of romantic disarticulation, the film inserts Annie's faltering debut as a nightclub chanteuse. As Alvy looks on, she performs the romantic standard 'It Had to be You', a song evoking the values and certainties of old-fashioned romance. Competing with the ringing of a telephone, the chatter of a disinterested audience and the clatter of glasses, Annie fails to engage a contemporary audience for the song's romantic ethos – which also serves as an ironic counterpoint to Alvy's own hesitant courtship. The film's most conventionally roman-tic moment is similarly undercut: as soon as Alvy utters the word 'love', he must compulsively subject it to a string of punning disavowals and deformations that translate it into the pregnant signifiers 'loathe' and 'laugh'.

Annie Hall is a collection of scenes and fragments organised not by the familiar co-ordinates of romantic comedy narrative but by the more disorderly flow of Alvy Singer's reminiscences, which mix together memory, desire and compulsive gagging. As he combs through the chaotic jumble of his life, Alvy seeks to rearticulate the fragments of experience to make sense not just of his failed relationship with Annie but also of his more long-standing problems with reconciling the claims of self and other. As Kathleen Rowe points out in her book *The Unruly Woman*, the focus upon the melodramatised male in the nervous romances serves to eject women from the central place they generally enjoy in romantic comedy (1995: 197). But although it speaks of the crisis besetting heterosexual romance and romantic comedy from a male perspective, abandoning the genre's traditional dual-focused narrative, *Annie Hall*'s critical dismantling of its narrator-protagonist prevents an easy scapegoating of women. Especially revealing is an early flashback where his second wife, Robin (Janet Margolin), an aspiring writer, drags him to a party full of New York literati. Retreating to the bedroom to watch a baseball game on television, Alvy tries to cajole Robin into having sex: 'No, it'll be great, it'll be great – because all those PhD's are in there, like, discussing modes of alienation and we'll be in here quietly humping.' This wisecrack is not simply an attack on intellectual pretensions, it also targets Robin's desire to gain acceptance in a world beyond his control. As Robin charges, Alvy uses sex to express hostility: a quiet hump in the midst of, and in defiance of, the professional intelligentsia, would also enable the subjugation of (her) mind to (his) body.

Employing sex as a prop to shore up the fragile barriers of self, any victory Alvy achieves is not merely temporary, it is also at the expense of his female partner. The film continually exposes his obsessive need for control and reassurance, highlighting the possessive and destructive components of his love for Annie. As Rowe notes, Alvy's neurotic overinvestment in sexual fantasy serves as a means of asserting his masculine competence (1995: 196–7). This is brought to the fore when he challenges Annie over her inability to enjoy sex without the aid of marijuana. With sex, as with his professional work as a comedian, Alvy needs to believe in the authenticity of the response (orgasm, laughter).[7] In both cases, however, the authentic reception is also a surrender, a willing subjugation to Alvy Singer's performative skill. While he criticises Annie for using cannabis as an emotional crutch, the film implies that this is precisely the role that sex itself plays for him.

At the heart of all romantic comedy is the fantasy of the transcendent couple, achieved through mutual learning, negotiation and exchange. Tracing the process by which a man and a woman move from their separate emotional and psychic spaces to embrace the space of the other, the genre shapes the union as an idealised reorganisation and redistribution of their individual differences. As Steve Neale emphasises, however, the ideal of the couple rarely surmounts the established gender hierarchy: although the genre may be expressly committed to an ideal of 'equal partnership', in most instances it is the woman who has most to learn (1992: 293–4). In *Annie Hall* the heterosexual learning process does not promote the unification of the couple but directly provokes its disintegration. Alvy's self-appointed role as Annie's mentor is repeatedly undermined. Neurotically exploiting the intellectual gap between himself and Annie as a controlling stratagem, he tries not merely to make her like him, but also to *be* more like him: to read the books he recommends; to see his preferred angst-ridden movies (Ingmar Bergman, *The Sorrow and the Pity*, 1969); to share his obsession with psychoanalysis. Demanding that the other functions as a mirror for the self, Alvy searches for an 'authenticity' shaped exclusively by his own chaotic needs.

As the relationship begins to founder, the contradictions within Alvy's desire for Annie become increasingly explicit. When she returns from her first visit to the analyst, Annie tells Alvy of a dream in which Frank Sinatra attempted to smother her with a pillow, a dream he analyses with breezy authority: 'Sure, because he's a singer and you're a singer. You know, so it's perfect. So you're trying to suffocate yourself. It makes perfect sense. It's a perfect analytic kind of insight.' This kind of insight may suit Alvy, enabling him to locate the roots of her anxiety within her 'misguided' ambitions, but Annie's psychiatrist offers a different reading of the dream: 'she said *your* name was Alvy *Singer*'. Shortly after, Alvy's authority is further satirised: he encourages Annie to take up evening classes, and the film cuts immediately to a scene in which he proclaims that adult education is junk (he suspects she is having an affair with her tutor). The more Annie grows, the more she grows apart from him. Her desire to pursue a vocation which literally allows her voice to be heard displaces Alvy as the centre that gives her meaning.

While romantic comedy is founded on the promise that the differences between the man and the woman will ultimately be overcome, the relationship between Alvy (New York, Jewish, death- and sex-obsessed intellectual) and Annie (Mid-Western, WASP, 'yo-yo') founders because they cannot find common ground without risking a damaging loss of self. Towards the end of the film Alvy watches a rehearsal of his first play, based on his time with Annie. We witness a scene that recreates the moment of their parting, at a health-food restaurant on Sunset Boulevard. Alvy has added a significant reversal, however: as the man begins to leave, the woman suddenly decides to abandon her new life in Los Angeles to return with him to New York. Rather than bidding one another farewell, they embrace. After this fantasy twist, Alvy turns to the camera: 'You know how you're always trying to get things to come out perfect in art because it's real difficult in life . . .'. Alvy's experiences with Annie provide him with the raw material to shape an art-work that aids his release from the pain of romantic disillusion, providing a means by which it can be dealt with, ordered, meaningfully rearticulated. Abandoning, with regret, the mutuality of heterosexual coupledom, the film cautiously validates the power of art as a process of catharsis. Alvy's aesthetic rescripting enables him both to renew his friendship with Annie and to come to terms with the transience of heterosexual attachments.

SEEMS LIKE OLD TIMES?

Where *Annie Hall* dislocates and disassembles the signifiers and structures of heterosexual romance and romantic comedy, *When Harry Met Sally*, like many of the new romances, strives to realign and rearticulate them. The film follows Harry Burns (Billy Crystal) and Sally Albright (Meg Ryan) from college graduation in the late 1970s' era of nervous romance to mature adulthood in the reconfigured intimate culture of the late 1980s. *When Harry Met Sally* differs from traditional romantic comedies in the chronological range of its narrative, but although it covers a twelve-year period the story of Harry and Sally eschews the chaotic temporal and subjective flux of *Annie Hall*. With its linear, carefully signalled shifts in time, the film is able to suggest that events are actually leading somewhere – to the 'inevitable' pairing of Harry and Sally. The film manoeuvres them through a convoluted range of relational permutations – antagonists, friends, regretful bedfellows, married couple – but contains this plurality by asserting and prioritising the values, the language, the scenarios of the 'whole romantic thing'.

The connection to Allen's film is triggered from the very start: the credits are accompanied by a bouncy instrumental version of Annie's audition song. In *Annie Hall*, 'It Had to be You' registers the discrepancy between the values of old-fashioned romance and the uncertainties of modern love, but *When Harry Met Sally* uses it to underscore Harry's conversion from hesitancy to romantic commitment. Towards the end of the film, he walks aimlessly through the streets of Manhattan, wrestling with the conflict between his feelings for Sally and his fear of emotional entanglement. In a further evocation of *Annie Hall*, a montage of visual and aural flashbacks replays highlights from Harry's long relationship with Sally. This is followed swiftly by a reflective version of 'It Had to be You' – performed, significantly enough, by Frank Sinatra. With the appearance of this distinctive voice on the soundtrack, Harry begins his dash through the streets to find Sally at the New Year's party where he will declare his love for her.[8] As the lovers meet, Sinatra sings 'For nobody else gave me a thrill/ With all your faults, I love you still/ It had to be you, wonderful you/ It had to be you'. Annie Hall may have feared Sinatra's suffocating embrace, but *When Harry Met Sally* tactically reclaims the authority of the crooner once described as 'the love voice of America' (Shaw 1970: 252).[9]

As Steve Neale has considered, romantic music recurs in many of the new romances as part of their 'persistent evocation and endorsement of the signs and values of "old-fashioned romance"' (1992: 295–6). 'It Had to be You' is one of a large number of romantic standards featured on the soundtrack of Reiner's film, the voices of Sinatra, Louis Armstrong, Ray Charles, Ella Fitzgerald, Bing Crosby and young pretender Harry Connick Jr summoning a nostalgic vision of romantic certainty to guide the stumbling but inescapable progress of Harry and Sally towards coupledom. A similar role is played by the citation of familiar romantic narratives: for example, *Roxanne* (1987) reworks the story of Cyrano de Bergerac; *Pretty Woman* (1990) revisits the Cinderella tale; *Sleepless in Seattle* (1993) makes extended reference to Leo McCarey's 1957 romance *An Affair to Remember* (Neale 1992: 296). Across the years of their friendship, Harry and Sally repeatedly discuss the ending of *Casablanca* (1942), the transformations in their reading of

this romantic melodrama's emotional logic mapping the shifting terrain of their own relationship.[10] The film also mobilises the discourse of
old-fashioned romance through a series of 'documentary' interviews, in
which married couples – including, ultimately, Harry and Sally themselves – tell of the difficulties and uncertainties they had to overcome in
order to find one another. These 'non-fictional' interruptions take the
place of Alvy Singer's monologues to the camera: instead of one man
speaking of his failed relationships, *When Harry Met Sally* showcases
men and women testifying to the value of the heterosexual love-
match.

The film's romantic project is most clearly affirmed by its determined
return to the formal convention of the dual-focused narrative. Harry
Burns resembles the Allen protagonist in terms of his morbidity and
his compulsively cynical wisecracking, but Alvy Singer's narrational
dominance is denied him. The film consistently balances scenes devoted
to Harry with scenes that privilege Sally, and draws numerous structural
parallels between their separate lives. For example, the 1977 section of
the film begins with Sally first catching sight of Harry as he kisses her
friend Amanda (Michelle Nicastro), his girlfriend; at the start of the
1982 section Harry observes Sally kissing her boyfriend Joe (Steven
Ford), his former college pal. The breakdown of Sally's relationship
with Joe is similarly synchronised with the collapse of Harry's marriage
to Helen (Harley Kozak). The effect of such structural parallels, which
recur throughout the film, is to forge a sense of the compatibility of
Harry and Sally, their ultimate rightness as a couple, in the face of their
individual differences.

Validating love as a traversing of borders, romantic comedy moves
each partner from the territory of the known to the sexual and emotional space of the other. On occasions, the motif of boundary-crossing
is directly visualised. The *locus classicus* is found in *It Happened One Night*
(1934), where the unmarried protagonists, forced to share a bedroom,
erect a rope-and-blanket partition to demarcate their respective spaces.
This barrier of convenience, which they christen the 'Wall of Jericho',
derives its strength from the symbolic power ascribed to it by the two
players of the game of love. Runaway heiress Ellie Andrews (Claudette
Colbert) and headstrong reporter Peter Warne (Clark Gable) require its
presence not just to affirm social propriety but also to 'screen' their
uncertainties about emotional involvement. Ellie and Peter are clearly

feted to be mated, but they may occupy a unified physical, sexual and emotional territory only when the less tangible barriers dividing them – differences in gender, class and economic status – can be toppled as a result of their mutual learning and negotiation. Variations of the 'Wall of Jericho' device recur throughout the romantic comedy genre. The Doris Day–Rock Hudson sex comedies *Pillow Talk* (1959) and *Lover Come Back* (1962), for example, use split-screen compositions to institute a similar play between proximity and distance: the man and the woman are visually yoked together at the same time as they inhabit distinct private spaces. *Annie Hall* redeploys the split-screen device against the grain of its conventional articulation. The two sequences that make use of split-screen compositions expose the gulf that separates Alvy and Annie: the first juxtaposes the incompatible worlds of the Hall and Singer families; the second places together their respective visits to the analyst, where they articulate divergent views of the quality and meaning of their sex-life.

In *Annie Hall* the split-screen device becomes but one further sign of the dismantling of romantic certainty, the visual continuity only sharpening the divisions between Alvy and Annie. *When Harry Met Sally*, however, returns the device to its conventional place. On the first occasion, Harry and Sally are shown together onscreen while they watch *Casablanca* in their separate bedrooms, discussing the movie over the telephone. The second instance occurs after they have sex. Unable to speak openly with one another following this dramatic change in their relationship, Harry and Sally confide in their best friends Jess (Bruno Kirby) and Marie (Carrie Fisher), now themselves a couple. At this moment of crisis, when the facility of communication established between the man and the woman is jeopardised, the film once more emphatically parallels them. A three-way split-screen composition securely centres the happy couple between the estranged lovers, placing Harry on the left, Sally on the right, with Marie and Jess in the middle.

The return to romance charted by *When Harry Met Sally* relies to a considerable degree upon the kind of formal realignments outlined above. Reconstructing romantic comedy out of *Annie Hall*'s disassembly and disarticulation, the film supplants Alvy Singer's impossible desire for 'authenticity' with a knowing embrace of the artifice of convention. As Norman Denzin points out, Harry (a political consultant) and Sally

(a journalist) are professionalised agents of a postmodern media culture 'where images and their manipulation constitute reality' (1991:
115). They may be too 'smart' to believe naively in the hoary old illusion
of romantic love, but they nonetheless come to embrace it with conviction – a sense of purpose motored not by idealism but by fear of its
alternatives. The film echoes the nervous romances in suggesting that
outside the protective shelter of a fantasised coupledom lies the horror
of emotional limbo, or the jungle of the singles scene, or – in the case
of Jess – a slavish subjection to work. Sally is warned by Marie that 'the
right man for you may be out there right now, and if you don't grab
him someone else will. And you'll have to spend the rest of your life
knowing that someone else is married to your husband'.[11] The desperation behind these words implies that what impels the film's validation
of heterosexual monogamy is not a genuinely romantic vision of transcendent union but the terror of isolation. When Marie finally escapes
from the sexual wilderness by marrying Jess, she gets him to promise
that she will 'never have to be out there again'. *When Harry Met Sally*
suggests that in the post-liberationist emotional landscape not being
'out there' is a more manageable goal than the illusion of the couple
who are 'made for each other'.[12]

LOVE IN AN AGE OF LOST INNOCENCE

As post-liberationist lovers, Harry and Sally face a predicament similar
to that confronting the players of an amorous scenario devised by
Umberto Eco. Eco suggests that new forms of communication are
required within a postmodern culture haunted by the overpresence of
the 'already said':

> the past, since it cannot really be destroyed, because its destruction
> leads to silence, must be revisited: but with irony, not innocently.
> I think of the postmodern attitude as that of a man who loves a
> very cultivated woman and knows he cannot say to her 'I love you
> madly', because he knows that she knows (and that she knows
> that he knows) that these words have already been written by
> Barbara Cartland. Still, there is a solution. He can say, 'As Barbara
> Cartland would put it, "I love you madly"'. At this point, having
> avoided false innocence, he will nonetheless have said what he

wanted to say to the woman: that he loves her, but he loves her in an age of lost innocence. If the woman goes along with this, she will have received a declaration of love all the same. Neither of the two speakers will feel innocent, both will have accepted the challenge of the past, of the already said, which cannot be eliminated; both will consciously and with pleasure play the game of irony . . . But both will have succeeded, once again, in speaking of love. (Eco 1985: 227)

To say 'I love you' is not simply to 'open one's heart', it is also to risk immediate engulfment in a swirling vortex of speech from elsewhere. However, through a recoded embrace of the exhausted and compromised language of love, Eco's lovers transform 'degraded' romantic discourse into a foundation, no matter how slippery, upon which to build discursive intimacy. Simultaneously acknowledging and transcending the debased currency of romantic language, the players of the game of love find one another through the otherness of Barbara Cartland.[13] Revisited with irony, the legacy of the past is made usable once more, and intimacy can be refound by speaking through the multi-forked tongues of inherited voices.

Like Eco's imaginary lovers, the contemporary romantic comedy film grapples with the difficulty of speaking of love in an age when the language, the conventions and the values of heterosexual union lack the integrity they once possessed. This is not essentially a new problem: the genre has always faced the challenge of how to deal with the formal and narrative conservatism that provides its basis, with how to effect a credible compromise between individual expression and the force of convention. But what distinguishes the new romances is the self-consciousness of their bid to revalidate and reconstruct heterosexual intimacy and the genre of romantic comedy. *When Harry Met Sally* is an exemplary new romance because it values aesthetic fabrication not as part of a process of critical self-awareness, as *Annie Hall* does, but as a necessary tool to achieve the reconsolidation of romantic illusion. The film reorders the repertoire of romantic comedy conventions to paper over the void exposed by Alvy Singer's brutally honest autocritique. Where Allen's protagonist fears romantic expression because it poses the threat of self-estrangement, of an/other-voicing, the new romancers manage a more comfortable *rapprochement* with old-fashioned heterosexual love by evoking and endorsing its signs and values with full awareness of their fantastical nature.

The new romances are not simply stories about love, they are tales of love and disavowal. The play of assertion and denial is illustrated succinctly by the ending of the phenomenally successful 1990 film *Pretty Woman*, an against-all-odds romance between a prostitute and a corporate raider which gratifies the Cinderella fantasy while simultaneously underlining its status as a worn-out myth (what one character terms 'Cinderfuckinrella'). As Vivian (Julia Roberts) is rescued by her charming prince, Edward (Richard Gere), the camera withdraws slowly from their kiss and a (black) male voice cheerily intrudes:[14] 'Welcome to Hollywood. What's your dream? Everyone comes here. This is Hollywood, land of dreams. Some dreams come true, some don't. But keep on dreamin'. This is Hollywood. Always time for dreams, so keep on dreamin'. Presenting the fulfilment of the fantasy of heterosexual union, while underscoring that it is only wish-fulfilment after all, this is the perfect solution for an audience disenfranchised from the constituency of old-fashioned romance yet wary of taking up citizenship in the disordered emotional territories explored by the nervous romances.

The ending of *Pretty Woman* neatly encapsulates the fetishistic splitting of belief and knowledge that drives romantic comedy in an era in which the metanarratives of both old-fashioned romance and 'sexual revolution' have lost their former powers of legitimation. In their attempt to rescue the protocols of heterosexual monogamy from the wasteland to which they were banished in the 1960s and 1970s, the new romances cannot easily ignore how precarious the 'whole romantic thing' has been rendered by the new perceptions of love, sex, marriage and gender identity that issued from this turbulent period in US intimate culture. But even though the old certainties have been tarnished, these films propose that it is better to believe in a myth, a fabrication, than have nothing. Contemporary romantic comedy suggests, moreover, that the mythology of love, now it has been removed from the social moorings which anchored it in the past (marriage, the secure hegemony of gender disequilibrium), must service its own aspirations and provide its own ground rules. As noted earlier, many of the films signpost the fabrication of romance by strategically remobilising the self-referential armoury of the 'already said' – old songs, old romantic narratives, poeticised speech (Neale 1992: 296). Even more suggestive, however, of the priorities of the new romance is the prominence it accords scenarios of deception.

While they are not uncommon in the genre, deception narratives have proliferated in recent years. For example, *Green Card* (1990) features a mutual fabrication, in which a man and a woman collude in a marriage of convenience to realise self-seeking desires. As in the pretend marriages of screwball-era films *It Happened One Night* (1934) and *Come Live with Me* (1941), the false basis for union facilitates the learning process that will transform them into a 'genuine' couple. A more provocative use of deception characterises *Housesitter* (1992), *While You Were Sleeping* (1995) and *The Truth about Cats and Dogs* (1996), which centre upon schemes initiated by the woman alone. In each case, she assumes a false identity in order to realise her wish not simply for the man himself but for the baggage he brings with him: a ready-made family for orphan Lucy Moderatz (Sandra Bullock) in *While You Were Sleeping*; a secure bourgeois lifestyle for urban nomad Gwen (Goldie Hawn) in *Housesitter*; a glamorous affirmation of self-worth for Abby Barnes (Janeane Garolfo) in *The Truth about Cats and Dogs*. Lucy, Gwen and Abby engineer masquerades that permit them access to forms of imaginative (and sometimes material) empowerment which may ultimately be accommodated within the bounds of a traditional heterosexual union but which are by no means fully contained by it. The subterfuge is an adventure which transports the desiring woman into an alternative realm of self-imagining. As mistress of the fabrication, she can reinvent herself as a wife (*Housesitter*), as fiancee to a handsome high-flyer (*While You Were Sleeping*), as a model superblonde (*The Truth about Cats and Dogs*). Although the heterosexual resolution inevitably requires the woman to renounce dissimulation, the ritualistic embrace of Truth leads not to the abandonment of her wishes but to their fulfilment, albeit with a degree of compromise. Thus, Lucy Moderatz gains access to her beloved Callaghan family but ends up not with Peter Callaghan (Peter Gallagher), her initial object of desire, but with his brother Jack (Bill Pullman).

The extended play with masks and dissimulation in these films makes it difficult to accept the formal resolution as unproblematically 'authentic'. Even if they do ultimately posit 'real' relationships growing out of pretend ones, the deception narratives overtly frame romance as the construction of a representation, consolidating the couple through a blatant manipulation of signs and identities. For Lucy, Gwen and Abby heterosexual unification is not the goal so much as the alibi, a cover story for other forms of satisfaction. These are not wide-eyed innocents questing idealistically for the perfect match but women who know that in order to get what they want they must lead others to believe they are other than what they are. This is illustrated by an especially provocative scene in *When Harry Met Sally*. In a crowded restaurant, Sally takes Harry to task for the lies he tells women when he sneaks from their beds in the morning. Responding to her accusation that he is 'a human affront to all women', Harry argues that the sexual pleasure he provides makes everything fair ('I think they have an okay time'). But Sally points out that he has no way of gauging the veracity of the evidence he invests so much faith in. She wins her point by acting out a convincingly demonstrative orgasm that climaxes with her shouting and banging the table – a performance that stuns Harry and the other diners into silence.

Sally's impromptu simulation of female ecstasy challenges Harry's unquestioned belief in his own sexual prowess. But the implications of the scene cut much deeper: as Pam Cook puts it, 'Why fake orgasms should even exist is the awkward question lurking beneath the film's light-hearted veneer' (1989: 377). Sally reveals to Harry that the expression of female pleasure he so treasures may be little more than a manipulation of signs. 'You don't think I could tell the difference?', he asks incredulously just before she demonstrates the art of faking orgasm. But Sally's masquerade of erotic self-transcendence makes it plain that he cannot *know*, he can only *believe* that his female partner is not performing. Norman Denzin argues that this scene from *When Harry Met Sally* points to the falsity at the heart of the film's embrace of traditionalist heterosexual union:

> Underneath this system of romantic love and its renewal of the traditional meanings of family and marriage lurks the hyperreal, the lie, the simulation, the faked orgasm, and the sexual truths about male and female sexuality . . . The new sexual order is based on lies. It is a marriage of convenience. It reflects not what is real, or truthfully felt, but what is pretended, what is thought to be appropriate, not what is. (Denzin 1991: 122)

Denzin's protest echoes Brian Henderson's complaint about 'false presences in the sexual dialectic' (1978: 19), but he neglects to pay sufficient heed to the very fact that, even if it is ultimately to be disavowed,[15] the lie is *flaunted* instead of being simply ignored. *The Truth about Cats and Dogs* presents a similarly daring scene which goes even further in parading the aporia that lies at the heart of postmodern romance. Abby and Brian conduct a highly charged telephone conversation that culminates in their synchronised orgasms.[16] As they masturbate, stimulated by one another's voices, the other is rendered a prop, a trigger, for an erotic satisfaction that is self-fulfilling. Although Brian is enticed by Abby's voice, as he masturbates he envisions Noele (Uma Thurman), the alluring blonde Abby has persuaded to impersonate her. False presences do not necessarily signify the decay of the sexual dialectic, of romantic comedy. Post-liberationist new romancers, these films suggest, must learn to love, learn to lie, learn to love the lie.

NOTES

1 As Steve Seidman points out, the post-liberationist critique spanned the ideological spectrum but was hijacked by a conservative sexual politic which readily scapegoated the sexual and social liberalism of the 1960s for provoking the decline – economic, moral, cultural – of the United States (1992: 59–63).

2 The following discussion of the nervous romance reworks arguments from Krutnik 1990: 63–70.

3 Steve Neale (1992: 287) dates the emergence of the new romance to 1987, with the release of *Blind Date, Roxanne, Who's that Girl?, Moonstruck* and *Overboard*; he also points to significant post-liberationist precursors like *Splash!* (1984), *The Sure Thing* (1985) and *Murphy's Romance* (1985).

4 *When Harry Met Sally* was a critical and commercial success, and many of those associated with the film went on to further work in the romantic comedy genre: scriptwriter Nora Ephron directed the equally successful *Sleepless in Seattle* (1993); Meg Ryan starred in *Sleepless in Seattle* and *French Kiss* (1995); Billy Crystal directed and starred in the remarkably conflicted *Forget Paris* (1995); Rob Reiner directed *The American President* (1995).

5 Some sampled moments: 'Reiner borrows a lot of his style from Mr. Allen, including a sunny view of New York City and a bouncy jazz-and-pop score' (Sterritt 1989: 11); 'This is the year's best Woody Allen film

made by somebody else' (Buckley 1989: 484); 'this Manhattan-based talkfest, with Gershwin on the sound track and upscale, self-scrutinizing New Yorkers on the menu, has a distinct Woody Allen flavor' (Benson 1989: 1); '*WHMS* will be immediately recognizable as directly out of Woody Allen' (Brown 1989: 68).

6 For a consideration of this narrative model, see Neale and Krutnik 1990: 26–38.

7 When Alvy visits Los Angeles, he is horrified to discover that his actor friend Rob (Tony Roberts) is prostituting his talents to the television industry by dubbing an artificial laugh-track over an unfunny sitcom scene.

8 Harry's run through the streets evokes the endings of both *Manhattan* and *The Apartment*, Billy Wilder's 1960 precursor of the nervous romance.

9 Sinatra recorded this Isham Jones–Gus Kahn composition for Capitol Records in the 1950s and for his own company Reprise in the 1960s. The film selects the Reprise Records version, rather than the more swinging Capitol take. With a voice that seems gravelled with experience, Sinatra exudes the mellow romantic authority he exhibits on other Reprise numbers like 'It Was A Very Good Year' and 'My Way'.

10 In *Play It Again Sam* (1972), based on Woody Allen's play, Allan Felix (Allen) is obsessed by the Humphrey Bogart hero from *Casablanca* as an ideal of romantic masculinity. *When Harry Met Sally*, by contrast, is more concerned with the choice that Ilsa (Ingrid Bergman) faces, between the bruised romantic she loves (Rick/Bogart) and the political idealist (Victor/Paul Henreid) to whom she is married. The film thus rearticulates *Casablanca* as a romantic drama rather than a template for individualistic hero-worship, substituting Ingrid Bergman for the Ingmar Bergman beloved of both Alvy and Woody Allen.

11 In *Frankie and Johnny* (1991), Johnny (Al Pacino) offers a similar warning to Frankie (Michelle Pfeiffer): 'Chances like this don't come along often. You gotta take 'em. Because if you don't, they're gone. Forever. And you may wind up not only . . . screwing some other person you meet, thinking you're in love with this person, and marrying him.'

12 *Village Voice* reviewer Georgia Brown identifies 'couple envy' as one of the film's principal obsessions (1989: 68).

13 Evoking the empress of bargain-basement romance as the prime signifier of a degraded 'already said', Eco's meditation on postmodern irony privileges a regime of self-reflexive 'cultivated' discourse at the expense of the 'baser' articulations of the popular. His theorisation implicitly excludes and demeans the cultural experience of those consumers of Cartland's fiction whose social disempowerment effectively blocks their access to such literate language games.

14 The exclusion of ethnic difference is a general feature of the new romances. Old-fashioned romance is often invoked alongside a nostalgia for a more orderly, whiter America – most explicitly in the Capraesque small-town communities of *Housesitter* (1992) and *Groundhog Day* (1993). *Green Card* provides an especially blatant testament to ethnic containment. The film starts with a black youth pounding a drum in an urban market: a signifier of the vibracy and emotional 'primitivism' resisted by the self-repressed heroine, Bronte (Andie MacDowell). These positively valued connotations of otherness are subsequently transferred to a much safer embodiment of alien culture, the French musician Georges Fauré (Gérard Depardieu). Georges usurps the signifiers of racial otherness: he first meets Bronte in the Afrika Café; he pretends to have returned from a field-trip to the 'dark continent'; and African rhythms accompany the build-up of sexual tension as he sleeps in Bronte's apartment.

15 After Sally sleeps with Harry the camera shows her aglow with sexual satisfaction. This scene of post-coital rapture, a still from which adorns the cover of the film's videocassette release, amounts to a significant containment of the implications of her expertise at 'faking it', implying that she will not have to do so with Harry.

16 The sequence's use of split-screen knowingly riffs off a moment from that earlier phone/sex movie, *Pillow Talk*: Doris Day and Rock Hudson speak to one another while taking baths in their separate apartments, and the film splices the two together so it appears as if they are sharing the same tub.

WORKS CITED

Benson, Sheila 1989. 'Review of *When Harry Met Sally*', *The Los Angeles Times* 'Calendar', 14 July: 1

Brown, Georgia 1989. 'Review of *When Harry Met Sally*', *Village Voice*, 18 October: 68

Buckley, Michael 1989. 'Review of *When Harry Met Sally*', *Films in Review*, October: 484

Cook, Pam 1989. 'Review of *When Harry Met Sally*', *The Monthly Film Bulletin*, 57, 671 (December): 377

Denzin, Norman K. 1991. *Images of Postmodern Society: Social Theory and Contemporary Cinema*. London: Sage

Eco, Umberto 1985. 'Postmodernism, Irony, the Enjoyable'. In *Modernism/Postmodernism*, Peter Brooker, ed. London: Longman 225–8

Henderson, Brian 1978. 'Romantic Comedy Today: Semi-Tough or Impossible?', *Film Quarterly*, 31, 4 (Summer): 11–23

Krutnik, Frank (1990): 'The Faint Aroma of Performing Seals: The "Nervous" Romance and the Comedy of the Sexes', *The Velvet Light Trap*, no. 26 (Fall): 57–72

Leo, John 1984. 'The Revolution Is Over', *Time*, 9 April: 48–53

Maslin, Janet 1979. 'Review of *Starting Over*', *The New York Times*, 5 October: C8

Neale, Steve 1992. 'The Big Romance or Something Wild?: Romantic Comedy Today', *Screen*, 33, 3 (Autumn): 284–99

Neale, Steve and Frank Krutnik 1990. *Popular Film and Television Comedy*. London: Routledge

Rowe, Kathleen 1995. *The Unruly Woman: Gender and the Genres of Laughter*. Austin: University of Texas Press

Seidman, Steve 1992. *Embattled Eros: Sexual Politics and Ethics in Contemporary America*. New York: Routledge

Shaw, Arnold 1970. *Sinatra*. London: Hodder

Smilgis, Martha 1987. 'The Big Chill: Fears of AIDS', *Time*, 16 February: 26–9

Sterritt, David 1989. 'Review of *When Harry Met Sally*', *Christian Science Monitor*, 2 August: 11

Chapter 3

'I THINK I COULD FALL IN LOVE WITH HIM': *VICTOR/VICTORIA* AND THE 'DRAG' OF ROMANTIC COMEDY

Steve Cohan

Victor/Victoria: *Deconstructing the gender system: Victoria (Julie Andrews) impersonates the impersonator*

Midway through Blake Edwards's *Victor/Victoria* (1982) a dance number performed at the nightclub Chez Lui stages the utopian ideal of gender mobility driving the film's comedic plot. Two of the four dancers are in recognisable drag as 'females'. Their faces are theatrically made up to resemble a woman's, and they wear low-cut evening gowns, the décolletage concealed yet defined by a bejewelled butterfly, its wings spread out across the manufactured bosom. When viewed from behind, however, these dancers appear to be 'male', dressed in white tie and tails, with a mask on the back of their heads substituting for a man's face. The other two dancers are dressed in the same costume but turned around; sporting short haircuts and thick moustaches, they are made up as 'male' in front and masked as 'female' in back. After all four dancers step on to the stage in their 'female' guise – their entrance alternating face and mask in sequence – they present the flip side of their gender impersonations. Then the dancers pair up as the Fred and Ginger of the drag world, and their swirling movement causes face and mask, 'male' and 'female', to dissolve into each other's image as the two couples spin around the stage.

The drag act's playfulness with cross- and same-sexed masquerades evokes the deconstruction of gender that has characterised both feminism and queer theory since the 1980s. As Judith Butler writes in *Gender Trouble*:

> The presumption of a binary gender system implicitly retains the belief in a mimetic relation of gender to sex whereby gender mirrors sex or is otherwise restricted by it. When the constructed status of gender is theorized as radically independent of sex, gender itself becomes a free-floating article, with the consequence that *man* and *masculine* might just as easily signify a female body as a male one, and *woman* and *feminine* a male body as easily as a female one. (Butler 1990: 6)

The drag act has the obvious effect of making 'gender itself a free-floating article'. For instance, with hands on hips or buttocks, all four dancers shimmy as 'females' but then turn around to perform the same 'feminine' gesture as 'males'. At another point, as two dancers lean forward in their 'male' costumes – imitating a conventional dance position meant to highlight the line and form of the female body – they are actually bending backward, with the hands of their 'male' partners resting suggestively on their buttocks, not their hips. Likewise, the 'males' lift their 'female' partners, whose swinging movement in the air exhibits the reverse side of their costume, turning the lift into another scene of same-sex partnering. Repeatedly, the performers blur the line between imitation and parody, revealing a decidedly queer underside to the gender conventions that dance celebrates.

A comparable blurring of cross- and same-sexed dressing occurs in the plot of *Victor/Victoria*, a result of Victoria Grant's (Julie Andrews) transformation from unemployed singer into the celebrated gay female impersonator 'Victor'. But while the slash mark in the film's title suggests the same gender reversibility that the dancers display, Victoria's transvestism does not efface her biological sex for she remains, as she puts it to her mentor Toddy (Robert Preston), 'a woman pretending to be a man pretending to be a woman'. Formulated in this way, the term 'woman' occupies two distinct positions in the syntax, the authentic female as opposed to the theatrically manufactured one. When the drag act at Chez Lui disturbs the referential ground of gender in a biologically sexed body, it collapses that distinction. As William Luhr and Peter Lehman comment, the dancers' cross-dressing violates the otherwise privileged viewpoint of non-diegetic spectators, placing them 'where most of the film's characters constantly stand' with regard to Victoria's gender impersonation (1989: 47). The biological sex of the four dancers is never visibly determinate; they all read as *men* in drag, 'male' as well as 'female', but there is no definitive proof that they are (not even in the cast list, which omits them). To compound this perceived ambiguity, during the number a tuxedoed Victoria – recognised as 'Victor' by the diegetic audience – enters the club with Toddy, her employer and agent André Casell (John Rhys-Davies), King Marchand (James Garner) and the latter's bodyguard Bernstein (Alex Karras). The nightclub owner Labisse (Peter Arne) greets this esteemed party and leads them to their table. All are dressed, like the four dancers in their 'male' personae, in white tie and tails. As they parade single file through the club, the long shot of these six characters obscures – for the non-diegetic audience, too, even though we *know* that Julie Andrews is playing the part – Victoria's visible identity as a *woman* pretending to be a man, heightening the implied parallel between her masquerade as a male/female impersonator and the dancers'.

The romantic comedy of *Victor/Victoria* pivots around the recontextualisation of gender in the kind of sexed performance that, as in the drag act at Chez Lui, illuminates how easily '*man* and *masculine* might just as easily signify a female body as a male one, and *woman* and *feminine* a male body as easily as a female one'. The resulting detachment of gender from biological sex produces the dilemma complicating King Marchand's attraction to Victoria, motivating his determination to prove that 'Victor' is not a gay man but a woman. King seeks to restore the ground of womanliness in the female body and to disavow the homoeroticism raised by Victoria's gender imposture, which makes it as easy for a heterosexual man to become excited by a male as by a female, at least when both wear the sign 'woman' on their bodies. King therefore has to view Victoria's naked body before he can act upon his desire; but while he is allowed relief from his initial anxiety, his dilemma raises as much uncertainty about a body's stable relation to sexuality, which the film does not resolve for him as easily. In this regard, the drag act at Chez Lui provides an unforgettable point of reference for the romantic couple of *Victor/Victoria* – indeed, for all the couples populating its diegesis. Condensing the problematic of gender and sexuality organising the entire film, the act typifies how, even in its closing moments, *Victor/Victoria* actively works against the heterosexual imperative of romantic comedy, notably the congruence the genre typically fashions between the masquerades instigating the disturbance of a comedic plot and the marriage motivating its resolution through the romantic couple.

'THERE'S A DIFFERENCE, FOR CHRIST'S SAKE'

At first glance, since Victoria pretends to be a gay female impersonator out of expediency, her cross-dressing motivates what Marjorie Garber calls a transvestite progress narrative, which allows for transgression of gender norms but 'as an instrumental strategy rather than an erotic pleasure and play space . . . The ideological implications of this pattern are clear: cross-dressing can be "fun" or "functional" so long as it occupies a liminal space and a temporary time period' (1992: 70). Broke, unemployed, and starving, Victoria agrees to Toddy's outlandish scheme that she pose as a gay female impersonator because she has no other options available to her; but she quickly finds that, as well as offering the success that eluded her as a woman, the imposture liberates her. 'I find it all really fascinating', she tells King to explain why she does not want to give up her 'Victor' persona. 'There are things available to me as a man that I could never have as a woman. I'm emancipated.' This declaration invites us to see Victoria's transvestism turning her initial economical need into psychological growth, simultaneously complicating and enriching her personal life until she has to decide between work and love. The antithesis set up by this conflict then naturalises her later choice, by basing it in her biological sex as a female, of abandoning her career and its pretence in order, as she puts it to Toddy, 'to celebrate my womanhood one day as Mrs King Marchand'.

Victoria's decision to celebrate her womanhood through marriage signals the plot's turn to closure, marking her transvestism as a liminal and temporary stage in her progress towards the expected end of romantic comedy. However, her imposture also has the effect of denaturalising the congruence of sex, gender and sexuality that her marriage to King will supposedly celebrate, as made evident when the couple first meet at the opening night party in her dressing room. Their conversation is worth quoting in full.

KING: Well, I – I just find it hard to believe you're a man.
VICTORIA: Because you found me attractive as a woman.
KING: Yes, as a matter of fact.
VICTORIA: It happens frequently.
KING: *Not* to me.
VICTORIA: It just proves the old adage. There's a first time for everything.
KING: I just don't think so.
VICTORIA: But you're not a hundred per cent sure.
KING: Practically.
VICTORIA: Ah, but to a man like you, someone who believes he could never under any circumstances find another man attractive, the margin between 'practically' and 'for sure', must be as wide as the Grand Canyon.
KING: If you were a man I'd knock your block off.
VICTORIA: And prove that you're a man.
KING: That's a woman's argument.
VICTORIA: Your problem, Mr Marchand, is that you're preoccupied with stereotypes, I think it's as simple as you're one kind of man, I'm another.
KING: And what are you?
VICTORIA: One that doesn't have to prove it – to myself or anyone.

Just how are we to interpret this exchange? Victoria reiterates what Toddy has told her: 'Contrary to the popular conception of how a man acts, there are all sorts of men who act in all sorts of ways'. Nevertheless, the audience, aware of Victoria's deception, has to hear the dialogue from King's perspective, too, knowing he is right to be suspicious. Victoria, furthermore, misstates her difference from King when she claims that she does not need to prove her masculinity. With Toddy coaching her how to sing 'just low enough to be a touch masculine' and to make her dancing 'broader, with tons of shoulder', the ultimate burden on her opening night performance has not been her female impersonation during 'Le Jazz Hot', but her subsequent unveiling as a 'man' when she removes her headpiece and tricks the audience into believing the illusion that she and Toddy have manufactured. Finally, for all her outward hostility, immediately after the conversation Victoria confesses to Toddy that she thinks she could fall in love with King, confirming that there has been a strong heterosexual undercurrent to this exchange after all. The conversation consequently has the same defensive edge as King's later avowal of attraction to Victoria, when he says, 'I don't care if you are a man' before kissing her and, after she reveals 'I am *not* a man', adds, 'I still don't care', his transgression recuperated by his knowing full well that she is female.

When contextualised in the 'truth' concealed by Victoria's double impersonation, that she is always 'a woman pretending to be a man pretending to be a woman', her introduction to King appears to reinforce the authenticity of his machismo, to validate the heterosexual drive of his erotic interest, and to efface the homophobic panic arising from the fact – so his mistress Norma (Lesley Ann Warren) declares upon meeting Victoria – that 'King's tongue was hanging out a foot'. But upon closer inspection, the context supplied by the audience's awareness that Victoria is female ends up substantiating what she says. Far from disproving her argument, knowing her biological sex measures the impact of her cross-dressing throughout the film, how her masquerade as both 'Victor' and 'Victoria' challenges King's presumption of the symmetry between sex, gender and sexuality. Just as Peter Pan is always played by a cross-dressing actress, Garber explains, 'because a woman will never grow up to be a man' (1992: 168), Victoria's being 'a woman pretending to be a man pretending to be a woman' means that 'Victor's' masculinity is indeed different from

King's, precisely because she is really female. Victoria points out, 'it's as simple as you're one kind of man, I'm another', and that other kind is the transvestite, whose function 'in culture is to indicate the place of . . . "category crisis", disrupting and calling attention to cultural, social, or aesthetic dissonances' (Garber 1992: 16). Victoria's transvestism widens 'the margin', as she puts it, 'between "practically" and "for sure"', causing King to doubt his eyes. When he interprets that doubt as the comparable margin between hetero- and homoerotic desire, Victoria's being a woman may confirm the 'normality' of his attraction, but because she speaks to him here as a transvestite her impersonation of maleness *and* femaleness throws the binary logic of those other categories into crisis too. After all, King *is* disturbed by his attraction to Victoria, extremely unsettled, as she realises, by that slight margin of error about her biological sex – uncomfortable enough, it turns out, to be rendered impotent with Norma later that evening.

Victoria's tranvestism, then, is not simply the function of a progress narrative leading her to renewed appreciation of her feminine place in a heterosexual relation. Rather, her imposture establishes transvestism as an alternative position from which to view the male/female, heterosexual/homosexual binaries that marriage institutionalises for the romantic couple. The plot complications arising once Victoria and King consummate their mutual sexual attraction in the middle of the film knot together the questions about gender and sexuality raised by her double masquerade. Victoria is perfectly willing to live with King openly but as 'Victor' since that is her job and she does not want to give it up. 'I'm a big star now. I'm a success', she declares, and King mutters dismissively, 'oh *that*'. 'Well, do you think it would be fair for me to ask you to give up your job?' she asks. 'It'd be ridiculous', he replies: 'There's a difference, for Christ's sake'. 'Right', Victoria states, 'but there shouldn't be'. King defends his position by shifting the terms of his argument to accuse her of dishonesty: 'Look, I'm not the one pretending to be someone else'. Imagining what their relationship will look like if he accepts Victoria's conditions, King then identifies what really bothers him: 'If you think I'm worried everyone'll think I'm a fag, you're right'.

KING: And while we're living and sleeping together, what's everybody going to think?

VICTORIA: I guess they're going to think that you're living and sleeping with a man.
KING: How do you feel about that?
VICTORIA: Well, they're going to think the same thing about me!
KING: But you're a woman.
VICTORIA: Yeah, but they don't know that.
KING: You do.
VICTORIA: And you know you're a man. I don't see the difference.

With these turns in their argument, the couple's dialogue moves back and forth between basing their disagreement in problems arising from Victoria's transvestism which are related but not synonymous: public misperceptions of the lovers' gender and their sexuality. Because homosexuality and effeminacy are synonymous in King's mind, he thinks that being perceived 'as a fag' threatens his gender status as a man by indicating what he does in bed and with whom. The dialogue recognises – to King's discomfort and Victoria's indifference – how her transvestism has the potential effect not only of collapsing two different sets of binary categories (male/female, heterosexual/homosexual), but of then inscribing that confusion on the appearance of the romantic couple, despite their straight orientation, which consequently cannot determine how the world sees them. Given King's anxiety about what the world will think, Victoria concludes, 'we have a problem', and the couple decide to separate. 'Sooner or later I'll probably ask you to stop being a gangster because I'll be worried everyone's thinking I was your moll', she concedes. To his insisting 'I am not a gangster', she counters: 'A business man who does business with gangsters and claims he's not a gangster sounds a lot like the kind of act I do . . . I think we're both pretenders.'

Victoria's comparison of King's professional persona to her own gender impersonation accurately forecasts what happens after he reconsiders and agrees to appear in public as 'Victor's' gay lover: begrudging recognition not only that gender is all acting, but that it bears no direct relation to sexuality either. Actually, this point has already been made clear to King immediately before this conversation. When Bernstein discloses his homosexuality upon finding his employer in bed with 'Victor', King's shock at this unexpected revelation has to do with the discontinuity his bodyguard reveals between homoerotic desire and a big, burly male body. 'I never saw a meaner, rougher, tougher, son-of-a-bitch football player in all my life!', King exclaims the next day in the gym. The bodyguard's body may connote virility but its outward appearance does not guarantee heterosexuality. Neither does the lean, diminutive body of the French prizefighter whom King antagonises into fighting at the gym. 'Don't worry', Bernstein ironically reassures him, 'he's gay'. But that doesn't stop the fighter from giving King a black eye.

King, in fact, sports a black eye in the film twice, the second time following his effort to recover from his sense of lost virility after going dancing with Victoria at a gay club. Entering a working-class bar, he bonds with the men there through a performance of masculinity that aims to reverse the dissonance between gender and sexuality which Bernstein's body – or the fighter's – represents. King cockily steps up to the bar, orders a glass of milk, insults the men's wives and mothers when they make fun of him, starts a fight that quickly escalates into a brawl and ends up sitting with the group, singing 'Sweet Adeline'. For King, brawling with the guys gives an appearance of restoring the congruence of his heterosexuality in his gender. Ironically, however, as Luhr and Lehman note, seeking 'to rid himself of the disgusting taint' of the same-sex intimacy that overwhelmed him at the gay dance club, King 'virtually re-creates himself in the same image . . . of an all-male environment with men with their arms around each other' (1989: 53). Although the bruises may convince him otherwise, his macho display fails to reinstate the congruence of gender and sexuality, but instead maintains their dissonance.

'I GUESS THE PROBLEM IS WE'RE NOT REALLY TWO GUYS'

King's aggression in the bar follows from the film's deliberate embedding of the romantic couple in masculine and feminine stereotypes in order to widen the margin between gender and sexuality. When Victoria throws up during a boxing match that excites King, or when she sobs uncontrollably at a performance of *Madame Butterfly* that bores him, these stock responses follow long-standing movie shorthand for showing a couple's intrinsic sexual difference as opposites that attract by displaying their conformity to the most orthodox of gender norms, as if to suggest that, beneath her man's suit, Victoria is as inherently feminine as King is outwardly masculine. In this montage of public scenes, however, far from taking the risk in the diegesis of 'drawing attention to herself by allowing her "natural" self to emerge' (Luhr and Lehman 1989: 53), Victoria's implicit unmasking as a woman through her 'feminine' responses inverts what she does on stage at the end of her act, when she removes her wig to identify herself as 'Victor'. Because the couple have to hide their heterosexuality, as far as the diegetic audience at the fights or the opera is concerned, what Victoria displays is not her inherent womanliness but the effeminacy of a gay man consorting with his more virile counterpart. Viewed through the lens of gender, the stock responses of both characters represent their pretended homosexual relation as an 'inversion', as an unnatural or poor copy of the binarised masculine and feminine roles structuring heterosexual subjectivity. This representation is a misrepresentation, though, so the straight couple's outward appearance of being gay has much the same effect that Butler attributes to 'butch' and 'femme' lesbian personae, which 'shift, invert, and create erotic havoc of various sorts' by disturbing binarised figurations of gender from their seem-ingly secure ground in heterosexual coupling (1990: 215). As Norma puts it to the couple, upon finding lipstick and a nightgown in King's bedroom, 'What do you do, take turns playing the woman?'

Norma, of course, means to deride the 'real' man as well as the impersonator. She can understand gay sex only as an inversion of the straight norm, with 'masculine' and 'feminine' positions still in place. Yet in hinting at the erotic play enabled by the imposture – and in evoking the drag act at Chez Lui, where the dancers do 'take turns playing the woman' – Norma's question conjures up an image of gender mobility that aptly summarises how *Victor/Victoria* deploys its opposition of gay and straight to satirise heterosexual presumptions about gender rather than to represent homosexuality. For King and Victoria are, of course, *not* a gay couple. As Victoria says to Bernstein, after King goes off to reclaim his masculinity at the workers' bar, 'I guess the problem is we're not *really* two guys'. Despite the many layers of gender pretense beclouding it, her coupling with King always refers to its concealed heterosexual ground. The outward appearance of their being two homosexual men does not imitate gay sexuality but parodies the straight presumption that binarised gender identities manifest, while determining, 'normal' sexual relations.

The two couples that King and Victoria's relationship replaces – he with Norma, she with Toddy – bring out this parodic dimension even more directly. With her bleached platinum hair, glamorous gowns and furs, temper tantrums, mispronounced words, and urban, working-class accent, showgirl Norma is modelled after 1930s' star Jean Harlow, just as King's macho persona resembles that of Harlow's screen partner, Clark Gable ('The King'), moustache and all. Although she was in fact initially mistaken about Victoria's sex too, and jealous of King's interest, Norma boasts afterward: 'I knew he was a man right away. I don't care how clever those costumes are, there are just some things you cannot fake. I mean, even with all those hormone shots and everything, a real woman can always tell.' Not only is Norma wrong, since she could not tell the difference during Victoria's performance, but her more 'real' womanliness is just as faked, an imitation that has its own unmistakable parodic quality. Norma's femininity may consist of just a single note but she comically – and skilfully – draws out every variation within that limited range. She calls King to their bedroom, announcing 'Yoo-hoo, I'm horny', but not before carefully posing her body seductively in the doorway and making a deliberate show (for the film's spectators, not King) of draping the fur collar of her négligé over her bare shoulder to achieve the proper siren's look.

In exaggerating her gender performativity, Norma's broad characterization as the 'femme' to King's 'butch' parodies the sexual binary that structures their erotic relationship. With her own lipstick and nightgown, Norma plays the woman's part and King the man's; they just don't take turns. Even though Norma believes that 'there are just some things you cannot fake' when it comes to gender, because 'a real woman can always tell', her sexuality is another matter. Trying to comfort King after he cannot get an erection, she reassures him: 'It's no big deal. It happens to everyone, men I mean. We're lucky, women I mean. We can fake it, if we have to. Oh, don't get me wrong, I never have with you, faked it I mean.' The logic of this 'norma-tive' reasoning inverts the significance of the penis in marking sexual difference on the body; rather than indicating female lack, here the absence of the penis marks the female's greater luck. After Norma announces her horniness, King rushes her like a bull in heat, throwing her over his shoulder and carrying her into their bedroom, where he cannot get his penis to perform its 'natural' function; and it is just as obvious at this point that he *is* trying to fake it. For what explicitly prompts his 'butch' response to Norma's 'femme' charms, and what then prevents him from following through on his vigorous display of manliness in bed with her afterwards, is King's glancing out the window and catching sight of 'Victor' and Toddy embracing across the way.

The interaction between King and Norma is constructed and edited to establish how Victoria's double imposture serves as the film's central trope for satirising heterosexual anxiety about gender. King is initially paired with one gender performer, 'femme' Norma, but ends up coupled with another, the closeted 'butch' Bernstein: after King punishes Norma for calling attention to his impotence by washing her mouth with soap, she furiously charges the pair with a lance, driving King and Bernstein into the latter's bedroom for safety. During this scene, too, the editing counterpoints the action in King and Norma's hotel suite to that in Victoria and Toddy's. Victoria confesses that 'pretending to be a man has its disadvantages' because she would not mind having an affair with King, and Toddy replies, 'you've just said a cotton-pickin' mouthful'. The next shot shows King at extreme disadvantage, unable to perform and unable to fake it, while Norma prattles on about the greater luck of women when it comes to their orgasms. Victoria and Toddy, meanwhile, are in bed, drinking champagne, reading magazines, and singing 'Home on the Range' ('where the deer and the antelope are gay') – acting, in short, like quite a 'gay' couple in both senses of the term.

Whether in the privacy of their own rooms or in the public eye as a gay couple themselves, Victoria and Toddy play with the 'butch' and 'femme' gender stereotypes of the straight pair. Toddy is effeminate but not exactly 'femme' – he performs professionally in a tuxedo and does not do drag until the finale – so his campy gestures, jokes and references to himself as 'an old queen' have the effect, like that of a transvestite, of collapsing the categories 'masculine' and 'feminine'. Victoria's gender reads the same way when in his presence; with her slicked back hair and business suits, she appears 'butch' in so far as she plays the boyish 'straight man' to Toddy's campier 'queen'. Once Toddy puts his plan into action, he treats Victoria as if she *were* Victor, referring to her always as 'he', and Victoria conforms to his lead whenever in his presence. She returns from breaking up with King following their unsatisfactory attempt to go out dancing at a gay club, and announces: 'I'm a bachelor again . . . Oh Toddy. I'm very much in love. And I don't know what to do'. 'Here', Toddy replies, handing her a handkerchief, 'I can't stand to see a grown man cry'.

The intimacy and warmth of their relationship puts Toddy in the position of serving as King's rival, triangulating the couple according to romantic comedy convention. After performing 'Crazy World' in male drag, Victoria tosses a flower to King in public acknowledgement of their affair, but only after Toddy blows her a kiss from the wings first. Of course, Toddy poses no direct sexual competition for King. Toddy points out to Victoria that his bed is a more comfortable and safer place than the bathtub in his flat, or reminds her that they have to take a one-bedroom hotel suite after their success in order to keep up their appearance as a gay couple, and these jokes reiterate the asexuality of their bonding, which is to say that they are not really two guys, either.

Toddy is himself not asexual, though, nor does his homosexuality correspond, not even as a parodic inversion, with the 'butch' and 'femme' binary of straight coupling. He is a man attracted to other men, as the opening shot of him in bed with his naked bisexual lover Richard establishes immediately. To be sure, the camp inflection of Toddy's homosexuality draws on Hollywood convention for represent-ing it as a gender inversion – a tradition of popular entertainment going back to what began as the 'pansy craze' of 1930s' cabaret and Broadway as well as the screen (Chauncey 1994: 314–29) – but his camp also has a more contemporary frame of reference to the sexualisation of gay identities. 'You're kidding, you really are queer?' Norma asks when she meets Toddy on Victoria's opening night. His correction – 'we prefer gay' – overlays the 1930s' diegesis with a post-Stonewall consciousness of the gay rights movement as a sexual liberation from heterosexual hegemony. Toddy's camp dialogue thus turns straight norms around so that the joke is heterosexuality, not his own homosexuality.

NORMA: I think the right woman could reform you.
TODDY: You know, I think the right woman could reform you.
NORMA: Oh! Me give up men? Forget it!
TODDY: You took the words right out of my mouth.

Before leaving, Norma laments, 'I still think it's a terrible waste', and

Toddy reassures her, 'Well, if it's any consolation, I assure you it's not wasted'.

At this point in the film, though, it is going to waste, at least as far as we can tell, since Toddy appears to have given up men momentarily in the interest of furthering Victoria's career. His affair with Bernstein, which follows a parallel course with Victoria and King's, seems to arise out of convenience and to depend upon the fortunes of the straight couple. After Victoria announces that she is a bachelor again, Toddy replies, 'It's just as well. Mr Bernstein was beginning to make a permanent dent in the mattress'. According to Robin Wood, 'Toddy's casual and brutal reference' minimises the gay couple so that it 'is allowed no real importance whatever', in contrast with the straight one, which 'is presented in terms of a commitment deserving sacrifices' (1986: 243). However, that view applies only if one invokes heterosexual monogamy as the standard for evaluation. Whether with reference to the plot's 1934 setting or the film's own production in an era right before the AIDS epidemic set constraints upon gay culture, Toddy's remark just as likely recognises the casual sex and multiple pairings that characterised homosexual behaviour as different from heterosexual – even, to some, as a liberating alternative to its oppressiveness. If his relation to Bernstein lacks the romantic gloss of Victoria and King's, that only makes the same-sex couple all the more carnal in its motivation. They *are* a couple of guys, horny ones, and they don't dance to the same tune that straights do.

The homosexual coupling of Toddy and Bernstein presses the limits of the film's overall strategy of using what are otherwise just intimations of gay sexuality to satirise straight assumptions about gender. Wood is thus right to conclude that the gay couple works overtly as a comic foil to the straight romantic one (1986: 243), just as the other couples do. Setting the pairing of Victoria and King against a backdrop of comparable gender masquerades and less conventionalised sexualities, *Victor/Victoria* multiplies couples; almost each major character is paired with one another at some point in the plot, if only momentarily and provisionally. The only two characters not paired at any time in the film, in fact, are King and Toddy, who barely have any dialogue with each other. Yet Toddy, it appears, would not be adverse to their coupling, suggesting his potential role as Victoria's rival as well as King's.

TODDY: What did you think of King Marchand?
VICTORIA: King Marchand is an arrogant, opinionated, chauvinistic pain in the ass.
TODDY: I think I could fall in love with him.
VICTORIA: I think I could too.

The other side of King's apparent attraction to a female impersonator is not his latent homosexuality but his own attractiveness to a gay man, which he cannot disavow or prevent. *Victor/Victoria* slyly allows Toddy to make the declaration that romantic comedy invariably gives to the woman: 'I think I could fall in love with him'. But a Toddy–King pairing would have to uncouple Victoria and her heterosexual lover, so it would also push King's homophobic panic and his later passing as 'Victor's' lover to a logical if, for mainstream romantic comedy, most unorthodox conclusion. *Victor/Victoria* nevertheless works around this injunction through the pairing of Toddy and Victoria, whose bond takes centre stage away from the romantic couple in the film's closure.

'THE GREATEST DISGUISE I HAVE EVER SEEN!'

Most critics agree that *Victor/Victoria* works towards a closure that, perfectly consistent with the outcome of romantic comedy, uses the heterosexual romantic couple to contain the transgressions (transvestism and homosexuality) allied with the unmooring of gender and sexuality from their common ground in the body's biological sex. 'This is drag as high entertainment', Butler comments, with the cross-dressing 'providing a ritualistic release for a heterosexual economy that must constantly police its own boundaries against the invasion of queerness' (1993: 126). Wood draws the same conclusion, arguing that the film follows a typical 1980s' strategy of separation, recognising heterosexuals and homosexuals but as 'two distinct species', effectively subordinating gays and women to the authority of straight men (1986: 241). Bruce Babington and Peter William Evans likewise claim that the film's closure removes 'the heterosexual female from the setting . . . of sexual experiment, reversal and metamorphoses of sex and identity' by redefining that setting as a marginalised, stereotypically queer space (1989: 296–7).

The ending of *Victor/Victoria*, however, is not that fully recuperative.

Given the funereal air of Victoria's black clothing (Luhr and Lehman 1989: 54) and the awkward, constrained 'lady-like' way that Julie Andrews holds her body throughout the finale, if the ending does rein-state the heterosexual regime that Victoria's gender impersonation has disturbed, it does not do so easily or happily, certainly not in the way that romantic comedy traditionally ends. As Luhr and Lehman demonstrate, the ending is far from 'unifying' but '[riddled] with dis-turbing elements' (1989: 54). They point out, for instance, that when Toddy performs Victoria's number, 'The Shady Dame from Saville', she is mouthing 'the words to the song that was once hers but which Toddy now sings' (Luhr and Lehman 1989: 54), indicating her disem-powerment through silence. The cut to Victoria miming the lyrics, in fact, occurs at the line 'The rest of the tale's not a pretty one'.

As important, the ending fails to close the plot logically. Although Victoria's sacrificial gesture gives an impression of resolving the legal complications arising from her impersonation, which amounts to fraud and misrepresentation, abandonment of her 'Victor' persona along with her career by no means saves her from facing charges for the scam she and Toddy have perpetrated. True, they have momentarily fooled the police inspector sent by Labisse to investigate. But Victoria and Toddy are still liable to be arrested for fraud after the performance – that is, unless she is still being viewed in the diegesis as a transvestite, which seems highly probable: the clubgoers must recognise her as the famed gay female impersonator Victor, as happened earlier when she entered Chez Lui during the drag act, and they must also know full well that Toddy is not 'Victor' but an impersonator of that impersonator. Somehow Toddy's outrageous camp of Victoria's act means to resolve any question, legal or otherwise, of criminal misrepresentation, but it is not immediately clear how or why since it simply compounds one misrepresentation upon another.

What Toddy's camp closes is a series of gag scenes focused on the body as the determination of gender. Initially, his scheme to pass Victoria as a gay female impersonator is premised on the way a body signifies its gender through context. 'People believe what they see', he explains to a doubting Victoria, so 'to create an illusion a magician creates a plausible diversion', in this case 'Victor's' background as a Polish count. 'They'll know he's a phoney', Victoria replies, and Toddy declares that is his very point: 'They'll know *he's* a phoney'. King's confusion about Victoria's gender, which causes him not to believe what he believes when he sees her perform, arises because he arrives too late to read the club's programme, which provides the proper context for fixing her body to its intended meaning as a gay female impersonator: full-page photos of 'Victor' and 'Victoria' displayed side by side, telling the audience what to see.

When, to prove that Victoria is female, King hides in the bathroom closet and watches her undress, this scene reinvests the body with its superior status as the authentic origin of gender difference, but it is followed by comparable scenes that call this authenticity into question. Suspicious of Victoria's impersonation because he recognises her voice, Labisse hires a detective, who eventually makes his way into the bathroom to learn of Victoria's sex just as King did, though in this case not by seeing her naked but by hearing her tell Toddy that she hopes one day to celebrate her womanhood as Mrs King Marchand. As the setup for the ending, Labisse, now armed with this information, brings the police inspector to Casell's club in order to expose 'Victor's' fraudulence, so the film gets to stage the revelation scene yet again, albeit this time off screen. Behind closed doors, Toddy drops his pants and takes Victoria's place, finally allowing for the delayed rebuttal to Norma's comment that men cannot fake it. 'That's a man', the inspector announces, emerging from the dressing room. 'When I walked in, the person in that room was naked from the waist down, and if that was a woman, then she was wearing the greatest disguise that I have ever seen!' The inspector's exclamation rings true in two different senses, first as sarcastic confirmation of the penis, since the body he views is undoubtedly male, then as ironic affirmation of its fakery, since the body he views is a substitute for Victoria's, so it *is* the greatest disguise he has ever seen. With each repetition of the original scene of King spying on Victoria, the body's authority is made increasingly suspect – to the point that, in the dressing room, the penis functions as just another prop in Victoria's impersonation.

Toddy's camp reprise of Victoria's earlier number then takes this 'greatest disguise' out of the dressing room. His drag act parodies the mimetic objective of her female impersonation; making no effort to act or look like Victoria, Toddy cannot hit her high notes, has trouble standing up with the dancers, always seems ready to fall out of his costume. Although he quite broadly appears to play the woman's part, his drag performance does not characterise homosexuality as a poor copy of gender, since the part he plays is not exactly a woman's but Victoria's impersonation of one. Burlesquing the normative view that a gay man is a 'femme' male, Toddy's camp style incorporates his middle-aged body and raspy voice into his performance so that it is legible as drag in a way that Victoria's never is, juxtaposing signs of masculinity and femininity in reiteration of the drag act at Chez Lui. And as in that act, Toddy's camp performance sexualises the number, also in a way that Victoria's impersonation does not, as when he gooses two of the male dancers with his fan, falls on the lap of the bullfighter and gets a big kiss, or at the end, tosses a rose to Bernstein in the audience, suggesting the renewal of their relationship as a romance on par with the straight couple.

Cut throughout Toddy's number are shots of Victoria watching, her face glowing with what can only be described as rapturous spectatorial pleasure. A shot of her applauding even terminates the narrative, marking the point at which the end-credits begin to unroll extradiegetically. During the film every character but Victoria is a spectator, so her finally attaining this position carries with it a force of closure that surpasses the romantic comedy plot. As she mouths the words to what is now Toddy's song, Victoria achieves spectatorship but through identification with the gay male performer who has taken her place on stage, in effect serving as her stand-in just as he did in the dressing room when the inspector came to investigate. Furthermore, Victoria joins a diegetic audience that, from Toddy's first number at Chez Lui to his camping of her act in the finale, represents a utopian ideal of gender and sexual heterogeneity. Whenever she or Toddy perform, shots of anonymous spectators often make it difficult to determine whether they are straight, gay, lesbian, male, female or transvestite, creating the impression of mainstream and queer cultures happily mingling.

In historical hindsight that representation of cultural integration, particularly as achieved through the shared pleasure of watching queer entertainment, seems either naive or, more likely, since the audience at Chez Lui invariably breaks up into free-for-all brawls which require police intervention, acknowledged as a utopian fantasy, one that can be staged within the privileged, carnivalesque space of the theatre but not sustained there. Released in 1982 to general, but not overwhelming, critical and popular success, *Victor/Victoria* found its own audience at the moment in American culture when the New Right marshalled its political forces to attack and reverse the gains of 1970s' gay, lesbian and feminist activists (D'Emilio and Freedman 1988: 344–53). At that time, too, in a specific inflection of this shift to the right, cinematic images of 'hard body heroes' (Jeffords 1994: 22) began to establish an iconography of determinate maleness that sought to maintain, as the measure of national identity, the very gender boundaries that *Victor/Victoria* collapses through drag. The ease with which *Victor/Victoria* can yield recuperative interpretations of its closure, as its more unsympathetic critics charge, registers the pressure of that historical juncture on the film's decentring of its romantic couple, but then so does the film's refusal to relieve that pressure by ending with the image of Victoria watching Toddy perform and not one of her embracing her straight lover. That final image reiterates how her alliance with Toddy, cohering first around her cross-dressing and then around his, gives *Victor/Victoria* the perspective from which to resist – by exerting a weight, or drag, as it were, on its romantic comedy plot – the heterosexual coupling that drives the genre towards marriage as its inevitable end.

NOTE

All quotations from *Victor/Victoria* (1982; dir. Blake Edwards) are my own transcriptions of the dialogue from the MGM/UA videodisc version of the film.

WORKS CITED

Babington, Bruce and Peter William Evans 1989. *Affairs to Remember: The Hollywood Comedy of the Sexes*. Manchester: Manchester University Press

Butler, Judith 1990. *Gender Trouble: Feminism and the Subversion of Identity*. New York: Routledge

Butler, Judith 1993. *Bodies that Matter: On the Discursive Limits of 'Sex.'* New York: Routledge

Chauncey, George 1994. *Gay New York: Gender, Urban Culture, and the Making of the Gay Male World 1890–1940*. New York: Basic Books

D'Emilio, John and Estelle B. Freedman 1988. *Intimate Matters: A History of Sexuality in America*. New York: Harper & Row

Garber, Marjorie 1992. *Vested Interests: Cross-Dressing and Cultural Anxiety*. New York: Routledge

Jeffords, Susan 1994. *Hard Bodies: Hollywood Muscularity in the Reagan Era*. New
    Brunswick, NJ: Rutgers University Press
Luhr, William and Peter Lehman 1989. *Returning to the Scene: Blake Edwards,
    Volume 2*. Athens, Ohio: Ohio University Press
Wood, Robin 1986. *Hollywood from Vietnam to Reagan*. New York: Columbia
    University Press

Chapter 4

MURPHY'S ROMANCE:
ROMANTIC LOVE AND THE EVERYDAY

Deborah Thomas

Murphy's Romance: *Role reversals in the context of modern romance*

'What kind of a community have I *come* to here?'
(Ranse Stoddard in *The Man who Shot Liberty Valance*, 1962)

'What kind of town *is* this?'
(Emma Moriarty in *Murphy's Romance*, 1985)

'Do I hear wedding bells? When can I print the story?'
'Don't rush me, mister editor, don't rush me.'
(Dutton Peabody and Tom Doniphon in
The Man who Shot Liberty Valance)

'I think you should get married again.'
'When I'm ready.'
(Emma Moriarty and Murphy Jones in *Murphy's Romance*)

'I haven't been to a movie since the Duke died.'
(Murphy Jones in *Murphy's Romance*)

As this book is intended to address the specific issue of romantic comedy, it seems sensible to begin by making explicit my use of this term. I have argued elsewhere that romance and comedy – along with melodrama – are the three constituting modes of American cinema: that is, they are far broader categories than genres (such as musicals, horror films, and so on), and their complex interactions play over the various narrative spaces – the geographies – of the vast majority of Hollywood films. Romantic comedy is thus a hybrid which combines two broad types of fantasy for its viewers: a fantasy of mutual erotic desire, which is what I understand by romance, and a fantasy of a 'magical' and sheltering place, which is the essence of what I mean by the comedic, and which keeps at bay the contrasting repressiveness of the melodramatic (whose narrative world is a place of strict social hierarchies and jockeyings for power). In this context, the comedic and the comic, while they may often overlap, are quite different things. Films belonging to particular comic genres (like screwball or slapstick, for example) may make us laugh, but I am suggesting that they are only truly comedic, as well as comic, if, in addition, they offer us a narrative world – or a space within it – which feels safe in two ways: in terms of its generosity to those who inhabit it (its characters) and in terms of the sorts of cinematic pleasures it offers us (its viewers). No harm will come to either them or us. But if we can answer the question 'Safe *from* what?' by seeing the comedic as a sort of refuge from or transformation of a threatening melodramatic world, we have a further question to consider: safe *for* what? In the case of romantic comedy, the answer may come down to no more nor less than the following: safe for the playing out of a fantasy of reciprocal desire. That is, if romance is understood in terms of a mutuality of erotic desire – the couple meeting up, or ending up, as equals (at least within the private romantic space, if not the larger world outside), their desires of equal standing and of equal motive power – then, in contrast to the melodramatic narrative world, which takes this undoing of male pre-eminence as a threat against which all its forces must be rallied, comedy welcomes romance and offers it a home.

I don't wish to repeat the detailed analyses of particular films which I've made elsewhere and which have led me to these conclusions and to my acceptance of the usefulness of such an understanding of romantic comedy as a supra-generic hybrid. Rather, I would now like to turn to *Murphy's Romance* to see how well these conclusions hold up with respect to what may appear an unlikely choice of film and in what ways they may need to be modified or expanded. Of course, if the status of *Murphy's Romance* as a romantic comedy is not a matter of genre, the film is nonetheless embedded at the same time within familiar generic terrain, and the genre to which it most clearly makes reference is the Western. The modern-day setting is small-town Arizona, the central character, Emma Moriarty (Sally Field), has a ranch where she boards and trains horses, various characters wear Western dress, and so on, but the connections go deeper than this, as the counter-pointed lines of dialogue from *Murphy's Romance* and John Ford's *The Man who Shot Liberty Valance*, with which I prefaced this account, are intended to suggest. Of course, *The Man who Shot Liberty Valance* is not just *any* Western, and its meditations on the passing of the Old West are paralleled by Murphy's (James Garner) comment – 'I haven't been to the movies since the Duke died' – which implicitly expresses his regret at the passing of *a way of making movies* about this self-same world and the passing of certain values from the standpoint of a later time. Both films, while firmly set in the West, are nonetheless aware of how its legends take shape and to a certain extent – at least, through some of their characters – appear to endorse this process. And yet the differences between the two films are substantial.

While it is implied that the consumers of Western legends in the Ford film (as opposed to their purveyors) accept such legends as fact, there is no evidence offered to suggest that Murphy does the same. The town in which he lives has explicit continuities not so much with the Old West of legend and John Wayne, but with modern American small-town life in all its everydayness which the film's audience can readily recognise and take as their own, or at least as a part of a world which is continuous with their own. Ranse Stoddard's (James Stewart) question as to the sort of community he has found in Shinbone is a rhetorical one to which he has already discovered the answer, and it represents his outraged response to the frontier violence he experiences first-hand and to the absence of Eastern law. Emma's question to Murphy about the nature of the town to which she's moved with her son Jake (Corey Haim), in contrast, is motivated by genuine curiosity and receives a much more modern response: 'Oh, it's small, friendly, nosy. You can carry a gun, but you can't get an abortion.' When Emma replies that she doesn't particularly want to do either, Murphy asks her where she's from. Her answer – that 'this time' she's from Modesto, California – both sets her up as a 'wanderer' from further west and leads into their first sustained conversation in the film, the beginning, if you like, of their romance, though not yet perceived as such by either one.

> MURPHY: Then you know the rules.
> EMMA: The rules? You mean like keep the front room picked up? Don't sit around in your bathrobe after ten o'clock in the morning? Don't mess with a married man?
> MURPHY: That's part of it. The rest of it is, uh, we got a Rhodes scholar, we got a homosexual, we've got marijuana growing in with the tomatoes, we've even got a man who wears his wife's nightgown. We're the mainstream.
> EMMA: [she laughs] Actually, not yet. Just today I got called "honey", uh, "missy", I think there was a "little lady" in there somewhere.
> MURPHY: Well, they're not too familiar with the ERA. If it's consciousness-raising you're looking for, you'll have to head East.

If Shinbone is seen to change in the course of Ford's narrative from a place with too few rules to one with too many, Murphy's home town is simultaneously rule-bound and tolerant of deviations from its norms, with no signs of either the uncontrollable violence nor the sterile lifelessness which characterise Shinbone's two extremes.

A further complication in comparing the two films is that, although the opening quotations seem to link Ranse and Emma as newcomers to the town, and to link Tom and Murphy, in contrast, as native inhabitants with a resistance to marriage, it is not that simple. Like Tom, Emma is a rancher, both of them living on the outskirts of their respective towns, while both Ranse and Murphy are associated with beliefs and ideas which single them out (Murphy's liberal causes – 'No nukes' and 'Reforest America' – are proclaimed openly on the signs he props up in the windscreen of his car, and in the conversation just quoted he distances himself from the townspeople by his use of 'they', not 'we', when referring to their unfamiliarity with the ERA). In addition, Ranse and Murphy are both seen dressed in aprons and serving up food (in Murphy's case, he wears an apron at the barbecue at Emma's ranch, and he regularly serves up food in the drugstore which he owns). But whereas Ranse's 'feminisation' provokes more widespread critical comment, and he is attacked by the outlaw figure of Liberty Valance who mocks his appearance in the restaurant as well as threatening his life, Murphy is a popular and well-respected citizen with no enemies. The villainous figure of Liberty Valance has no equivalent in *Murphy's Romance*, though Emma's ex-husband, Bobby Jack (Brian Kerwin), who turns up almost halfway into the film, has hints of Liberty's dandyism and a similar desire for freedom without responsibility (although, in Bobby Jack's case, it surfaces not in the form of unrestrained violence but of irresponsible sex), and he too comments on what he sees as Murphy's 'feminisation' when Murphy openly admits to being able to sew a dress, Bobby Jack asking, 'You one of those funny fellows?' But Murphy's look and intonation when he replies – 'No-o-o. The only son of a widowed mother' – suggest a criticism of Bobby Jack for his small-minded prejudices, rather than a defensive reaction to his insinuations. In the main, however, even Bobby Jack is seen as good-natured and well-meaning, if clearly prejudiced and morally weak as well.

So *Murphy's Romance* presents us with a very different world from that of *The Man who Shot Liberty Valance* in two key respects: first, it is tolerant of difference and, second, both of its central characters, Emma and Murphy, who are to form its romantic couple by the end of the film, incorporate within themselves aspects of both Ranse and Tom (John Wayne), of both liberal and more traditional values, and of both 'feminine' and 'masculine' traits. The fact that, in *Murphy's Romance*,

both difference and its dissolution are presented as wholly unthreat-
ening and safe is confirmation of the essentially comedic orientation of
the film. A final significant difference between the two films, of course,
is that, whereas Tom Doniphon's insistence that he not be rushed into
marriage makes him leave it too late and lose Hallie (Vera Miles) to
Ranse, Murphy is able to ready himself for the prospect of marriage to
Emma in time. Nonetheless, his reaction to the death of his first wife is
described in terms not so different from Tom's reaction to the loss of
Hallie, when Tom gets drunk and burns down his house in a suicidal
gesture of despair: as Murphy's friend, Margaret (Georgann Johnson)
tells Emma, 'Oh, honey, that man was a wreck. Drunk the first year,
never spoke to a soul the second. Crazy about his wife.' Similarly,
Emma's regrets ('I've done a lot of dumb things in my life. I married
too young. I married the wrong guy. I never went to college.') may
remind us both of Hallie's lack of education and of our sense that she
too, like Emma, has married the wrong man. But a crucial difference
remains: where Tom dies a lonely and purposeless man, a virtual
stranger in his own town, and Hallie grows old in a marriage that is
clearly sterile and emotionally dead, both Murphy and Emma get a
second chance. To repeat what, by now, should be obvious, the melodramatic relationships of *The Man who Shot Liberty Valance* are replaced
by those of romantic comedy in *Murphy's Romance*.

More specifically, the fact that both Murphy and Emma have been
married before gives their romance some of the qualities of what Stanley
Cavell calls a 'comedy of remarriage'. Although such films generally
involve the splitting up and coming back together of the *same* married
couple, Cavell allows for a case like Frank Capra's *It Happened One
Night* (1934), where a woman married to one man – but whose marriage her father is threatening to annul – comes to realise that she's
falling in love with another. Thus, such a film

> shifts emphasis away from the normal question of comedy,
> whether a young pair will get married, onto the question whether
> the pair will get and stay divorced, thus prompting philosophical
> discussions of the nature of marriage. We might accordingly say
> here that the issue of remarriage is present but displaced. (Cavell
> 1981: 85)

That the words to the song which accompanies Emma's arrival in Murphy's home town, in the credit sequence, include the phrase 'maybe I'm coming home' suggests a return to something familiar which she has encountered before. Cavell approvingly cites Freud's claim that 'The finding of an object is in fact the refinding of it' (1981: 68), and this is relevant too. In moving to Arizona and taking up ranching, Emma is returning to something she has known all her life, in contrast to her husband's ignorance of ranching when he turns up and stays with her later on, which implies that her marriage was a *break* in the continuity of her life from which she is now trying to find her way back home.

Murphy's first openly admiring looks at Emma are in the scenes when he watches her at work in the corral, riding and training the horse which he has bought in order to board it with her and push some much needed work her way, having previously refused her a loan. Her competence and self-sufficiency are what seem to attract him, not the chance he could have taken to secure her dependency upon him by the loan. The film is unusual – in relation to mainstream American films generally, if not in relation to Ritt's films overall – in the visibility and screen time it gives to women's manual labour, such work presented not in terms of traditional housekeeping jobs, but through the 'masculine' jobs which Emma performs in order to get her ranch in good repair and to keep it going: thus, we see her repair heavy fences and machinery, while more domestic tasks like window-washing and washing-up are shared in by her son and Murphy respectively, and she gives the most menial tasks (like shovelling up after the horses) to Bobby Jack, as a kind of sweet revenge.

Another indication of the film's belief that traditional roles and expectations are not binding but are subject to change is in Murphy's belief in individual moral responsibility and its necessary precondition, free will, which the film seems to support. Thus, when Emma asks Murphy whether he has lived in the town very long, and he answers, 'All my life', and she goes on to ask if he likes it, his reply – 'Well, I must have or I wouldn't have stayed' – asserts his freedom to choose his life rather than merely choosing how to respond to what life dishes out to him, as Emma's words suggest. Yet Emma too has chosen to make a new life for herself and her son, and in this act of self-assertion she shows herself to be Murphy's match.

Murphy's belief in free will is further emphasised when Emma's son
Jake tells Murphy that he had noticed his father cheating at cards when
they were all playing for matchsticks earlier on, and Murphy replies:
'Take after him or not – it's up to you'. This second example is even
clearer than the first in suggesting that free will, in this film at least, is
a matter of making moral choices: that is, Murphy, Emma and Jake are
all seen to be responsible for constructing their own identities and the
values that go with them in full awareness (at least to the extent of
having learned from past mistakes) of precisely what is at stake. Free
will is thus seen as a process of judicious weighing up, of taking
responsibility for one's actions in an ongoing process of moral self-
education based on experience rather than the received wisdom of
others. In this respect it is in contrast to the 'freedoms of the id' which
characterise versions of liberty in so many other films, and, indeed, in
this film too through Bobby Jack's debased sense of freedom – from
marriage, from work – in terms of what Robin Wood, in another context, has called the lure of irresponsibility. The contrasting visions of
freedom as moral responsibility, on the one hand, and unrestrained
impulse, on the other, are ironically juxtaposed in *The Man who Shot
Liberty Valance* when Dutton Peabody (Edmund O'Brien), the editor of
The Shinbone Star, having stood up to Liberty Valance through the
headlines and editorialising in his newspaper, returns to the office to
find Liberty and his men materialising from the shadows. As Liberty
strikes a threatening pose, the offending newspaper displayed in his
grasp, the cadences of Peabody's words – 'Liberty Valance taking *liber-
ties* with the *liberty* of the press?' – play with the ambiguities to which
the concept of freedom gives rise. As Peabody is beaten up and left for
dead, the brutality of Liberty's version of freedom is met by the coura-
geous resistance of Peabody's version, and of Ranse's matching version
elsewhere in the film.

What Ford's film makes clear is that *Murphy's Romance* has no
monopoly on the representation and endorsement of freedom as
moral responsibility, nor on the structural opposition of such a vision
of freedom with its counterpart as freedom from restraint. However,
the melodramatic versions of such themes are much more pessimistic
than their comedic equivalents, not only in representing unrestrained
impulse more negatively, but in presenting the melodramatic world as
a place where social factors such as class, race and gender determine

behaviour and choices in ways to which its protagonists are symbolically blind. Thus, when melodramatic characters believe themselves to
be free, they are often presented as self-deceived, the illusion of such
freedom being part of their plight. Where they are more aware of their
entrapment, their appropriation of moral responsibility may still feel
like an intervention by the hand of fate: a good example of this occurs
in another film directed by Martin Ritt, *Hombre* (1967), where John
Russell (Paul Newman) knowingly goes to his death in order to do
what he *has* to do in order to save a woman's life, the moral decision
to do this coming across as his destiny, rather than an act which is, in
any but a heavily qualified sense, a free choice. Of course, comedic
films frequently undercut their characters' freedom as well, through
such devices as coincidence, chance meetings, magical resolutions, and
the sense they often give of a benevolent directorial presence offscreen.
However, in such cases, the manipulation of the central characters – or,
at least, the ones we are encouraged to like – is in their own best interests and rarely fatal. *Murphy's Romance* is unusual in avoiding both the
entrapments of melodrama and the 'magical' interventions which are
such a commonplace of the comedic. This is part of what I mean by the
'everydayness' of the film (its causality lacking any strongly marked
sense of intervention from an offscreen director or of a broader background context of restriction or disapproval). The Existentialist version
of freedom which the film seems to embrace – the sense that we
choose our destinies and our selves – is befitting to such a world of the
here and now.

Nonetheless, it is a twentieth-century platitude that we are not as
free as we think we are, and the legacy of Marx and Freud which has
flooded film theory on this issue has produced enormously influential
accounts not only of the blindness and ideological entrapment of
characters within certain kinds of films, but of the passivity and lack of
freedom of viewers in consuming mainstream narrative texts.

George Wilson describes what he calls 'this "prison house of movies"
thesis':

> It is often maintained, roughly, that the strategies, forms, and
> techniques of classical narrative cinema lock members of an audi-
> ence into an epistemic position that makes it impossible for them
> to criticize either their own habits of perception in film viewing or

the modes of perceptual intelligibility that the films themselves display. (Wilson 1988: 191)

In this context, it is striking that the scene where Murphy and Jake discuss Bobby Jack's cheating at cards occurs at precisely the point where Jake has followed Murphy out of the local cinema, both of them choosing not to sit through the exploitative horror film on offer. Their active refusal of the movie's vulgar manipulations – and they are joined by Emma moments later, though Bobby Jack remains inside – is a further indication of the alliance of *Murphy's Romance* to a vision of freedom which, in encompassing movie spectators within the film, may extend to its own audience as well.

This commitment not to patronise its viewers but to allow them a substantial degree of freedom in choosing what to look at and to take as significant is evident throughout *Murphy's Romance*. A good example of this occurs in the sequence of the barbecue at Emma's ranch which Bobby Jack has orchestrated and to which Emma, somewhat reluctantly, has agreed. We have already noted that Bobby Jack represents a morally debased version of freedom as unrestrained impulse, but because his impulses lack the dangerous edge of those in more melodramatic films, their hospitable and generous aspects – when he invites what seems like the whole town to Emma's ranch for a party – are salutary correctives to Emma's too puritanical adherence to an ethic of hard work and self-denial, and the film seems to extend its affection towards him on these grounds. Indeed, his explanation for the party – 'Life's short!' – is a variation on a motif which can be found in numerous comedic films: a sort of fleeting and light-hearted *memento mori* which suggests the film's awareness of a darker world outside its frame which in some way provides a justification for the festivities within. From this point in the film onward, the scenes of strenuous work and financial anxiety on Emma's part are increasingly replaced by those of relaxation and of the growing integration of Emma and Jake into the community through a series of convivial events (the barbecue, a dance in town, the surprise birthday party for Murphy).

After a few establishing shots of various outdoor activities, with Bobby Jack playing the congenial host amongst the guests, the barbecue sequence shifts indoors to Murphy and Emma washing up together in the kitchen of her house as the party carries on outside. Although they have placed themselves at one remove from the events around them, opening up a space of relative calm and intimacy within the larger space of the party, the connectedness of the two areas outweighs their separation. The kitchen is an airy space with a series of screen-doors and windows around the periphery of the room, giving us glimpses of running children and groups of people chatting outside, as Murphy and Emma talk, and letting in both the muted sounds of the party and a breeze which plays about in Emma's hair. At one point, as Emma stands at the kitchen sink washing up, while Murphy dries, Bobby Jack can be seen through the window with a young woman who had looked at him admiringly earlier on, though Bobby Jack is less than engrossed as he turns to look in Emma's direction (and later finds an excuse to come into the kitchen to see more clearly what's going on) instead of at the pretty – but not *too* pretty – blonde. It is a background detail, no more, which is in no way insisted upon by the rhetoric of the film, and the viewer can either notice it or not, concentrating as we are upon the pleasing way that Emma and Murphy have fallen into an easy domestic intimacy, their words circling around – but stopping short of acknowledging – their growing mutual interest and desire.

Thus, Emma takes an oblique approach to the subject of love and romance by asking Murphy what kind of husband he's been, suggesting that, having had one good marriage, he can have another, while he answers with equal circumspection that good marriages are rare, adding that he was surprised to find a woman in love with him. The conversation ends with Emma pulling back abruptly from discussing marriage in terms of affection by stating as evidence of Murphy's suitability as a husband, 'You're a big help in the kitchen', as Murphy looks at her, unsmiling, over the top of his coffee cup, reacting with evident dissatisfaction to her sudden change of direction, but saying nothing in response. Such tentative and indirect approaches and withdrawals are characteristic of their conversations throughout most of the film, as are the lingering shots of one or the other of them reacting with surprise, bemusement or dissatisfaction with which many of these sequences end.

Later on, in the final moments of the barbecue, Murphy again looks serious as he sits on the edge of the porch with Jake and Emma, listening to Bobby Jack as he sings and plays the guitar for the other guests a short distance away. It is a moment which sets Bobby Jack off at his most attractive and effortlessly seductive, the dust which blows around him producing a soft-focus effect, and it is suddenly easy for us – and Murphy – to imagine how Emma could have fallen for him in her youth. Emma, now anticipating and reacting to Murphy's possible feelings for her as well as her wish to express her feelings for him, though still unable to do so directly, leans towards him and comments softly, 'Sometimes it felt like I had two kids', thus finding a way to reassure Murphy, who smiles in response, while their mutual desires continue to remain unacknowledged.

Murphy's withholdings seem a deliberate strategy of biding his time (especially now that Bobby Jack is on the scene, clearly eager for a reconciliation with his former wife), though they suggest not so much reluctance on his part as a wish to give Emma enough time to make up her mind for herself. Emma, in contrast, as we've seen, appears to be trying to find a language to express her desires and get the romance underway without risking the embarrassment of having her declarations met with indifference or rejection on Murphy's part. As each waits for a sign of commitment from the other, the romance hits a stalemate which is only resolved in the final moments of the film. So *Murphy's Romance* is not so much about the vicissitudes of a romantic relationship whose problems are finally resolved as it is about the problem of kick-starting the romance into existence to begin with. Lacking the forthrightness of a Hawksian woman like Feathers (Angie Dickinson) in *Rio Bravo* (1959; 'I'm hard to get, John T. You're going to have to *say* you want me'), Emma can only fall back upon heavily coded expressions of her desire.

An earlier example of such circumlocutionary strategies is to be found in the scene where Murphy looks in on Emma in the hospital after she's been accidentally driven off the road by an uninsured teenager. A tearful Emma lists her problems to Murphy, ending up with her mournful declaration that 'I'm 33 years old, and I'm living like a nun'. Murphy's reply – 'You're thirty-three? That's seasoned, not sagging. You . . . uh . . . you're living like a nun? Next time you're asked, say yes' – completely misses the point. That this is a wilful misunderstanding of her fairly evident wish to say yes to *him*, and not just to anyone who asks, is amply confirmed by the consistency with which he refuses to solve her problems for her, from his turning her down for a loan, as noted earlier, to his response to her demands for advice in the film's penultimate scene: 'You want advice? Write Dear Abby. You got problems? Take 'em to your local minister. Your head isn't on straight? The mental health fund is in the phone book. I'm not a life guard, and I don't put up bail, and I'm not your damn Dutch uncle'. The fact that this impatient tirade is followed by his first unambiguous indication of his feelings for her, as he kisses her for the first time, confirms the sense that he is not so much resisting her as he is insisting upon the terms of the sort of relationship he wants: a relationship of equals.

This is particularly important in view of the age gap between them – Murphy's refusal to tell Emma his age until the very last scene constituting a running joke between them – since romantic relationships across a gap of almost thirty years are rarely the stuff of romantic comedy, figuring more commonly either as melodramatic relationships between powerful older men and naive, victimised women, or as comic (but not comedic) relationships between fond older men and the women who reject or exploit them. Of course, comedic romances between characters played by *actors* of very different ages – at least in the form of an older man and a younger woman – are common enough, but any narrative awareness of this gap tends to be somewhat uneasily suppressed, rather than dramatised as a thematic concern. In contrast, not only is Murphy's age a continuing theme, but the gap between Murphy's age and Emma's is exaggerated by a good nine years beyond the actual gap between James Garner's age and that of Sally Field. The point, however, is that the film refuses to use Murphy's age to set the relationship up in terms of Emma's dependence upon him and his dominance over her, but, rather, his more advanced age is seen to give him the opportunity to slow down and appreciate life. Thus, when Emma asks him, 'Don't you ever work?', he replies, 'I'm getting other interests at this time of life', though he admits that he needs something more – 'Like loving somebody?', in Emma's words – to put the heart back in things. He presents himself to Emma not only as a romantic lover, but as a safe and dependable friend who appreciates her strengths, and his eventual declaration of 'how things are', in the final scene, is couched in these terms where, at last, he helps Emma to find the right words:

EMMA: Are we talking about the *weather*?
MURPHY: *You* are.

EMMA: That's not what I wanna talk about.
MURPHY: Take another tack, Emma.
EMMA: I don't know what tack to take.
MURPHY: I'll help you. Separate the men from the boys, Emma. I show some wear, I don't deny it. If the fruit hangs on the tree long enough, it gets ripe. I'm durable, I'm steady, I'm faithful. And I'm in love for the last time in my life.
EMMA: I'm in love for the first time in my life.

At last the film can draw to a close and the romance proper can begin.

This process of finding the right words – that is, of articulating a shared understanding of the right sort of basis for their relationship – has been an ongoing theme, but only now are its terms explicit. Earlier, their feelings found expression by following a more indirect route, not only in roundabout discussions of their past marriages and present lives, but through reconstruing offers of sex and affection as offers of hospitality and food, especially on Emma's part. This is most humorously developed in the sequence of invitations she extends to Murphy to join her, Bobby Jack and Jake for supper each time he comes out to the ranch to ride his horse, the various occasions linked by dissolves.

The sequence begins with Emma asking Murphy if he can help fix the stopped-up toilet which Bobby Jack has broken, Emma explaining Bobby Jack's continuing presence in the house to Murphy while he works: 'He's out of a job. That's why he's here.' When Murphy comments that he remembers how people would come to the door during the Depression and his mother would feed them all, Emma replies with a raised eyebrow and an expression of mock defiance: 'That's all I'm doing'. So, in the case of Bobby Jack, offering him food is simply offering him food, but in the case of Murphy himself, Emma's invitations express a desire for much more. This promise is delivered at the end of the film when the couple finally know how things stand between them and Emma, once more, invites Murphy to stay for supper.

MURPHY: I won't do that unless I'm still here at breakfast.
EMMA: How do you like your eggs?

Here, the meaning of her offer of breakfast is clear, just as was Murphy's reply, much earlier in the film when she had asked about his sex life, and he had told her about a lady in Phoenix whom he visited from time to time and who would give him dinner and breakfast (and, by implication, everything in between).

The sexual implications – whether in the form of a present fact or a future likelihood – of Emma feeding Murphy are also acknowledged in the comments his friend Margaret makes to Emma in the restroom at the bingo hall, Margaret observing that Murphy seems to have put on weight and that Emma must be a good cook. When Emma responds that her cooking wouldn't win any contests, Margaret continues, 'Well, he probably just comes up to your place for the company. He sure seems cheered up.' On the occasion of the surprise birthday party for Murphy which Emma and Margaret plan together later on, Murphy too expresses his awareness of what Emma has provided – 'You know, Emma, this has become sort of a second home to me. You've kept me fed and warm. I want to thank you for it.' – and Emma responds, again with only an indirect indication of her own desires, by suggesting he get married.

Just as Murphy seeks warmth and food in Emma's company, so too does Emma seek something similar from *him* on the occasions when she turns up at Murphy's drugstore and asks him to fix her something to eat or drink, from a lemon Coke at the beginning of the film to a chocolate soda near the end, the progression from lemon to chocolate suggestive of the richer and more self-indulgent pleasures she is increasingly prepared to allow herself as the film goes on. It is clear not only that she too seeks his company as much as his food ('Make me something, Murphy. Talk to me.'), but that the two forms of sustenance and comfort are closely linked. Hunger and food are not displaced representations of repressed desires, mere metaphors for sexual hunger and its satisfaction, as in so many other movies, but are experienced and offered – at least implicitly – as part of the same package. Both sexual pleasure *and* shared domesticity are interconnected aspects of what Murphy and Emma seem to want to offer and to receive from one another, rather than desire and domesticity being at odds, as is so frequently the case in other films.

Despite the growing domestic ease and intimacy between Murphy and Emma as the film proceeds, none of their meetings takes place in a completely private place. We have already seen how the washing-up scene at the barbecue takes place in a portion of the larger space which is both continuous with it and yet whose privacy – except for Bobby Jack's brief incursions – is respected by the community around them. Similarly, their other conversations often take place in a public or social setting: the drugstore, a bench in the middle of town, the horse auction, a hospital room, the kitchen of Emma's house with Jake and Bobby Jack or the birthday party guests in the next room – rather than while alone in Emma's house or behind closed doors. Their first hug takes place in the bingo hall when Emma wins two hundred dollars, and their first kiss in Murphy's drugstore during working hours. The possibility is always there that they will be interrupted or overheard, and yet neither of these things ever seems to occur. The overall effect is to embed their romance within a community which, while wishing them well, is never intrusive nor judgemental.

Even during the period when Bobby Jack is living at Emma's ranch and Murphy is a frequent guest, public speculation about the situation is benign. As Murphy puts it when Emma asks what the ladies in town are saying, 'They do like something to chew on . . . They think . . . uh . . . three's a real interesting number.' If the gossip is motivated by curiosity rather than by malice, so too are the film's rivalries good-natured rather than antagonistic, and they are easily defused. Margaret's remark to Emma about her having taken Murphy out of circulation, a comment which might at first seem to be a preamble to jealous insinuations and underminings of Emma's position, proves to be nothing of the kind, and when we next see Margaret, it is at Emma's house during the surprise birthday party for Murphy which they have concocted together. Not only have Margaret and Emma joined forces, but we learn from Murphy's thank-you speech at the party that he has known Margaret since they were children, and that he had kissed her long before they both went on to marry other people. So their relationship is that of lifelong friends, and it is unlikely that this will change now that Emma is on the scene, except to broaden, as has already begun to happen, to include Emma within the friendship as well, if not to include Margaret within the romance.

More unexpectedly, perhaps, during the scene where Murphy and Bobby Jack keep cutting in on each other as they take it in turns to dance with Emma, and she tells them with exasperated impatience to dance with each other, Bobby Jack takes us by surprise by holding out his arms in invitation to Murphy:

BOBBY JACK: Care to?
MURPHY: I'll lead. Watch your toes.

The prevailing spirit of benevolence extends to Bobby Jack in the film's final moments as well. Rather than being left adrift as Murphy and Emma pair off, he is providentially supplied with a (potential) wife and children when a casual girlfriend turns up with their twin boys and they all leave together to settle down into their own version of domesticity. That Bobby Jack does not experience this as unalloyed good fortune is certainly true, but we are encouraged by the atmosphere of good will to anticipate that he will somehow grow into his new responsibilities and that they are not altogether a bad thing: 'Well, at least he likes kids', Emma muses hopefully, and the film encourages us to share her guarded optimism.

What makes *Murphy's Romance* a romantic comedy, in my terms, should by now be apparent. The mutuality of the central romantic relationship between Emma and Murphy (their mutual respect and the shared appropriation of traditionally gendered roles like breadwinning, on the one hand, and the provision of food and domestic comfort, on the other, as well as a self-evident mutuality of sexual desire) contributes to our sense of a romance worth waiting for, as its conditions and terms are gradually and tentatively spelled out. Equally, the tolerant benevolence of the community which shelters them in its midst gives a ready comedic welcome not only to the film's romantic couple, but to those on the sidelines of the main narrative events. In producing this sense of an integrated and emotionally bountiful narrative world which is so central to its project, the film nonetheless maintains its distinctiveness from many other romantic comedies in one key respect: as indicated earlier, it refuses the 'magical' qualities of so many comedic films whose resolutions seem to come from elsewhere than the characters themselves. Such a sense of external causality may manifest itself either in the form of social determinants or serendipitous interventions on the part of a director, whether as magic, coincidence or implausible good fortune, and generally involves a fairly blatant acknowledgement that what we are watching is only, after all, a movie, its characters mere puppets in someone else's scheme.

Here, in contrast, the characters seem to be in charge of their own destinies and of the consequences which follow on from their behaviour,

and our sense that Ritt, as director, is pulling the strings is more suppressed. Thus, the ready-made family who appear for Bobby Jack
towards the end of the film are not produced like rabbits out of hats (as
with the twins who resolve a much earlier romantic comedy, Preston
Sturges' *The Palm Beach Story of 1942*), but are a predictable result of
his errant and irresponsible relationships with women, a clear case of
a past of his own making catching up with him at last. Similarly, Emma
and Murphy themselves have to choose each other – and to find the
words to do so explicitly in the process – rather than waiting passively
to be chosen or to be thrown together by destiny or chance. This is a
film which, in taking feminism on board, is clear-sighted enough to
realise that, in Simone de Beauvoir's words, 'What woman needs first
of all is to undertake . . . her apprenticeship in abandonment and transcendence: that is, in liberty' (1961: 670). In its insistence on a model of
freedom based upon individual moral responsibility for both women
and men, the narrative world of *Murphy's Romance* is simultaneously
optimistic and grown-up.

WORKS CITED

Beauvoir, Simone de 1961. *The Second Sex*. New York: Bantam Books
Cavell, Stanley 1981. *Pursuits of Happiness: The Hollywood Comedy of Remarriage*.
    Cambridge, MA: Harvard UP
Wilson, George M. 1988. *Narration in Light: Studies in Cinematic Point of View*.
    Baltimore: Johns Hopkins UP
Wood, Robin 1981. *Howard Hawks*. Revised edn. London: British Film Institute

Chapter 5

SOMETHING WILD:
TAKE A WALK ON THE WILD SIDE
(BUT BE HOME BEFORE MIDNIGHT)

Constanza del Río

Something Wild: *Trapped between two sources of anxiety, Charlie (Jeff Daniels)
momentarily settles for the male bond, while Lulu (Melanie Griffith)
looks on powerless*

There is a moment in Jonathan Demme's film *Something Wild* (1986)
when Charlie (Jeff Daniels), after being beaten by Ray (Ray Liotta) and
having lost his girl – Lulu (Melanie Griffith) – returns to the High
School Reunion locale to collect his car. He finds the scene deserted,
and the banner formerly announcing the '76 Reunion, 'The Spirit of '76

75

Revisited', appears partially unhooked so that only the word 'Revisited' can be read. What is it, then, that this film revisits? Fredric Jameson (1989) has seen *Something Wild* as a historical rethinking of American culture in generational terms, as a nostalgia film portraying an allegorical encounter between the oppositional 1950s (Ray) and the conformist 1980s (Charlie) via the countercultural 1960s (Lulu). My intention is to explore the generational and love triangle the three protagonists engage in, a triangle narratively framed and coded by the conventions of classical screwball comedy of the late 1930s and early 1940s. I will focus mainly on the interaction between the apparently progressive aspects of *Something Wild*'s cultural, ethnic and social politics and its gender politics by analysing the two romantic leads' trajectory, trying to demonstrate that the changes undergone by Lulu and Charlie, which seem necessary for their final reunion, respond to different strategies, and that Lulu's metamorphosis into Audrey is not sufficiently moti-vated and argued by the text, so that the ambivalence in the narrative's treatment of the heroine works to undermine its social and cultural revisionings.

Maurizio Viano (1987: 12) has remarked that *Something Wild* seems to respond to a tension between an 'urban population uneasily strad-dling the dropout ideal of the sixties and the join-the-rat-race spirit of the eighties'. To a certain extent, the film attempts to explore the ways in which the liberal and liberating social, ideological and political agendas of the 1960s can be incorporated into the 1980s. This project is complicated through Ray, a character that, as Jameson (1989: 531) has remarked, encapsulates the genuine rebellion, genuine violence and genuine consequences of the oppositional 1950s as well as the romantic representations of such rebellion. The appearance of Ray provokes a dramatic generic shift in the film, which veers from comedy to melo-dramatic thriller, and takes the spectators away from the zany world of screwball into a Hitchcockian paranoid fantasy.[1] *Something Wild*'s generic hybridity attests to its status as postmodern cultural product and also to contemporary difficulties and obstacles for the creation of the heterosexual couple, a point commented on by most recent theo-rists on contemporary romantic comedy.[2]

The irruption of violence and destruction in the film's narrative threatens its humanistic project and the final reunion of the couple, but the existence of this obstacle represents a menace that *Something Wild* consciously acknowledges as a contemporary possibility, as the price that has to be paid for historical patriarchal violence and social exploitation. What seems more questionable is the film's interest in channelling social and cultural contemporary issues through a romantic love-story highly indebted to classical Hollywood screwball comedy of the late 1930s and early 1940s.

As explained by Tina Olsin Lent (1995: 319), classical screwball comedy attempted to redefine gender relations by supporting a more egalitarian relationship between men and women. Yet it also supported the ideology of domesticity by transforming the desirable heterosexual marriage into a utopian space of resolution of social, economic and gender tensions and conflicts. For Steve Neale and Frank Krutnik (1990: 154–5), what was at stake in the 1930s' romantic comedies was the reaffirmation of male authority at a time when patriarchy felt endangered by economically and socially independent women.[3] The 1980s and early 1990s have seen a revival of the genre which responds to the increasing problematisation of marriage and gender relations – the aftermath of the 1960s' 'sexual revolution' – and to the feeling that patriarchy is declining.[4] In this sense, the prosperity of the genre intensifies the desire 'to return to heterosexual romance in the contemporary era of sexual revisionism' (Neale and Krutnik 1990: 172). Krutnik has elsewhere historicised the genre, investigating the ways in which romantic comedy has adapted its conventions and narrative formulas to changing socio-cultural discourses and circumstances, but he has also stressed that the genre is 'concerned with the normative and permissible forms of heterosexual union in specific conjunctures', that it 'has a firmly ingrained conservatism' and always 'pushes forward and seeks to relegitimize a *sanctioned* heterosexual union – marriage' (1990: 62).[5] The romantic comedies produced in the 1980s and after, among them *Something Wild*, have been termed 'new romances' by Neale (1992: 287), who again asserts the cycle's commitment to old-fashioned values of traditional heterosexual romance. What I intend to investigate in the following pages is precisely the way in which Demme's film revisits and revises classical screwball comedy, and the way in which the conservative pull of romantic comedy affects the otherwise progressive agenda of the film. The discussion will be centred on Lulu/Audrey and Charlie's trajectory, on the sentimental education that they both undergo so that their final union is – however self-consciously – realised.

In Jeff Evans's view (1996: 12), the development of the narrative and its culmination in Lulu/Audrey and Charlie's final meeting seem to indicate that both characters have changed. For him, the ending of the narrative suggests 'the leads' similarities in dress, demeanor, and presumably, destination, and purpose as they drive off together', and works to put forward a gender politics based on individuality, compromise and mutual respect. Yet I will argue that the treatment given to the two protagonists' trajectory differs greatly and appears quite unbalanced. At the end, and in spite of the fact that the whole narrative is self-consciously put into question or bracketed, a point I will return to later on, one feels that Charlie has indeed gained valuable knowledge but that Lulu/Audrey has undoubtedly lost equally valuable qualities, and the necessity for her loss seems quite elusive.

Something Wild is centred on Charlie's maturation, reflecting a current cultural preoccupation with the redefinition and relocation of masculinity, a necessary step after the redefinition and relocation of femininity brought about by the second wave of feminism.[6] As Bruce Babington and Peter William Evans (1989: 280) have argued, the central issue of contemporary romantic comedy might be said to be the enigma of masculinity rather than the enigma of femininity. Jonathan Demme himself (in Smith 1991: 34) has stated that *Something Wild* deals with Charlie's awakening, 'a total shades-down bonehead', whom Lulu takes for a wild ride that opens his eyes 'to the life out there'.

The first half of the narrative falls within the world of screwball. Charlie is the conventional white male, a yuppie stock analyst who carries an umbrella on a sunny summer day – just in case – owns an estate car and a suburban house, is a little too self-satisfied about his impending job promotion, and leads an utterly predictable and boring life.[7] He is self-conscious about his own body and displays a comic stiffness and awkwardness that makes him prone to pratfalls, following the example of illustrious predecessors, such as David (Cary Grant) in *Bringing up Baby* (1938) or Charles Pike (Henry Fonda) in *The Lady Eve* (1941). Demme's choice of Jeff Daniels for the male lead in *Something Wild* encodes the Charlie character as malleable. Clean-shaven and placid-looking, Jeff Daniels projects an image of masculinity that Demme would later use in the male lead of *Married to the Mob* (1988), Matthew Modine. Demme's preference for sensitive and vulnerable male characters expresses his conviction that the feminine inhabits the masculine and *vice versa* (Smith 1991: 30), and it can also be inscribed in a more generalised cultural need to provide kinder and gentler – 'feminised' – forms of masculinity, forms that depart from a patriarchal paradigm no longer suited to the demands of the liberated woman – the patriarchal masculine myth, based on rationality, strength, mastery and control, theorised by Anthony Easthope (1986).

Charlie's potential for redemption, for rescue from dullness, self-centredness and conformity is signalled in the first scene at the café. His life may be pathetically boring and he may be a stodgy yuppie, but he is not free from the occasional misdemeanour: he enjoys sneaking out of bars and restaurants without paying his bill. Charlie's petty gesture of rebellion immediately attracts Lulu's attention, who realises that Charlie's weakness may offer the possibility of fun. As Lulu ironically says, he is a 'closet rebel', a loaded remark covertly introducing the possibility of homosexual desire in Charlie. In the café scene, Lulu takes the narrative lead by initiating the look and by following Charlie out of the bar, hailing him while she impersonates the offended bar waitress claiming payment. After delighting in Charlie's embarrassment and confusion, she offers him a lift and he obeys her. He seems to be taken aback and intrigued, for Lulu is full of promise: adventure, excitement and sex. Lulu kidnaps Charlie and soon starts to make sexual overtures to him. Their crazy and dangerous ride – Lulu drives drunk – ends in a motel in New Jersey, where Charlie learns a very instructive lesson in kinky sex.

Up to this point, Lulu and Charlie's relationship is not yet a pure romantic attachment, and one of the purposes of the film will be precisely to transform it – and tame it – into such a bond. In these first stages, their involvement is mainly characterised by sexual ardour and urgency – 'Loco de Amor' is the song that opens the film. On the other hand, Lulu and Charlie's first encounter seems also to be 'love at first sight', an encounter in which both seem intuitively to grasp qualities in the other that they lack, so that each can complement the other in a narcissistic relationship that combines freedom and self-realisation, which is one of the particularities of romantic love (Giddens 1992: 40). Lulu and Charlie's attachment could have remained a merely sexual encounter if Charlie had not decided to cut loose and go to Pennsylvania with her. His decision introduces the possibility of romance, or, as Giddens says (1992: 39), the telling of an individualised story which inserts 'self and other into a personal narrative' oriented towards the future. But, what is it that leads Charlie to make such a decision? He probably sees that his extreme conventionality can interact with, and be healed by, Lulu's unruliness. As for Lulu, her motives are not so clear in my opinion.

As in other romantic comedies, among them *Ball of Fire* (1942), *The Lady Eve*, *Housesitter* (1992), *Into the Night* (1985), *Green Card* (1990) or *Pretty Woman* (1990), in *Something Wild* social conflict is channelled through the romantic love-story and is encapsulated in the heroine's unruliness (Rowe 1995: 118). What is interesting in Demme's film is that the 'difference' inscribed in the Lulu character through clothes, behaviour and music is an index, not so much of social difference, but rather of cultural and ethnic diversity. Furthermore, difference is not circumscribed to her persona, but spills over into the rest of a narrative that makes a point of repeatedly calling attention to the presence of such difference in US society. The film encodes two ways of approaching American society and culture: the 1980s' homogeneity of urban white middle-class Charlie and the 1960s' diversity of marginal provincial white – but Africanised – Lulu. Both ways, however, will be threatened by the oppositional 1950s, by the bitterness and anger embodied in Ray.

The Lulu character is a truly 'unruly woman' as described by Rowe (1995), and she most resembles the heroines of *Bringing up Baby*, *Ball of Fire* and *The Lady Eve* in her impulsiveness, spontaneity, zest for life, energetic force and ability to turn a straight white middle-class man's life upside down. Her sexuality, nevertheless, is not as virginal as Ellie's (Claudette Colbert) in *It Happened One Night* (1934), Sylvia's (Katharine Hepburn) in *Sylvia Scarlett* (1936) or Susan's (Katharine Hepburn) in *Bringing up Baby*. Lulu is a thoroughly sexualised female whose sexuality is bluntly expressed and coded in terms of the 1960s' liberated and available woman. After all, there is little of the androgynous in Melanie Griffith's body, so that the Lulu character combines features of the voluptuousness of Mae West, the allure of Barbara Stanwyck and the vulnerability of Katharine Hepburn, especially as the victimised Audrey of the second part. She is deliberately provocative and offensive when she declares that she likes big things between her legs or when she claims to be pregnant in front of Charlie's workmate, Larry, and his wife Peggy. She is excessive in looks, and her fetishised African-American 'satanic' jewellery, black dress and behind keep Charlie in a trance, 'fixation or no fixation', as Susan (Katharine Hepburn) would say. Her behaviour is anarchic, yet markedly different from Ray's lawlessness. The spectator does not indeed see her as a criminal, and this is one of the reasons why her domestication seems unnecessary. She can show little respect for private property or drive people crazy but her transgressions belong in a carnivalesque, playful and comic space, and whatever dangers she may pose to Charlie's integrity are gradually diluted by the narrative itself to be replaced by the threats embodied in Ray. Yet, for the first part of *Something Wild*, Lulu is the woman on top, the female who makes patriarchal gender roles capsize and dominates the male sexually and narratively, for it is her inventions and fantasies that keep the narrative moving until the High School Reunion takes place.

Lulu is drawn towards Charlie precisely because she thinks he is a predictable and orderly type: married with children and carrying the family photographs in his wallet. His conformity and acceptance of mainstream values can balance Lulu's excessive tendencies. It could also be that for Lulu his married status represents a protection against more serious and long-lasting emotional involvement. Yet Lulu and Charlie's fake marriage is her fantasy, a female fantasy betraying her dream of a gentle and sharing husband getting the kids' room ready and a suburban house with garden and estate car at the door. When she learns that Charlie is separated from his wife, her resentment does not so much stem from his lies – she has also lied to him – as from the fact that her fantasy has crumbled. If Charlie does not have a supporting wife and kids awaiting his return, he may not own an estate car or a suburban house either. In some way, the film seems to be reluctant overtly to contain Lulu's excesses in marriage or coupledom, since *Something Wild*, as has been argued above, claims a certain progressiveness. Yet it also introduces the idea of marriage, or life together, as Lulu's desire in the first place, a desire fulfilled through a story of romantic love in which both partners are compelled to abandon their extreme positions.

For his part, what Charlie undergoes from the moment he meets Lulu is a comic process of male divestment whereby he is gradually stripped of the external signs of his conformist and deficient phallic masculinity: umbrella, newspaper, business telepager, wallet and clothes. He subjects himself willingly to Lulu's invigorating treatment, following and imitating her as a child does his/her mother. In this, again following screwball conventions, Charlie is masochistically attached to Lulu. Kathleen Rowe (1995: 155) has argued that the relationship between the unruly woman and the male hero in comedies of gender inversion is informed by masochism. Rowe bases her arguments on Gaylyn Studlar's (1988) conceptualisation of masochism, who has grounded her theories in Deleuze's masochistic aesthetics, and not in Freud's view of this perversion as originating in Oedipal conflict and as complementary to sadism. For Deleuze (Studlar 1988: 9–28), masochism is not just a clinical perversion, but a ritualised way of perceiving and relating to different experiences. That is, it is an aesthetics whose origin has nothing to do with the Oedipal father but is located in the pre-Oedipal oral stage, in the child's perception of the mother as an all-powerful figure, lacking in nothing and representing plenitude. In Deleuze's terms, masochism amounts to a disavowal of phallic power and to the rejection of the father, the latter being replaced by a mother who is powerful in her own right – and not in relation to the phallus – and to whom the masochist submits in a nonphallic sexual relation. The masochist's desire is for total merging with the mother's body and that is a merging that can only be realised in the masochist's death, an 'unhappy ending' whose prospect provokes both pleasure and fear. That is why masochism is ambivalent (Rowe, 1995: 155) and masochistic male heroes are repeatedly drawn towards and repelled by their objects of desire, enacting the attraction and anxiety that the unruly woman embodies.

I do not claim that masochism is fully explored and pursued to its ultimate consequences in *Something Wild*, yet it is true that a popular and vulgarised form of masochistic behaviour and iconography is inscribed in this film: Charlie's initial submission and consent to Lulu's dictates – even if they imply an assault on his masculinity – Lulu's black underwear, her use of handcuffs for 'imaginative' sex and the 'sweet' torture she inflicts on Charlie, turning him on while simultaneously forcing him to concoct an excuse for his absence at work. In this sense, the first part of the narrative deals with Charlie's fantasy of his encounter with Lulu, the all-powerful mother whom he is unable to figure as a girl: 'I can't imagine you growing up', he says. This is also an encounter with his own femininity which amounts to Charlie's coming to terms with gender, social, ethnic and cultural difference.

What happens frequently in romantic comedies attempting to portray a relationship based on equality between the sexes is that the subversive, nonphallic sexuality of masochism has to be abandoned and the divested romantic hero, once familiarised with the feminine, has to be empowered. His masculinity has to be restored to him if both romantic leads are to meet on equal footing. There are cases, though, such as *Bringing up Baby*, *The Lady Eve*, *I Was a Male War Bride* (1949) or *Monkey Business* (1952), in which masochistic male attachment and humiliation are sustained and envisaged as a valid structure for the couple's future relationship. In Demme's film, Charlie will be empowered but his empowerment will not be Lulu's responsibility and will be, at least narratively, effected at her expense.

The initial masochistic structure starts to change when, after an elliptical but presumably second 'wild' session of sex and alcohol in a Pennsylvanian motel, Charlie manages to impose his authority on Lulu and persuades her out of drinking a 'morning cap' and into trying an anti-hangover remedy instead. The process goes on with Lulu's gradual stripping away of the external markers of her power and unruliness, and also of her difference: jewellery, black dress, dark wig and name. She becomes Audrey, the blonde, sweet, next-door-girl wearing a shoulder-strapped white dress, a most dramatic change that seems to please Charlie. Once the carriers of danger and threat have disappeared, Charlie and Audrey can come closer to each other and pretend that their relationship is one of conventional domestic and romantic bliss. Although Peaches, Audrey's mother, is the excuse that Audrey provides for their fake marriage, the truth is that Peaches is at no point deceived, and as has been argued above, marriage appears as Lulu/Audrey's fantasy, which she is now given the opportunity to enact maybe in an attempt to see what it feels like and to rehearse their future relationship. The High School Reunion marks the turning point in the film's narrative. Just when Audrey and Charlie's romantic involvement seems to have triumphed, as they embrace and kiss while dancing slowly, the film temporarily shatters the promise of their future happiness with Ray's perverse plot: 'Hi baby, surprise'. He now takes the narrative lead, making the story drift from romantic screwball into melodramatic thriller, while reproducing a similar pattern to the one followed by Lulu in the first part. He assaults a drugstore and kidnaps the couple, driving them south into Virginia, thus thwarting the circular plot that ensures the couple's final reunion in other comedies. In *Bringing up Baby*, both Baby and the wild leopard are extensions of Susan's unruliness, respectively indicating fun and threat (Rowe 1995: 153). Likewise, Ray Sinclair embodies the dangers to be met if one engages in genuinely asocial and anarchic behaviour, dangers which the transgressive Lulu, and by extension her disciple Charlie, introduce in the narrative in the first place. *Something Wild* seems to be saying that there is a frontier that should not be crossed, the frontier between wildness as pre-Oedipal fun and wildness as asocial, and thus pre-Oedipal, aggressiveness directed against others, between Charlie's face smeared with lipstick or with blood, between consent and brute force. This is a line that Lulu – probably through previous involvement with Ray – seems to be able to draw, yet Charlie will have to learn to picture it through a painful ordeal of violence. But I would argue that this frontier is far more easily imagined symbolically than perceived in real terms, since frequently violence and laughter or fun appear together, as when, for example, spectators cheer the death of a bad guy – Robert de Niro as evil incarnate in *Cape Fear* (1991) or Ray Liotta in *Unlawful Entry* (1992) – or when violence is so exaggerated that it makes us laugh, however hysterically – the orgy of blood, bites and torn limbs in Robert Rodriguez's *From Night to Dawn* (1996).

Like Lulu/Audrey, the Ray character is loaded with meanings. He personifies aggressive masculinity, a violent and untrammelled pre-Oedipal father, a primal father whose return has been imagined by Laura Mulvey (1989: 199) as haunting 'relations between men, generating homophobic anxieties and an attraction bonded by physical violence'. Both Lulu as the all-powerful mother and Ray as the violent primal father can be seen as Charlie's sexual fantasies, and also as the way in which the narrative historicises the masculine 1950s and the feminine 1960s as pre-Oedipal spaces and times of, respectively, aggression and fun. However, Ray's extreme anger and violence are not presented as the consequence of individual development but rather as the product of his socio-cultural circumstances, for example, during the 'confession scene' at Ray's place – when Audrey learns that Charlie is separated and Charlie learns that Audrey is not divorced the film insists on Ray's marginal status by unexpectedly cutting out to show the squalor in which he lives. His anger is socially justified to some extent, and he addresses it towards Charlie, whose 'damned TV show' image he shoots at the drugstore, for it probably reminds him of what he could have been if he had been given a chance. In this sense, Ray is also a product of American society, of disillusionment with and failure of revolutionary hopes. As Jeff Evans (1996: 11 and 12) has stated, Ray dramatises the 'politics of underclass anger' and 'shows Charlie the real-life consequences of Charlie's moonwalk on the wild side'.

Fredric Jameson (1989: 531) has linked the Ray character with the romantic rebel heroes – Brando and James Dean – of the 1950s. In fact, Ray's iconography combines features of the cowboy 'desperado' and the 1950s' rebel: cowboy boots, tattooed arm, cowboy leather black jacket, animal aggressiveness and sexuality. In the film, he is associated with hard-edged rock 'n' roll and night shooting (Evans 1996: 6). He is also linked to the 1950s through the gang of bikers who appear twice in the second part of the narrative, although these are given a placid, unthreatening aura that contrasts with the stereotype and with Ray. As Juan A. Suárez (1996: 151) has explained, bikers emerged as a manifestation of post-war youth discontent and angst, as a form of 'oppositional youth style, often allied to violence and deliquency'. Their sub-culture was glamorised in the 1950s' youth picture, with titles such as *The Wild One* (1954), *The Blackboard Jungle* (1955) and *Rebel without a Cause* (1955). Tough bikers' iconography was then appropriated by gay culture, an appropriation that still persists today (Suárez 155–6). In *Something Wild*, a film which makes a point of portraying social, cultural, ethnic and gender difference, homosexuality seems to have been conspicuously suppressed. Yet I would say that it emerges in the second part of the film, encoded in the Ray character, a figure that, as well as pre-Oedipal violence, signifies the final obstacle that Charlie has to confront if his heterosexual romance is to succeed: Charlie's fear of homosexuality.

For Constance Penley and Sharon Willis (1993: viii), straight white masculinity is frequently trapped between two sources of anxiety: women and homosexuality. Similarly, Anthony Easthope (1986: 6) has argued that contemporary masculinity 'is defined mainly in the way an individual deals with his femininity and his desire for other men'. The

double plot of *Something Wild* seems to illustrate Charlie's double effort
to define his masculine identity. The different way in which his two
endeavours are coded – comedy and thriller – suggests in some way
that the threat posed by the sexually liberated woman is more easily
assimilated and coped with, while Ray and homosexuality are no
laughing matters.

Through the concept of 'male homosocial desire', Eve K. Sedgwick
(1985) has hypothesised the existence of a continuum between social
relationships among men, which may be characterised by homophobia
and fear of homosexuality, and homosexual desire. Her aim is to
demonstrate that homophobia and homosexuality are historical constructions, intensely concerned with each other yet maintaining a
shifting relation of meaning. In Demme's film, Charlie and Ray's relationship is initially one of male bonding, but connotations of sexual
desire are slowly introduced, thus backing the potential existence of a
continuum between the homosocial and the homosexual. From the
moment Ray appears in the film, Lulu/Audrey's narrative and visual
relevance starts to die down and her transgressiveness and power are
transferred to Ray. As Ray tells Charlie, 'It looks like it's you and me,
pal'. Audrey is fully aware of the dangers implicit in Ray, and tries to
talk Charlie out of getting involved with him, but Charlie now ignores
her and follows Ray in the same way as he followed Lulu in the first
part. Charlie and Ray's initial bonding – before Charlie is confronted
with Ray's violence at the drugstore – follows typical forms of male
exchange centred on Audrey as the object of such exchange. Ray jokes
about Audrey's sexual prowess at school and Charlie takes Ray's
banter as a compliment to his own virility, but soon banter gives way
to obscenity when Ray, leaning towards Charlie, insists on knowing
what Audrey is like in bed. He surely knows what she is like, since he
has been married to her, so what he really wants to know is what
Charlie and Audrey are like together. When the conversation gets too
hot, Charlie reacts in a gentlemanly way, refusing to discuss such
improper matters. This last part of the scene in the car is rendered in
shot/reverse shot close-ups of Ray and Charlie's faces, a cinematic
device that has previously been used in Charlie and Lulu's 'love at first
sight' encounter outside the café.[8] Initially, male bonding, centred upon
the exclusion of Lulu, seems to draw Charlie towards Ray, but a current
of homosexual desire that shuts the woman out as well starts to flow

between them. Whether homosocial or homosexual, Charlie and Ray's mutual involvement bears similar consequences for Lulu: she is left out. Male bonding combines with erotic desire, violence and homophobia in Ray and Charlie's final fight, when both are facing each other in the bathroom and their disbelieving and horrified faces are dramatically sustained in extreme close-ups.

Jonathan Demme (Smith 1991: 36) has stated in interview that in *Something Wild* he wanted to convey how terrible violence is. In the film, Charlie's conviction that he can win Audrey back without confronting Ray directly is finally undermined, while Ray's certainty that Charlie will have to fight for her is proved right. The scene at Charlie's Stony Brook house is brutal indeed but it also appears inevitable. This scene is very ambivalent, since Charlie and Ray's struggle is at the same time repellent and compelling. It represents an intensely dramatic and symbolic moment – it could be said that this scene *is* the ending of the film – even charged with tragic beauty when Ray, shocked and incredulous, looks at himself in the mirror and combs his hair with his blood-tainted hand. His death symbolises the death of a pre-Oedipal victimiser, a victimiser of both women and men, and Charlie's rejection of aggressive masculinity and of the primal father's dangerous homosexual seductions. Yet it also symbolises Charlie's empowerment through confrontation with historical patriarchal violence and social disaffection, and his assimilation or acceptance of his own complicity in and responsibility for such violence and disaffection. When Audrey asks him 'What are you going to do now that you know how the other half lives . . . The other half of you?', Charlie's other half is both Audrey and Ray, the female oppressed and the male underclass oppressor, both victims and products of a sexist and classist system whose mechanisms Charlie has so far ignored.

However, in terms of gender politics, Charlie's empowerment can be questioned, since it involves Lulu's transformation into Audrey and her subsequent loss of power. It would appear that Lulu has just been an instrument to allow the making of a new identity for Charlie. His learning process has been depicted as a gradual development in which the climax comes when he faces social and psychical violence, assimilating its consequences. The accumulation of his experiences with Lulu and with Ray transforms him into a different man, aware of difference and not so willing to accept mainstream values. He learns to look around, quits his job, shifts to more casual and relaxed wear, pays his bills and is ready to meet Lulu/Audrey again. For Lulu/Audrey, on the other hand, there seems to be no such process to justify her transformation. The fact that she changes is mainly coded as a change of style and looks, a usual device in screwball applied to both Lulu and Charlie in *Something Wild*. Yet the narrative grounds Charlie's metamorphosis and new identity on a more solid basis as well, while Lulu/Audrey's new-self is shallow and evanescent. In this, the Lulu character seems to be a carrier of postmodern identity, an identity constructed and defined by image and style, and marked by shallowness, instability and performance.

The night culture of violence and aggresion that so shocks Charlie is nevertheless not something new for Lulu/Audrey. It is true, as Celestino Deleyto (1994: 350) has remarked, that for the second part of the film, Lulu stops being the comic unruly woman and becomes a helpless victim of male aggression, a melodramatic heroine who is finally rescued by the male hero. However, it can be assumed that Lulu was already familiar with victimisation because of her previous emotional involvement with Ray. So, what is it that makes her relinquish her power, and when does her readiness to compromise become evident? Although I still consider that her trajectory is not as motivated and justified as Charlie's and that her new identity remains to be defined in a less ambiguous way, it is clear that Lulu's visit to her mother and family home prompts her decision to change. In this sense, her transformation is linked to affection and family life, betraying a desire informed by nostalgia for the past. In the last instance, the force that changes her is that of romantic love, a force that seeks to tame her into 'an "old-fashioned", "traditional" and ideologically conventional position' (Neale, 1992: 297).

The conventional and old-fashioned values that Neale (1992) attributes to 'new romances' are self-consciously displayed at the end of the film, first in Audrey's new disguise – elegant spotted outfit, wide-brim white hat, gloves and handbag – and then in the wooden-pannelled estate car. Both elements, on the other hand, allude to the world of classical screwball, in particular to *Bringing up Baby* and its refusal to abide by patriarchal standards. In this sense, Charlie's acceptance to drive again with Audrey without knowing their destination has been interpreted by Jeff Evans (1996: 13) as indicating Charlie's 'positive recognition and acceptance of the more spontaneous and open-ended stance toward life she embodies along with its implied rejection of his old values'. Audrey's new image can just be taken as a new disguise, as yet another signifier of her playfulness and endless drive to perform, so that the ending, as Viano (1987: 12) has suggested, could be taken 'as an ironic return to the beginning'. But how do spectators who are familiar neither with screwball conventions nor with artistic self-conscious devices read this ending? What they see is that Audrey is smartly dressed, her clothes now embodying the values that she was previously supposed to oppose, and that, although the car is a bit quirky, Charlie is going to drive it. A similar argument can be applied to the film's metafictional bracketing or suspension of its central narrative. Lulu and Charlie's romantic love-story is framed by a shot and a scene that signal both the film's interest in difference and the fact that what we are going to watch is just a fictional construct, subject to the manip-ulations and conventions of any story. The first bracketing shot takes place after the initial tracking shots of New York from the river, the frame moving from left to right. The sequence of tracking shots stops and there is a cut to a low-angle shot of the top part of a building, then the camera tilts down to include a black teenager who moves from right to left in the frame, stops and looks at the camera. In the last scene of the film, the camera disengages itself from the romantic couple and their fortunes and focuses on the Jamaican waitress, reggae per-former 'Sister Carol', who looks again at the camera, not as waitress but as 'Sister Carol', and ends *Something Wild* singing 'Wild Thing' in celebration of the film's happy ending. As Deleyto (1994: 354) has suggested, the final gaze and the final voice in *Something Wild* are female and black, and they represent the film's vindication of margin-ality and difference, once the signs of difference have completely disappeared from Audrey. But, what if the spectator is not aware of postmodernist intertextual and self-referential games?

The most progressive formal and ideological aspects of the film, and also the ways in which *Something Wild* revisits and updates screwball, are its preoccupation with the cultural, ethnic, social and narrative margins, its self-consciousness about the contemporary possibility of romantic love, and its use of intertextuality. These are all aspects that a spectator familiarised with cinematic conventions and history probably grasps but that could be missed by a less experienced and/or younger audience. What such a spectator will probably think is that *Something Wild* is a romantic love-story with a happy ending and with a very potent soundtrack in which a zany woman and a clownish man fall in love after some romping and violence and, at the end, the woman is far less zany and the man less clownish because love has worked its miracles.

The gender politics of *Something Wild* waters down its cultural and social revisionings because it introduces ambivalence by stripping Lulu's domestication of social and cultural content and by grounding it purely and exclusively in the demands of romantic love, assuming that romantic love is desirable for a liberated woman. This, of course, derives from the film's indebtedness to the conventions of romantic comedy, but not all romantic comedies, classical or post-classical, encode the romantic heroine's domestication in such drastic terms as *Something Wild*. *Desperately Seeking Susan*, for example, makes a point of presenting Roberta's (Rosanna Arquette) romantic attachment as liberating. Moreover, Lulu's new identity is based on her image and little else, and this is an image that has shed the signs of difference. Summarising, the film seems to be saying that genuine cultural, social and political opposition, represented here by the Ray character, has to be abandoned, since it can return with a vengeance, and the necessity to relinquish radicalism is conveyed through Lulu's transformation into Audrey. Lulu is the teasing but harmless, and aimless, embodiment of the 1960s, whose revolt is mainly an aesthetic one and does not represent any actual danger, not even as the 'woman on top' of the first half. Paradoxically, Lulu is much more forceful and compelling than Audrey, so that what both men and women probably remember of the film is not so much Audrey as the unruly Lulu, her eccentricity, playful wildness and peculiar approach to life, and it is ironic that the main outcome of the film was Melanie Griffith's, and not Jeff Daniel's, rise to stardom.

NOTES

1 Celestino Deleyto (1994) has analysed the thematic function of *Something Wild*'s references to *Marnie* (1964), and Jeff Evans (1996: 6) has pointed out the allusion to *Psycho* (1960) in the final confrontation between Charlie and Ray in the bathroom, while Lulu/Audrey watches from behind the shower curtain.

2 On this, see for example Babington and Evans (1989: 267–81), Krutnik (1990) and Rowe (1995: 191–200).

3 There are, though, glorious – and highly significant because of their impact – exceptions, such as *Bringing up Baby* (1938), a film that refuses to compromise with patriarchy.

4 Barbara Ehrenreich (1995) has argued that the decline of patriarchy, understood as both male power over and protection of women, does not necessarily entail the decline of sexism, misogyny or domination, but may give way to new forms of impersonal and corporate exploitation or individual male violence.

5 For Kathleen Rowe (1995: 96–7), romantic comedy has more liberating aspects, since it provides a space for the inscription of female desire and at least allows women to resist, although temporarily, male control.

6 From the 1980s onwards, the redefinition of masculinity, no longer considered a monolithic category, has occupied an increasingly wider slot in gender and cultural theory. In the case of post-classical romantic comedy, Kathleen Rowe (1995: 194–200) has denounced the appropriation of femininity and feminism by the increasing presence of suffering and melodramatised male heroes, and Manuela Ruiz Pardos (forthcoming) has investigated the 'new' type of romantic hero emerging from a group of contemporary comedies – *Pretty Woman* (1990), *Green Card* (1990), *Moonstruck* (1987), *Sleepless in Seattle* (1993) and *Ghost* (1990).

7 Emasculating male deficiencies, associated in such classical screwball comedies as *Bringing up Baby* (1938), *Ball of Fire* (1942) and *The Lady Eve* (1941) with professors, scholarship and men of letters, seem to have been displaced on to yuppie values and lifestyle in, for example, *Something Wild*, *After Hours* (1985), *Into the Night* (1985), *Pretty Woman* (1990), *Housesitter* (1992) and, more recently, *Box of Moonlight* (1996).

8 Following the conventions of classical comedy, a genre that, in order to promote the affective distance that the comic requires, does not favour short distances, there are very few close-ups in the first half of *Something Wild*. Close-ups become much more relevant and abundant in the second part, especially in the melodramatic confession scene at Ray's place and in the final psycho-thriller scene at Charlie's house.

WORKS CITED

Babington, Bruce and Peter William Evans 1989. *Affairs to Remember: The Hollywood Comedy of the Sexes*. Manchester and New York: Manchester UP

Deleyto, Celestino 1994. 'Parody, Feminism, and the Ending of *Something Wild*'. In *Proceedings of the 16th AEDEAN Conference*, José M. Ruiz, Pilar Abad and José M. Barrio, eds. Valladolid: Universidad de Valladolid, 347–55

Easthope, Anthony 1986. *What a Man's Gotta Do: The Masculine Myth in Popular Culture*. Boston: Unwin Hyman

Ehrenreich, Barbara 1995. 'The Decline of Patriarchy'. In *Constructing Masculinity*, M. Berger, B. Wallis and S. Watson, eds. New York and London: Routledge, 284–90

Evans, Jeff 1996. 'Something New: Music as Re-vision in Jonathan Demme's *Something Wild*', *Popular Music and Society*, 19, 3: 1–17

Giddens, Anthony 1992. *The Transformation of Intimacy: Sexuality, Love and Eroticism in Modern Societies*. Cambridge: Polity Press

Jameson, Fredric 1989. 'Nostalgia for the Present', *The South Atlantic Quarterly*, 88, 2: 517–37

Krutnik, Frank 1990. 'The Faint Aroma of Performing Seals: The "Nervous" Romance and the Comedy of the Sexes', *The Velvet Light Trap*, no. 26 (Fall): 57–72

Lent, Tina Olsin 1995. 'Romantic Love and Friendship: The Redefinition of Gender Relations in Screwball Comedy'. In K. B. Karnick and H. Jenkins eds, *Classical Hollywood Comedy*. New York and London: Routledge, 314–31

Mulvey, Laura 1989. *Visual and Other Pleasures*. Bloomington and Indianapolis: Indiana UP

Neale, Steve 1992. 'The Big Romance or Something Wild?: Romantic Comedy Today', *Screen*, 33, 3 (Autumn): 284–99

Neale, Steve and Frank Krutnik 1990. *Popular Film and Television Comedy*. London and New York: Routledge

Penley, Constance and Sharon Willis eds, 1993. *Male Trouble*. Minneapolis and London: University of Minnesota Press

Rowe, Kathleen 1995. *The Unruly Woman: Gender and the Genres of Laughter*. Austin: University of Texas Press

Ruiz Pardos, Manuela (1997). 'Male Images in the New Romances: Towards the Construction of a New Romantic Hero'. In Pedro Guardia and John Stone, eds. *Proceedings of the 20th AEDEAN Conference*. Barcelona: Universitat Central de Barcelon, 563–7

Sedgwick, Eve K. 1985. *Between Men: English Literature and Male Homosocial Desire*. New York: Columbia UP

Smith, Gavin 1991. 'Identity Check', *Film Comment*, 27, 1: 28–37

Studlar, Gaylyn 1988. *In the Realm of Pleasure: Von Sternberg, Dietrich, and The Masochistic Aesthetic*. Urbana and Chicago: University of Illinois Press

Suárez, Juan A. 1996. *Bike Boys, Drag Queens and Superstars: Avant-Garde, Mass Culture and Gay Identities in the 1960s Underground Cinema*. Bloomington and Indianapolis: Indiana University Press

Viano, Maurizio 1987. 'Something Wild', *Film Quarterly*, 40, 4: 11–16

Chapter 6

TIME TRIPS AND OTHER TROPES:
PEGGY SUE GOT MARRIED AND THE
METAPHYSICS OF ROMANTIC COMEDY

Bruce Babington

Peggy Sue Got Married: *Peggy Sue's (Kathleen Turner) wistful recollections of the past's bygone certainties*

Peggy Sue Got Married (1986) structures itself around a metaphysical speculation. Peggy Sue Bodell (Kathleen Turner) is a 45-year-old mother of two, separated from her husband Charlie (Nicolas Cage) and facing the prospect of divorce. Attending her 'Class of '60' Reunion, she collapses and finds herself back just before the 18th birthday on which she slept with Charlie and conceived her daughter, Beth. Although accepted by everyone in 1960 as a teenager, in her interactions with family and others she possesses the knowledge of the mature woman. Thinking she can rewrite her life, she investigates possibilities of relationships with other classmates while trying to distance herself from Charlie. However, after visiting her grandparents she surrenders to him, replaying Beth's conception. She wakes in hospital. She and Charlie come to a tentative reconciliation and the film closes with Peggy, Charlie and their daughter together.

This summary omits many comic moments, but also many melodramatic ones, as well as the intensely nostalgic atmosphere that pervades the film. Thus my original decision to discuss *Peggy Sue* as a major contemporary romantic comedy now seems doubtful as I wonder whether it actually is a romantic comedy. While this rethinking complicates writing about the film, it does not make it any less interesting, since in its wavering along the fault lines of romantic comedy, forms of romantic melodrama and the (unromantic) comedy and melodrama of the sexes, it tells us much about those modalities as well as the state of romantic comedy just before the still continuing wave of 'new' romantic comedies.

A topography of the genres where sexual relations are the primary subject (that is, not relegated as in other genres to a supplementary position) is dominated by three areas, clearly distinguishable in their most obvious operations, but fuzzy at the borders where they overlap and combine: romantic comedy, the large field of romantic melodrama (with its various forms, including the woman's film) and the (unromantic) comedy and melodrama of the sexes. The last is defined against the first two by its giving (to use Schopenhauerian terminology later adapted by Freud) precedence to the drive over the object of the drive, while the first two are distinguished from the third by their 'romantic' granting of precedence to the object over the drive. Both romantic comedy and romantic melodrama privilege monogamy over multiplicity and diffusion in the sexual sphere, but the attitudes of the protagonist of romantic melodrama are too extreme for romantic comedy, which occupies a median zone in which the love object is idealised to the point where the sexual drive is channelled into monogamous romance, but not to the point of a quasi-religious 'dyadic fusion' with its undertext of death and redemption through amorous suffering. While in many senses remaining faithful to the system of romantic comedy, *Peggy Sue* problematises this difference in ways which account for some of the most interesting changes occurring in contemporary examples of the genre.

ENDS AND MEANINGS

Peggy Sue's final time-travel experience is to repeat the sexual act on her 18th birthday through which her daughter was conceived. As Charlie declares with romantic absolutism 'I want this to be forever', Peggy comes to in hospital. In an exhausted coda a reconciliation takes place, but hardly an upbeat closure. Charlie, grieving, begs another chance. Peggy Sue eventually suggests a future reconciliation by inviting Charlie and 'your children' to 'your house' for a Sunday lunch at which the spirit of the grandmother (Maureen O'Sullivan) will preside. At her words 'I'll bake some strudel' the music associated with the past is fully sounded. The grandfather (Leon Ames) has earlier said that the only thing that has kept the family together is Lizzie's strudel. In the same scene the grandmother has instructed Peggy to choose 'the things you are proud of; things that last', a statement Peggy takes to mean her children. As Charlie is about to leave, their daughter Beth enters and the film ends with daughter and husband at Peggy Sue's bedside.

In his account of recent generic changes in romantic comedy, Steve Neale (1992: 298) argues that *Peggy Sue Got Married* ends with Peggy Sue 'regretting nothing at all'. However, even at the simplest level this ending is dominated by unanswered questions. Is Peggy's acceding to Charlie merely exhaustion? Will a reconstituted marriage last? Or will it founder in the abyss between Charlie's infinite will and confined execution? These obvious questions, products of the film's hesitations between romantic comedy and melodrama, presuppose an audience caught between desires for romantic closure and the inscription of scepticism.

One way in which *Peggy Sue* drifts away from romantic comedy is in its emphasis on family and children, notably absent in the genre, even in the 'comedy of remarriage' (Cavell 1981, Britton 1983, Babington and Evans 1989). By repeating her 18th birthday act of sleeping with Charlie the mature Peggy palimpsests on to the original coupling (romantically undertaken without children in mind) a retrospective replay in which Beth's conception becomes intentional rather than accidental. The end draws together a desire for stable romance (that fascinating oxymoron) and nostalgia for the family. In this it bears interesting relations to *Moonstruck* (1987) with its closing celebration of the extended family, its only slightly ironised toast 'alla famiglia!', its dwelling on generations of family photographs (cf. a similar trope in the grandparents' home in *Peggy Sue*) and the importance given to female–family relationships (paralleling those between Peggy Sue and her grandmother and her daughter). *Peggy Sue Got Married*'s dealings with the family are more hesitant than *Moonstruck*'s, but both share this address to an institution to which audiences remain stubbornly more committed than some radical critics would like. *Moonstruck* has the advantage of having been given a feminist reading which intertwines a positive view of the family with feminist thematics (Rowe 1995), but even here parallels exist, for the mother–daughter relationship that has been celebrated in the former is certainly highly prominent (doubled, even tripled) in *Peggy Sue*.

But the ending hardly invokes nostalgia simply, for the grandfather's statement about the grandmother's strudel is immediately preceded by Peggy's words, 'You know, when you and grandma are gone, the family's gone. I'll never see the cousins anymore'. Peggy's overtly oneiric return to the grandparents' house amounts to a dream within a dream, and unlike the space of Peggy's parents' home, also viewed through a subjective amber haze, the dream is unbroken by the kind of critique that plays around the Kelchers. This critique resists the simple accusation that the point of the time trip is to conflate the mid-1980s with the conservative late 1950s. Additionally, the idealised grandparents (Leon Ames, aged 83, and Maureen O'Sullivan, 75) represent not characters of the 1950s but people who would have been in their prime in the 1930s. As Peggy's remark indicates, by 1960 the extended family of which the grandparents are seen as the last exemplars, is all but dead, so what is given is not a statement of historical changelessness but a process narrowed down to the nuclear family by the end of the film. (By contrast, *Moonstruck* presents not just positive feeling for the family but feels able, by a charming but deceptive sleight of hand made possible by its Italian ethnicity, to give us the extended family alive and well.) The family at *Peggy Sue*'s end is, even in nuclear terms, depleted. As Charlie slumps in his chair at a distance from Peggy, Beth enters, responds to Charlie's touch, but then turns towards and touches her mother. On this image the film ends, and attentive viewers might register the dissymmetry of the grouping (the daughter–mother pairing, Charlie at a remove) compared with the earlier grouping after Peggy tells Lizzie that Beth is named after her. There, recognising the grandfather's exclusion, she holds his hand as well as her grandmother's. The invocation of the family registers not only its shrinking but a tension between the two linked parts of the conclusion, the affirmation of family and the affirmation of romantic love, as well as between the idealised grandparents (seen only in serene old age, not struggling with the socio-sexual changes and expanding divorce rate of the 1920s and 1930s) and the frailties of the next two generations. If we interpret fourth-generation Beth's relationship with the musician less as an avoidance of marriage motivated by what she has seen of her parents, than as an escape from too early marriage, then there is a portrait of four generations of couples, the furthest past idealised, the future one still unclear, the immediate past and present given in all their difficulties (symptomatic in the former, explicit in the latter).

The final grouping has the further dissymmetry that it lacks the Bodells' second child, Scott, mentioned at various points in the film, and here where Peggy invites Charlie to bring 'your children'.[1] Coppola's reworking of the screenplay after he took over direction excised Scott (who remains in the credits) from the film, strengthening the mother–daughter bond – in line, it has been suggested, with personal motifs in Coppola's *Rain People* (Chown 1988: 204). However, verbal references remain so that the viewer might well ask why he is absent. Whatever the cause, this presence-in-absence gives further incompleteness to the final tableau. Arguably there is a further curious effect intersecting the son's absence with the fact that for most of the film Charlie is not Peggy Sue's adult partner, but young enough to be her son, so that even the 'reparative' comedy of her revenges on him for the assumptions of 1950s' patriarchy has an undertow of maternal correction. Whatever accidents contributed to it, there is a fugitive logic about Scott's absence in that Charlie, the incorrigible eternally adolescent romantic lover, both heroic and grotesque, could be said to fill his place. Further, one might argue that both this absence and Charlie's marginalisation at the end, act out a micro-allegory of male displacement from the centre, about which the tone of the film is enigmatic.

A final paradox hovers round this ending. If it seems to place more emphasis on the family than the romantic couple, this is belated in utilitarian terms. Beth must be 26 and Scott (one guesses) 20–24. Thus the poignant regrouping is undriven by utility, no longer required for the nurturing of young children whom divorce might scar. Deprived of its fundamental social rationale, the family is invoked in terms of precious psychic bonds, as the ultimate site of close relationship, even a mild ancestral piety, that, whatever contradictions are displayed or implicit, is hard to conflate with either the crude 'family values' of mid-1980s' right-wing moralism (see Bartosch 1987: 4) or the simple desire to subjugate the heroine in terms of which it has been seen (see Neale 1992, Krutnik 1990 and Neale and Krutnik 1990). In talking about *Peggy Sue* I occasionally call on comparisons with *Moonstruck*, a film where one influential article has countered the automatic ease with which, in the rather rarified world of film analysis, positive feelings for the family are automatically equated with the most regressive sexual and other politics (Rowe 1995). The complex representation of such feelings, through contradiction as well as nostalgia, in *Peggy Sue Got Married*, demands a similar response.

COMPETING NARRATIVES

One way of clarifying *Peggy Sue*'s hybrid nature is to see it as torn between three competing narratives which give historical concreteness to the transhistorical relations of romantic comedy to melodrama. Narrative 1 follows the trajectory of romantic comedy in its troubled 1980s' form. Narrative 2 follows the trajectory of the 'woman's film' in its latest inflection in the few years before *Peggy Sue*. Narrative 3 uses the time travel trope less to clarify the meanings of 1 and 2 than to replay the 3rd act of Thornton Wilder's *Our Town* where Emily Gibbs, having died, returns to visit her family. Of course behind the late forms of 'nervous' and 'reparative' romantic comedy lie generic patterns that the hesitations of later comedies play against. *Peggy Sue* is conventionally seen as a romantic comedy and retains significant aspects of the classical 'comedy of remarriage' whereby the co-protagonists, after literal or only threatened divorce, re-establish their relationship. After a re-encounter in which Peggy resists Charlie – 'I may be crazy, but I'm not crazy enough to marry you twice' – the pair sleep together and are reconciled. Paralleling the classic prototype of one or both part-ners' entanglement with an unsuitable potential mate, she gets involved with but eventually rejects two men (the class boffin, Richard Norvick,[2] and the beatnik, Michael Fitzsimmons). But 'nervous' and 'reparative' elements substantially modulate older patterns. In *Peggy Sue* this is particularly visible in its ambivalent 'happy ending' and its situation of an 18-year-old Charlie being confronted by a Peggy Sue who is 17 going on 45 in a very clear situation of comic punishment in which the female possesses authority and knowledge. Though the structure of a revised 'comedy of remarriage' just holds together, the film finds it difficult to sustain. While divorce is averted after the sepa-rated pair interact in such a way as to lead to renewal, to do this, instead of proceeding forward (as, say, *His Girl Friday* (1940) does), the narrative moves backward into the past, becoming a teenage comedy of *pre*marriage, though observed from an adult perspective. Preserving Peggy's age as 45 sets up many possibilities but crucially distorts the 'comedy of remarriage' since the mismatched pair never meet on equal ground and the comedy of reparation enacted, though very clear to the audience, merely bewilders Charlie. Nevertheless, however compro-mised, the structure of a heavily problematised romantic comedy is visible (alongside many genuinely comic moments) and accounts for the conventional categorisation of the film (see, for example, Neale 1992: 298).

The second narrative recalls the new late 1970s' 'woman's film', the brief cycle headed by *Alice Doesn't Live Here Anymore* (1975), *The Turning Point* (1977) and *An Unmarried Woman* (1978). These films drew immediate analytical interest and some hostility, being perceived as Hollywood's attempt to incorporate (or 'inoculate') feminist problem-atics into the genre. *An Unmarried Woman* and *Alice Doesn't* share roughly the same narrative trajectory, as well as substantial similarities of theme with *The Turning Point*. I would christen this sub-genre 'The female *Bildungsroman*' or, more precisely, 'The delayed female *Bildungs-roman*', since the heroine must be, like the heroine of the 'comedy of remarriage', married and experienced. *Peggy Sue Got Married*, like the first two films above, centres on a middle-aged woman, released from marriage through the death or infidelity of her husband, who under-takes a journey of self-definition. Though female friendships are much more pronounced than in romantic comedy, there is a similar testing of new partners before, dissimilarly, one worthy of the woman is discovered (hence those strained images of tender virility built around Alan Bates and Kris Kristofferson) and allowed a supportive role. This narrative bears the clear imprint of feminism, centring on the dissatisfied wife who functions in 1970s' and 1980s' romantic comedy mainly as a problem for the hero. The monologic tendency, however, whether the protagonist is female or male, is a trait more of melodrama or the comedy or melodrama of the sexes than of romantic comedy, since the over-privileging of one party disturbs the couple focus of romantic comedy. Thus *Peggy Sue*'s drift from romantic comedy is signalled in its title, since names in romantic comedy titles are almost always those of the pair (for example, *Pat and Mike*, 1952), while the 'woman's film' often uses single names as titles (*Stella Dallas*, 1937; *Sylvia Scarlett*, 1935; or, in a male inflection, *Peter Ibbetson*, 1935). In the released wife's journey there are various opportunities for reparative action (for example, in *An Unmarried Woman* where Erica (Jill Clayburgh) refuses to take back her husband) and for reworking ideas of partnership. One major difference in *Peggy Sue* is that the new revised mate is actually the (reformulated) husband, so that the film follows at its end something between the patterns of the comedy of remarriage and the redemptive critical melodrama of a film like Dreyer's *Master of the House* (1925).

The imprint of these 1970s' films on *Peggy Sue* is self-consciously inscribed in various references (for example, Peggy's claim that she wants to be a dancer retreads Erica's fantasy dance in *An Unmarried Woman*, just as her words 'Still, if I knew then what I know now, I'd do a lot of things differently' allude to Deedee's statement about her daughter at the end of *The Turning Point*). But various elements interfere with the form's purity, especially the elevation of Charlie from secondary adjunct to the heroine's progress to something like the equal partner of romantic comedy. To say this is paradoxical since much of the time *Peggy Sue* produces radical imbalance rather than equality between the couple. In spite of this, the force and complexity of the meanings Charlie bears make him approach the status of co-protagonist, albeit in a deviant way. This is reflected in a number of narrative strategies. Though the film is narrated largely from Peggy Sue's point of view (that is, focalised through her by many means outside her literal point-of-view shots), the scenes where Charlie is present tend to be exceptional, for example the immediate point-of-view shot he is given when he enters at the Reunion. Several other scenes involving Peggy begin with the focus on him, for example the alfresco school lunch, his arrival at the Kelchers' house and subsequent conversation with Mr Kelcher, and his Nosferatu-like prowling outside Peggy's bed-room. When Charlie is rejected by the talent scout she is actually nowhere in the vicinity, having left the R & B Club with Michael. Scenes between Peggy and Charlie are shot dominantly in compositions that hold both of them in the frame, and point-of-view shots of Charlie from Peggy are avoided, as if to stress his paradoxical non-subjugation within the constant put-downs he suffers. This is dramatically illustrated by the way they are avoided in the Blood Donor scene where they would occur very naturally until the moment Charlie leaves, where-upon Peggy is immediately given subjective views of Walter.

The third competing narrative is the time trip conceit itself, or at least that part of it which evokes the wonder of revisiting the past, not to the exclusion, but certainly in excess of, any critical impulse. This is the part of the film that vies with its family feeling (and the two are connected, since the archaeology of the past for Peggy is situated in the family) as a scandal to some critics, for example the *Jump Cut* review which insisted that the time travel simply diverted attention from the film's real ideological work (Bartosch 1987: 3–4). A particularly pure moment in this narrative is Peggy's first visit to the parental home. Another, which actually quotes its source in *Our Town* (but turns it from a soliloquy to a direct statement to the mother) is where Peggy tells her mother that she never knew she was so young.[3] And, of course, there is the visit to the grandparents. This narrative's emotional force, built around universal desires, tends to diminish ideological perspectives. Concurrently, though, the time trip's metaphysics are sometimes sub-jugated to the physics of critical comedy which prevent a simple corre-lation between desire for one's past and its endorsement at every level. Thus the often critical view of the parents: Mr Kelcher (Don Murray) a parody of the suburban hunter-gatherer, standing underneath a moose's head, accoutremented with hat and pipe, practising gestures of authority; Mrs Kelcher (Barbara Harris) with her perky desperation lying to Peggy about selling her jewels for housekeeping money. Equally there is the terrible conformity of the schoolkids' attitudes to Richard and Michael ('First the geek and then the weirdo', as the terrible teen queen Dolores says); or the subtle criticism in which the limits of the radicalism of Michael's beat libertarianism are exposed by his plan to have Peggy and another woman support him; or the implication attached to one of the most liberating moments in the film, where the girls ecstatically applaud Charlie's band singing the Dion number, a moment that, for all its positiveness, is based firmly on a male as performer / female as audience division. Thus the background playing of the hit from *Kismet* (1955), 'Stranger in Paradise', in one scene, is a complicated thing, the past being both paradise and not-paradise. While it provides the trope that brings certain critiques into being, this narrative is also profoundly in tension with them.

The narrative proper is marked by indicators of worry about the problematics of narrating the story. For instance, *Peggy Sue* seems to register dissonances raised by feminist criticism of the time which accused the female centre of Hollywood films of being merely a ventriloquist's doll for patriarchal ideology. One moment viewable in this light is the brief appearance and abrupt exit of Rosalie Testa, the vibrantly attractive wheelchair-bound woman who, when she jokes intimately with Peggy at the Reunion and sits with Peggy's group, seems to be the heroine's closest friend. Scripting revisions may account for her unexpected later non-appearance, but, even more than with Scott, incomplete excision from the final cut invites interpretation. Because Rosalie sits in a chair and is something like the Director of the Reunion in her tracing of the graduates; because her crippledness makes her a watcher rather than a participant; and because she doesn't appear in the time warp where we are primed to expect her, she might well be seen as a self-conscious surrogate for the director, especially when her name (Testa = head) chimes italianately/cinematographically with Coppola (= eye), and the first choice director (that is, the preferred teller of Peggy Sue's story) was Penny Marshall.[4] It is as if Coppola is announcing his symbolic transvestism or else invoking a woman director who might keep an eye on proceedings.

This problematic might also be seen to be inscribed in the title sequence, shot to Buddy Holly's singing of 'Peggy Sue Got Married', the follow-up to his famous hit. In relation to the narrative, three things are striking about the song. (i) The lyric's statement that 'Peggy Sue got married not long ago' is elaborately complicated by layers of denial and agnosticism: ('Please don't say/ No, no, no,/ Don't tell that

I told you so/ I just heard a rumour from a friend./ . . . If you don't believe, I'll understand./ This is what I've heard./ Of course the story could be wrong . . .', and so on). Such effects might suggest that the greater narrative could also be complicated by doubts and conflicting sources, and also cede to its audience interpretative responsibilities ('I don't say that it's true/ I'll just leave it up to you').[5] (ii) The song is uttered by a male, so the obvious assumption is that the 'you' addressed are male listeners. Yet, actually, there are no gender markers in the lyrics, so that they could be addressed to both males and females. Thus it is too simple to think of Holly's male voice overriding the part-female voice and address of romantic comedy and melodrama in the film. (iii) Anyway, the auteurial signature of Holly's singing is, above all, its mixture of male and female elements, dips in register between falsetto and baritone, and extreme contrasts of delivery between a feminised lisping sweetness and a masculinised drive. Whether Holly's idiosyncrasies suggested the extraordinary voice assumed by Nicolas Cage, passing far beyond realistic mimicry of adolescent instability, is beside the point, which really resides in their shared instability and its relation to Peggy's and Charlie's switchback ride through gender roles and different historical conceptions of sex relations.

This opening uses the icon of Peggy Sue as majorette (itself highly ambiguous; connoting health, youth and nostalgia, but also female secondariness, since the drum majorette merely performs for the male sports spectacle). The icon is reduced, so that it looks like a stamp, as if Peggy, like Elvis or Jerome Kern, had been honoured by the US Mail. Here she is frozen just as the baton has been thrown up and floated beyond the frame. It is difficult not to relate this image of possession, control and loss of the baton, to questions of the degree to which Peggy is controller or controlled in her narrative (at least as far as anyone may be said to have that control). Towards the end there are two moments, very interesting in this respect, where Peggy is taken over into overtly male micro-narratives in ways which invite complex and rather con-tradictory readings. In the playfully fantastic scene at the Grandfather's Lodge (crossing *Sons of the Desert* (1934) with *Die Zauberflöte*) the Lodge members try to return Peggy to 1986. Comic as its outlandish costumes and ludicrous resurrection symbols (eggs and antic easter wings) are, it also contains language of great gravity in its address to the 'Lord of the Universe' and its appeal 'The name of your daughter is

Rebirth . . . Reclaim Thy Child of Light that her Soul may find its Home'. We don't actually know that this group of gentle, mostly aged patriarchs will fail, because Charlie interrupts them by fusing the lights, but presumably we share Peggy's smiling scepticism. The moment invites multiple interpretations. Do we see them as Peggy's fantasy of the benevolent patriarchy of her childhood, incapable, endearing as they are, of solving her problems in 1986? Or do we lay more positive emphasis on the Lodge members inviting a female into the closed male order of Enlightenment-derived misogyny, in such a way that Pamina is addressed as Tamino's equal? The second moment usurps the first as Charlie forcibly rescues Peggy, bundling her up in her cloak in such a way that, in a film of many literary allusions (Hemingway, Fitzgerald, Thornton Wilder, Yeats, Ginsberg, Bram Stoker, *Othello*, for a start), brings to mind the end of Henry James's *The Ambassadors*: 'Ransom, as he went, thrust the hood of Verena's long cloak over her head, to conceal her face and identity . . . she was in tears. It is to be feared that with the union, so far from brilliant, into which she was about to enter, these were not the last she was destined to shed' (1966: 389–90). Like much else in a film of jostling views and competing narratives, this is a highly ambiguous moment; leading both to a happy and an unhappy ending; to a successful taking over of events by Charlie, which is at the same time Peggy's fantasy, dictated by her for reasons (Beth's conception) of which he is unaware. My aim here is to demonstrate the complexity of the film's workings rather than to bring them into a (possibly specious) coherence. What I think is undoubtedly true is that this multi-levelled indecisiveness is some-thing that – if we think of *Peggy Sue* primarily as romantic comedy – tends to disappear in late 1980s' and 1990s' romantic comedy which seems to be produced in a period of greater consensus that assumes that the age of anxiety is in remission and that the genre can once more be seen as an optimistic project.

'CRAZY' CHARLIE

As the primary identification that has to be taken up for the narrative to be understood, Peggy Sue is defined in contrast to her girlfriends as a kind of paradigm of mid-1980s' womanhood, altered (if less than some would wish) by feminism; domestic, yet not oppressively so like

Maddy (since she runs her bakery); adventurous, but not as oppor-tunistic as Carol; defined by her 1950s' patriarchal upbringing, but not as corrupted by it as Dolores; both freer and more trapped than Rosalie whose serenity is probably beyond both her and the audience. This centrality demands the most median qualities from Kathleen Turner's semiotic store (blondness; the mix of babyface and a voluptuousness tending to maternal thickness – crucial to this role; middle-class artic-ulateness; an almost corn-fed air of physical wellbeing). Consequently the signs of the *femme fatale* (Maddy in *Body Heat* (1981), Irene in *Prizzi's Honor* (1985), inflected variously in *V. I. Warshawski* (1991) and *The War of the Roses* (1989)) are marginal, but sufficient to satisfy the assertiveness required of the heroines of the 'delayed *Bildungsroman*' and reparative comedy, most obviously in her put-downs of disadvan-taged males like the 'macho schmuck' Doug Snell, Michael when she pukes at his sub-'Howl' poetry, her father over the Edsel, and when the beleaguered Charlie shouts 'Woman humiliator!' after her. Her most meaningful acting characteristic – the facial kinesic of a plangent down-tugging at the corner of her lips, turning her slightly trembling mouth into, if not a tragic mask, a site of emotional vulnerability – adds depth to her as a figure of empathic identification (whether in the fortysomething female's entrapment in a failing marriage or her wonder at re-entering the past).

If Peggy is the centre of identification, Charlie, both for her and the audience, must be the most complex character, excessive and contra-dictory, played by Nicolas Cage at his most riven. This rivenness is staged in Cage's virtually tripartite entry into the narrative, each entry thickened with myth-alluding intertextuality. First, as 'Crazy Charlie, the Appliance King' on TV, in a white buckskin jacket that parodies the decline from frontiersman to businessman (Miller's *Death of a Salesman*) he cracks open fortune cookies to reveal only the price of videorecorders. Second, in the extraordinary moment at the Reunion, Cage, bearing bodily traces of the 1950s' rebel heroes Brando, Dean, Mitchum and Presley (see Dargis 1995: 6–9), and wearing with an open-collared shirt a white suit (*The Great Gatsby*, the homework for Peggy's literature class), looks out over the ballroom, a balloon (his soul? Peggy's? The audience's?) mysteriously floating up to him. Third, the teenage Charlie parodies Dracula ('I want your blood!') when Peggy wakes up at the Blood Drive, a moment establishing something vampirically predatory about his romanticism, a connotation taken up in the lighting of his eyes and mouth in the quarrel in the basement, and in the similar way Charlie's part-alter ego Michael (preaching romantic 'intensity') is imaged with Peggy. The second of these entries, Cage at his most postmodernist demotic myth-alluding, suggests that Peggy will find it hard to leave him (something abetted by suggestions that the looming divorce is not her choice). In fact she surrenders to him not once but three times: first, when she disastrously asks him to have sex with her; second, when she reconceives Beth; and third, at the film's end. In the first, where her response is uncomplicated by later motivations concerning Beth and the family, Turner is shot (from the waist, in youth-enhancing profile, with pink-bowed teenage hairstyle) so that in a moment unlike any other in the time trip the girl/woman duality breaks down to leave only the girl.

Peggy's come-on, distressingly for Charlie, reasserts the older woman, and what follows is structured around comic disparities in the theatre of sexuality between 1980s' gender roles and more inflexible 1950s' ones. Charlie, subjected to a barrage of role reversals, becomes almost hysterical. 'What the hell's going on, Peggy Sue . . . That's a *guy*'s line!' Here the contours of comic revenge are clear, but accompanied by more subterranean effects. Though Charlie's romanticism is chastised by Peggy's mundane sexual realism, it is his 'is, was and ever will be' romanticism that moves her to proposition him. This creates an extreme of instability in Charlie who moves between a reassertion of male ownership of the sexual sphere when he caps Peggy's talk of his 'Thrill-hammer' with 'You mean my Whang' and a traditionally ' feminine' position of fighting off seduction and defending an idealised love (encapsulated when he complains, 'You sure know how to spoil a mood, Peggy Sue') against Peggy's 'masculine' demands.[6] In fact romantic comedy, even in its 1980s' inflections, has to be uncomfortable with both their rhetorics, his too idealistic, hers too reductive. Yet a profound part of Charlie's more fugitive attraction, both for Peggy Sue and for the audience, lies exactly in what attracts laughter, his role of the suffering lover, rationally rejected but inwardly desired by that audience ('we', not 'they') De Rougemont characterises as having 'a secret preference for what is unhappy' (1956: 51).

Shaken by Peggy's infidelity with Michael, Charlie invokes 'The Book of Love'. The allusion to 'The Monotones' hit creates further bathos around Charlie's teenage rituals.[7] But while the girls giggle over a more pragmatic Book of Love, most probably Theodore van de Velde's *Ideal Marriage* with its vindication of the genital kiss,[8] Charlie invokes the line of texts proclaiming the exalted meanings of love in Western culture, from the *Vita Nuova* to the contemporary profanities of Roland Barthes' *A Lover's Discourse* (1990), with its exquisite catalogues of masochisms and narcissisms, self-pity and self-display, its cherishing of abysmal positions and its endless rewriting of the infant's unappeasable abandonment by the mother. For all the difference between the mandarin heir of Proust and the Hollywood film, the comparison suggests why we and Peggy might be so moved by 'Crazy Charlie', why his 'furore' so exceeds the comic critique of the adolescent male, for Charlie is that character almost totally absent from romantic comedy, the 'flayed man' (or woman), the purveyor of the 'sentimental obscenity' (Barthes 1990: 95 and 177), banned from a genre that at the same time depends on it (since romantic comedy paradoxically celebrates durable relationships founded on the vicissitudes of passion). Another connection between *Peggy Sue* and *Moonstruck* is that the latter also has a rare acting out of the forbidden role (again by Nicolas Cage) in Ronny's early extraordinarily melodramatic appearances which, however, more than Charlie's, drift into relative conformity by the end, with Ronny seemingly changed and marginalised. The depiction of Charlie's romanticism through his adolescent immaturity allows it to be consciously recuperated as critical comedy, but more interesting is the way this 'screen' makes respectable our attachment to his display of the 'mechanics of amorous vassalage' (Barthes 1990: 82).

The same mechanism that heightens the reparative comedy, Charlie's being put down by an all-knowing 45-year-old, also creates an Oedipal scenario in which Charlie becomes Peggy's eroticised child, especially as she utters the motherly 'Oh, Charlie, what am I going to do with you?' (a scenario echoed when, after Michael shouts 'No more Jell-o, Mom!', she finds herself identifying with his parents). In that for much of the film Peggy and Charlie are palimpsests of girlfriend and mother, boyfriend and son, one might read around them a series of variations on Barthes' epigram, 'The adult is imposed upon the child. I am then two subjects in one: I want maternity and genitality' (1990: 104). Charlie constantly breaks down the ideal of balanced amorousness (the lower case 'only you') of romantic comedy. For Charlie is a compellingly abysmal lover, unstably veering between romantic ideality ('Your eyes look like silver pools of moonlight when the tide rushes in'); self-pity ('I had a miserable time last night because of you'); narcissism (his appropriation of the traditional catalogue of female charms in 'I've got the teeth! I've got the eyes!'); desperate self-assertion ('I've got the car! I'm the lead singer! I'm the man!'); banal threats ('Nobody treats Charlie Bodell like this!'); even thoughts of ultimate violence as standing like Othello over Desdemona's bed, he momentarily thinks of stifling Peggy; and even a Tristan-like allusion to the goal of love in death ('I even wrote you in my will!'). All these are justified by his claim that 'Love is all that matters! It's the only thing that matters!' My point here (by way of De Rougemont's 1956 celebrated analysis of romantic love in *Passion and Society*) is that it is almost impossible for both Peggy and the audience not to empathise with Charlie at some preconscious level created by the profoundest myth of their erotic enculturation, whatever the corrective force of Peggy's riposte that it isn't enough. This is something that pre-empts any gender-divided identifications and cuts across heterosexual and homosexual categories, for the mystique of romantic love, of passion, of authenticity through erotic suffering, pervades the myths of homosexuality as well as heterosexuality. Charlie, late in the film, tells Peggy that he is 'tired of being the romantic fool', but we find him at the end perceptibly sadder, his rhetoric more muted, but essentially unchanged. It is easy to treat Charlie (especially when he is literally an adolescent for most of the film) as a simple critique of adolescent masculinity (his shrine to Fabian, and so on), for this text has a strong existence in the film, alongside the one that affirms his innate decency (for example, his respect for Richard, his singing in the black club, his vain attempt to resist his father's fate of the bored, adulterous small businessman, that fate Michael actually does manage to escape). I am not suggesting that these and other texts are cancelled by the one I have concentrated on, or less worthy of analysis, but what grips me is what is enacted within them, the higher craziness of 'Crazy Charlie'. Its grip is doubly powerful: first, because what Charlie represents is the secret mirror of both Peggy and the audience (so that in viewing him we confront deep-rooted aspects of the desiring self); and second, because for the theorist of romantic comedy, this craziness, which is the negative on which the genre's positives rest, is spoken here more interestingly than almost anywhere else.

NOTES

1 Peggy tells Carol at the Reunion, 'I've got two great kids' and then shows Richard's wife the locket with the pictures of the children, saying 'These are my children'. In reply to her grandmother she says, 'I'm proud of my children. I miss them so much. Beth. Scott and Beth'. When Charlie gives her the locket containing pictures of her and Charlie as infants, she is confused: 'Scott and Beth. Where did you get this?'
2 In the original screenplay Richard's role was larger and involved a sexual relationship with Peggy that is not in their 'partnership' in the film (see Chown 1988: 202).
3 The play text's semi-soliloquy reads, 'Oh, how young Mama looks! I didn't know Mama was ever that young!'
4 Coppola was apparently the third choice, behind Marshall and Jonathan Demme (Lewis 1995: 145).
5 See Laing (1971) on Buddy Holly as auteur and on the rock singer's 'ensemble of vocal effects' and the syntax of the lyrics of 'Peggy Sue Got Married'.
6 If we accept Freud's view that the 'overvaluation of the sexual object' is more marked in men than women, these interchanges of masculine and feminine positions become even more interesting (1981b: 250).
7 The Book of Love' (Davis/Patrick/Malone), sung by The Monotones (and also used in *American Graffiti* (1973)), contains the lyrics: 'Chapter One says you love her/ You love her with all your heart/ Chapter Two you tell her/ You're never never never never ever gonna part/ In Chapter Three remember/ The meaning of Romance/ [and quoted by Charley] In Chapter Four you break up / But you give her just one more chance.'
8 The reference to the 'genital kiss' makes Theodore van de Velde's *Ideal Marriage* (1930) a slight favourite over Dr Eustace Chesser's *Love without Fear* (1941). Both books were familiar objects in middle-class homes at least until the early 1960s.

WORKS CITED

Babington, Bruce and Peter William Evans 1989. *Affairs to Remember: The Hollywood Comedy of the Sexes*. Manchester: Manchester UP

Barthes, Roland 1990 (1977). *A Lover's Discourse*. Trans. Richard Howard. Harmondsworth: Penguin

Bartosch, Bob 1987. *Jump Cut*, no. 32: 3–4

Britton, Andrew 1983. *Cary Grant: Comedy and Male Desire*. Newcastle upon Tyne: BFI

Cavell, Stanley 1981. *Pursuits of Happiness: The Hollywood Comedy of Remarriage*. Cambridge, MA: Harvard UP

Chown, Jeffrey 1988. *Hollywood Auteur*. London and New York: Praeger

Dargis, Manohla 1995. 'Method and Madness', *Sight and Sound*, June: 6–9

De Rougemont, Denis 1956. *Passion and Society*. London: Faber & Faber

Freud, Sigmund 1981. 'On the Universal Tendency to Debasement in the Sphere of Love', *On Sexuality*. The Pelican Freud Library, vol. 7. Harmondsworth: Penguin, 243–60

James, Henry 1966. *The Bostonians*. Harmondsworth: Penguin

Krutnik, Frank 1990. 'The Faint Aroma of Performing Seals: The "Nervous" Romance and the Comedy of the Sexes', *The Velvet Light Trap*, no. 26 (Fall): 56–72

Laing, Dave 1971. *Buddy Holly*. New York: Studio Vista

Neale, Steve 1992. 'The Big Romance or Something Wild?: Romantic Comedy Today', *Screen*, 33, 3 (Autumn): 284–99

Neale, Steve and Frank Krutnik 1990. *Popular Film and Television Comedy*. London: Routledge

Rowe, Kathleen 1995. 'Comedy, Melodrama and Gender: Theorizing the Genres of Laughter'. In *Classical Hollywood Comedy*, Kristina Brunovska Karnick and Henry Jenkins, eds. London: Routledge

Chapter 7

WORKING GIRL: A CASE STUDY OF ACHIEVEMENT BY WOMEN? NEW OPPORTUNITIES, OLD REALITIES

Chantal Cornut-Gentille

Working Girl: *Looking the part: in her quest for the New Jerusalem, Tess McGill (Melanie Griffith) disowns the past in her fabrication of a new identity*

In the past few years, critical interest in romantic comedy has been re-awakened by Henderson's – now famously erroneous – presage concerning the imminent fate of the genre. The 'comedy of the sexes' or those films that 'celebrate heterosexual relationships' (as critics commonly refer to the genre) had, in his opinion, no place in a society imbued with the liberation ideology of the 1960s, with its new ethic of *personal* self-indulgence. Both Frank Krutnik and Steve Neale, among others, have refuted this assertion by insisting that romantic comedy, as a genre, is as fluid as any social force and, consequently, that it cannot be captured on a *permanent* basis. Using the period between the 1930s and the 1990s as a microcosm of change, Frank Krutnik offers scholars a blueprint for unravelling and analysing the complex historical forces that have shaped the ideological directions of romantic comedies. Likewise, after examining the correlation between structural and formal elements found in romantic comedy and the ideological function they perform, Neale draws out several consistent and distinctive features that characterise those films he labels 'new romances'. Thus, in their different ways, both critics highlight those historical changes in gender roles that have affected the narrative formulae of this 'game of love' – a game of love that has to mediate between 'the narrative/stylistic conventions of the "classical" era and the demands of an age . . . that has undergone substantial tranformation' (Krutnik 1990: 59).

With this in mind, Mike Nichols' 1988 film, *Working Girl*, can now be presented as a 'new romance' – a contemporary film with roots in the narrative forms of romantic comedy but which simultaneously offers a social commentary on the changing nature of work and gender relations. There is, of course, nothing new in a film featuring an autonomous and successful woman but the mild feminism, or even the trendiness of *Working Girl* derives from the two steps this particular film takes towards fostering more liberal and broad-minded images of women in society today: in the first place, it focuses almost exclusively on women, women's space and women's problems and, more importantly, the story outlines the working life of a *single* woman, which indicates (at first glance) that Tess McGill (Melanie Griffith) is deliberately established as the heroine of her own life rather than defined by the presence of a man. As such, the film comes close in line with the 'woman on top' narrative – a type of comedy analysed by Kathleen Rowe in *The Unruly Woman* (1995). While I am largely in agreement with Rowe's theoretical framework, her evident optimism concerning the rebellious potential of unruliness to undermine patriarchal norms and authority seems to lay claim to the author's liberal sympathies. Interestingly enough, Rowe's 'women *on* top' syndrome echoes, in caricatured or magnified form, the slogan 'woman *at* the top' which integrates the goals and aspirations of bourgeois or liberal feminism. In political terms, bourgeois feminism asserts that women, if they really want to, and try hard enough, can make it to the top. Basically, this political strand of feminism simply seeks a larger share of social power for women. In practice, bourgeois feminism accepts the world as it is; in other words, what men actually do is seen as the norm, which usually means that, from this ideological viewpoint, the *real* basis of power relations between the sexes remains concealed.

Hence, rather than simply extracting the positive (feminist) elements in the film, my goal here is to examine *both* sides of the coin. That is, although a feminist analysis will show that *Working Girl* as a 'new romance' is, basically, an exaltation of female empowerment in the public arena, I want to suggest, by comparing Tess's success story to a traditional fairy tale, that the film simultaneously works to keep women in their socially and sexually subordinate place. Either way, it is nevertheless important to note that the plot supplies many hooks for femininity and class as narrative for, if 'class' designates a position in the economic structure of society, it also nearly always signifies *inequality* (Jordan and Weedon 1987: 67). Lastly, the issue of 'class' ('any set of persons or things grouped together, or graded or differentiated from others especially by quality' (*The Concise Oxford Dictionary*)) will serve to demonstrate that *Working Girl* can be read as an allegory of the new aspirations boosted by 'Reaganomics' (Chafe 1995: 474). In effect, the problems the heroine – as a female entrepreneur of the 1980s – comes up against speak to a social formation in which the factors that enforce class identification are individualism, competition and economic prestige rather than family origin, education and social position.

The focus of the film *Working Girl* is the life of a young white New Yorker whose accent and physique immediately betray a low-strata, underprivileged background. Already in the very first scenes, the film departs from the conventional stereotype by directing attention to the heroine's tight timetable of self-imposed assignments (speech class; Emerging Markets Seminar) interfering with the more hedonistic side of life envisioned in the form of rendez-vous with friends and birthday parties. This, combined with the fact that the film narrative seems bent on representing a realistic image of a perfectly ordinary woman, immediately gives *Working Girl* the air of being a different, and more acceptable, film about women's experience in America.

Conveniently for the story, Tess McGill has no parents, sisters or brothers. This allows the audience to see her in isolation from family ties and only in relation to colleagues at work and friends and boyfriend at home. The plot outlines Tess's efforts to assert her own merits as an individual and worker in the business world of high finance. However, her journey to success is sprinkled with difficulties: a constant victim of sexual harassment, she is transferred from job to job until finally – and to her great relief – she is offered the opportunity of working for a woman. The scenes delineating Tess's uncertain 'progress' in the workplace are contrasted with displays of her, at home, as her boyfriend's sexual play-thing. Both in her relationship with Mick (Alec Baldwin) and in her job, Tess acts with perfect co-operative subjection until she discovers that her boyfriend makes the most of her absences from home to have sex with another woman and that her idea regarding Trusk Industries, which Katharine Parker (Sigourney Weaver) had tricked her into believing was a dead-end, was, in fact, being followed up by her boss – to her own credit and advantage. Outrage spurs the heroine to action and gives her the necessary confidence to shake herself out of her customary docility. From then on, the action in the film accelerates, tracing Tess's mutation into an impostor and her ever more daring ploys to bring the contract with Truck to good term as a means of undoing Parker's subterfuge. In the end, Tess not only 'gets the man' (Jack Trainer played by Harrison Ford) but her merits as a talented business woman are fully recognised by Oren Trask (Philip Bosco) in the form of a management post. This 'happy ending' can be said to break with romantic comedy conventions in that the last scenes do not depict the usual loving embrace between male and female protagonists, but show a flexible and liberal Tess establishing a spontaneous and natural association with her secretary. The conclusion of the film therefore seems to put more emphasis on work values, personality and work motivations than on standard male–female relationships.

From a woman-centred stance, Tess's experiences as a worker seem, at first, to be totally at variance with the message of hope in the lyrics of the introductory hymn: 'Let the river run/ Let all the dreamers wake the nation/ Come the new Jerusalem.' In the opening scenes, after an embarrassing situation in the men's toilet and after being informed that her application for an entry programme has once again been turned down, Tess, hungry for promotion, is tricked by her bosses into yet another kind of date-rape with Bob Speck (Kevin Spacey). The display of David Lutz's (Oliver Platt) and Turkel's (James Lally) offensive bantering produces in the audience an uncomfortable sensation of imbalance between male and female power – a sense of absolute male control and dominance over an apparently weak, compliant and rather unintelligent female. This said, Tess is very quickly shown to be quite capable of stereotyping men back in a retaliatory devaluing gesture, when she stomps into the secretaries' pool, to the sound of military music, and resolutely types out 'David Lutz is a sleazoid pimp with a tiny dick'. As could be supposed, her dramatic gesture may have served to discharge her indignation as a woman but it leaves her jobless as a worker. Hence, the suggestion lurking beneath the incipient narrative seems to be, as Judi Marshall has argued (1984: 14–24), that women's position in the workplace is severely affected by the existence of 'a double-bind': as workers, women are expected to comply with traditional female stereotypes. If they conform to these pre-ordained, male assumptions, they tend not to be taken seriously, if they don't, they are seen as a threat to organisational stability.

Tess's transferral to Katharine Parker's Fusion and Acquisition Department recalls the early stages of the women's movement when conciousness-raising groups represented safe spaces defended against men. The heroine's first encounter with her boss, the two women's small talk about their similar ages and sex and their comments about Tess's penchant for soft-toy animals open up for Tess a view of the workplace as an unadulterated feminine space, announcing her arrival in a place 'beyond' patriarchal tyrannies and impositions. The salient point the film makes, however, is that separation of women from men does not necessarily imply unpolluted female bonding. When the boss makes her striking and imposing entrance into the secretaries' marsh, there is no doubt that she, in Kathleen Rowe's words: 'wields power in multiple dimensions – power over men, financial power, celebrity power, sexual power. These words and images also acknowledge that she has achieved that power by cultivating a particular persona defined by gender inversion' (1995: 54–5).

The pertinence of Rowe's description derives from it providing such a neat outline of the bourgeois, 'women *at* the top' syndrome. This

feminist strand urges women to take charge of territories normally
seen as 'male' preserve – a feat which Katharine Parker has evidently
achieved, but, because of its acceptance of patriarchal status quo (with
more power for women), the liberal stress on individual effort also
tends to encourage a certain gender inversion in producing token
women who, like Katharine Parker, 'ape' men and are served by other
women; this means that bourgeois feminism has no interest in any
idea of solidarity or sisterhood – the reverse, since such an idea clashes
with the notion of *individual* self-advancement. Interestingly enough,
it is precisely Katharine Parker's overdose of egocentricity that will
eventually lead to her being cast aside as the typical, neurotically
eccentric 'wrong partner', which Steve Neale identifies as one of the
constant characteristics of 'new romance' (1992: 288). Having said this,
there are other facets of woman-to-woman bonding which a materialist-
feminist approach fails to capture. According to Kristeva, the 'self' is built
out of the interaction of two dispositions – the individual's unconscious
drives (semiotic) and social impositions (symbolic) – the result invariably being individuals whose identities are never fixed and finished.
Crucially for Kristeva, this continuous tugging and yanking between
semiotic and symbolic inevitably takes place *within the social order*,
which explains the author's radical adherence to the notion that, even
if the feminine can be expressed, woman – what she calls the *feminine-
feminine* – cannot *be*. 'Woman', for Kristeva, is therefore only a label for
varying degrees of the *masculine-feminine* (Duchen 1988: 85–7). From
this perspective, the 'bond' established between the two women
reflects Tess's candid attempt to withdraw from the symbolic, which
she associates exclusively with males/male power and patriarchal
rules, while at the same time, it highlights all the more vividly how she
is being duped by Parker's physique into believing that they are exactly
alike for, in the character of the boss, the presence of the symbolic has
clearly overridden any semiotic impulses. This is made plain when the
relationship is shown to be, at bottom, envisaged by Parker as a cold,
contractual association – one Marilyn French would describe as sustained by the ideology of 'power-over', so typical of patriarchy (1985:
538). Power, French argued, is not bad in itself, but only when it
appears as power-over. When it materialises as 'power-to' it is good
and humanising. 'Power-to', she writes, 'refers to ability, capacity, and
connotes a link of freedom', whereas power-over 'refers to domination'
(1985: 505) – a statement that seems to point directly to the contrasting

characters of Tess and Katharine, especially as the spectator recalls certain details such as Tess's five years spent at night school (over and
above work) and her getting an honour's degree – all to end up serving
coffee 'with no sugar'. The theme of domination is subtly reintroduced
in the scenes exhibiting Tess thawing amidst fumes behind a trolley
laden with Chinese knick-knacks (even though this delicatessen *was*,
originally, her own idea). During the cocktail party, both Tess's attractiveness as a female and her self-esteem as a potential business woman
are seriously undermined by her ruffled aspect and her position as a
waitress. By not remarking on the one and keeping her stationed as the
other, Katharine Parker is proscribing Tess's freedom of action, thus
leaving the field open for herself to use allure, enchantment and other
tantalising feminine tricks to secure her *own* position. Hence from both
a liberal-feminist and a subjective standpoint, the radical feminist idea
of sisterhood, which implies a *class* oppression – an oppression shared
by *all* women – gives way to a certain Hobbesian version in which
Katharine Parker maintains her superior position by *exploiting* her
employee.[1] But, quite apart from the arguable claim that women constitute a single class, the film provides an intriguing insight into the
kind of value-scheme of each female character. A rather cynical contrast is drawn between Katharine Parker, presented as the 'Queen-bee'
of a female community, whose aim is to make the Fusion and Acquisition
Department function on a (supposedly) co-operative basis – 'Remember,
it's a two-way system', she keeps reminding Tess – and Tess who,
initially at least, willingly sacrifices self-fulfilment and personal ambition
on the altar of sisterhood.

As with Katharine Parker, it seems that whenever Mick, Tess's
boyfriend, appears in the film it is to use and abuse her in defence of
his *own* interests: beneath his constant ogling and sexual innuendo is
the assumption that Tess is no more than his own erotic possession.
In virtue of his position within the class system, Mick represents the
typical macho-man from the social groups otherwise kept invisible and
inaudible by official capitalist society. He is a homely figure but, by
deliberatly removing him from the world where 'things happen', the
film explicitly classifies him and his over-virile attitude as antiquated
and unnatural – his notion of masculinity thus providing an important
site for humour in being, as Kathleen Rowe expresses it, 'as fossilised
and laughable as the skeleton' (1995: 147).

From the moment Tess discovers Mick's infidelity and Katharine

Parker's double dealing, both characters become cultural symbols and carriers of social values against whom the heroine directs her anger and frustration. To live through these feelings positively, Tess needs her own phase of separation, an opportunity to withdraw into her 'self' and ascertain her own strengths. This core aspect of 'self' must find its expression before the character can become fully realised, both in her individual personality and in her connectedness with the world of which she is part. On a more general level, the incorporation within the story of this 'quest for meaning' on the part of the main character also invalidates Brian Henderson's forewarning concerning the incompatibility of romantic comedy with the post-1960s' flowering of new, individualistic values.

Katharine Parker's home provides an ideal retreat for the ripening of such thoughts. The awareness Tess develops during this phase of coming-to-know involves the woman changing her perspectives on the world, values, opinions and even lifestyle. From the upheaval of these mental processes a new 'whole' emerges. Interestingly enough, the way the heroine has chosen to dress for work the next day is, in itself, a telling detail, for it reveals to what extent *dress* can acquire a symbolic function as 'status leveller'. From this perspective, Tess's appearance in one of her boss's neat suits (with its clear parallel to norms of dress for male executives) has a double significance: on the one hand, it indicates how women in high managerial posts must, first of all, 'look the part' to be taken seriously (proving one's competence comes after) while it also underlines how, in this case, Tess's budding sense of self-worth can only flourish behind a false or inauthentic public identity. On the other hand, the heroine's new, forged identity is evidently one of those legacies from classical comedies that, from now on, will guarantee a certain amount of suspense and frolic in the story (Neale 1992: 293). Even so, it seems that, in *Working Girl*, the visual allusions to a 'fabricated' self – a self that is 'not real' – are immediately muted by the film's subsequent presentation of Tess's first, rather blundered, encounter with Jack Trainer. It then becomes evident that the heroine's newly found self-acceptance is no longer solely contingent on everybody else's approval: 'I've got a mind for business and a body for sin. Is there anything wrong with that?' These words represent a crucial moment in the action for they embody a contemporary acceptance of *self* on the part of the ex-downtrodden female heroine. From then on, it is the combination of the 'fraudulent' woman and the potential female entrepreneur which gives the film its own peculiar and original essence, especially in its subtle evocation of Mary Daly's exhortation to women:

> instead of settling for being a warped half of a person, which is equivalent to a self destructive non-person, the emerging woman is casting off role definitions . . . this is not a mere 'becoming equal to men in a man's world' . . . it is, rather, something like the new identity of women. (Daly 1991: 41).

However, as noted before, circumstances only permit Tess to *dramatise* her true potential. Her total metamorphosis, as she emerges from her retreat, determined to 'usurp' a senior or Board level position not only serves to produce comic suspense (Neale and Krutnik 1990: 38) but also to bring the class issue very much into focus. With the whole story in mind, the scenes that show Tess exercising on a static bicycle in Parker's flat while training to emulate her boss's accent and intonation, and the ones exhibiting Tess and Cyn attempting to forge a new 'façade' for the heroine become much more important, for their purpose is precisely to underline those status signifiers that Tess needs in order to acquire a new 'class identity'. Proper diction exemplifies the *cultural signifier* she appropriates for herself by means of her potential as an actress (her constant clearing of the throat could be interpreted as sonorous inverted commas – a subtle way of 'punctuating' the performance she is staging[2] – while the 6,000-dollar dress she decides to wear for the party represents a significant *material signifier* that, from then on, she can procure for herself out of Parker's wardrobe (see Conroy 1996: 114–38). The irony, of course, is that these appeals to status prestige are wholly undercut by their sheer tenuousness, as when Tess automatically stands up at the mention of coffee during her all-important meeting with Jack Trainer. The unreliability of surface or 'cosmetic' status-claims is further underlined if comparison is made between what the two main female characters wear *beneath* the more visible material signifiers, as when we are given a glimpse of Tess hastily hoovering Parker's flat in high heels and tacky, black-laced underwear. The relevance of these garments is that they bear nodding acquaintance with the heroine's *legitimate* culture, especially when contrasted with the 'cachet' of Katharine Parker's *déshabillé*, which she purposefully wears to receive Jack Trainer on her return home. In a broader sense, it could be said that these allusions authenticate the film's representation of its contemporary cultural moment by indirectly reflecting on the precariousness of 'class identity' during the Reagan era which was based, above all, on cultural 'prestige economy' (Conroy 1996: 117, Kleinhans 1996: 251). On another level, however, these scenes also provide a vivid play on Coco Chanel's famous 'guess the women', quoted earlier by Katharine Parker, that again reinforces the 'class' conflict between different models of womanhood. The momentary but eye-catching, spirit-lifting display of Tess's freedom and sexuality could be interpreted as an indirect statement about the post-1960s' triumph of the female body. On the other hand, there is constant evidence of something calculating and self-conscious – something designed to bewitch and impress in Katharine Parker's elegantly attired (and care-fully enacted) nonchalance. This oozing of affectation on the part of the female manager yet again recalls the liberal-feminist stress on women's talent for making their way in a man's world. More particularly, it enhances how the right *pose* or *performance* in a woman will enable her not only to 'equal up' with men but to *dominate* them as well through flirtation and sexual allure. Seen in this light, Parker's excessive reliance on Coco Chanel's recommendation – 'the presentation of her self, especially her gendered self, as visual construct or image, created through the *performance* [my italics] of femininity' (Rowe 1995: 119) – results in a mock version of both the liberal-feminist slogan 'woman *at* the top' and Kathleen Rowe's 'woman *on* top' syndrome.

The heroine's momentary downfall, caused by Katharine Parker's unexpected arrival in the meeting room and her perfidious 'clarifica-tion' of facts bring to the fore the relationship between comedy and melodrama by introducing 'a dramatic (or "serious") issue into the terms of comic pleasurability' (Neale and Krutnik 1990: 133). The melodramatic hazard that suddenly threatens to separate the couple comes in the form of a class predicament – a problem of class position and class consciousness. Surprisingly, when accused of being a mere secretary, Tess almost immediately steps down: she abandons the negotiation table and leaves the meeting room, apologising once and again to everyone. Why, spectators ask themselves, does she surrender so easily and forsake all her projects in such a docile manner?

The classic exposition of the concept of class is, as is well known, Marx's prediction concerning the inevitability of increasing class polarisation 'into two great hostile camps . . . directly facing each other: Bourgeoisie and Proletariat' (Marx and Engels 1988: 80) – the bourgeoisie trying to increase their profits by intensifying exploitation; the proletariat resisting and pressing for improvements in wages and working conditions. Marx expected the conflict between these two fractions to expand until the proletariat as a block seized control of the means of production for itself, thus creating a society without a division between exploiter and exploited: a classless society (Marx and Engels 1988: 105). The central point here is the faith Marx placed in the industrial worker as a necessary agent of *revolutionary* change. This said, the history of advanced capitalism has evidently not followed Marx's augured one-way traffic from the economic to the political. However, there are two ways in which Marx's thesis may serve, and even validate, my interpretation of the momentary crisis in the negotiation room as the reflection of a wider 'class conflict'.

Since Marx's time, there has been a clear shift from an industrial to a financial form of capitalism. Theorists like James Burnham in the 1930s have argued that big corporations like General Motors or ICI (Investment Company Institute) are not really 'capitalist' in the traditional sense for 'no-one' actually owns the company and it is the managers who really run the corporation (Worsley 1990: 60). This line of thought would have us believe that Marxist precepts are now basically irrelevant to current social conditions. However, the counterarguments to such claims are that even multinational firms still have to make capitalist profits and exploit their workers to do so; that managers are normally recruited from the top social class and that, very often, in addition to their salaries, they have financial interests in the corporations they work for. For this reason, critics like Immanuel Wallerstein contend that the process of increasing dependence on wage labour has continued into this century, which means that Marx's 'polarization' remains 'a historically correct hypothesis, not a false one' (James and Berg 1996: 7). With this in mind, a simple, objective definition of class materialises: the bourgeois are those who receive surplus value and are in a position to reinvest it; all others are proletarian. Hence, the negotiation-table scene in *Working Girl* can be looked upon as a clear rendering of Marx's social polarisation. As members of the 'oppressor class', all those present around the table are astounded at the fact that a mere secretary should dare to have tresspassed into or invaded their privileged territory. Even Jack Trainer is rendered speechless and incapable of overcoming the gulf of incommunication and antagonism between the 'two hostile camps'. His reaction, or rather his lack of reaction, therefore, leaves Tess helpless and it is her consciousness of unequal power that induces her to withdraw from the board room without even attempting to put up a fight.

For its part, the proletariat or working class has also undergone serious changes since Marx's time, but it has not changed in the *way* prophesised by Marx for it is, nowadays, by no means a socially and culturally homogeneous body. Given that, today, the lowest-paid occupations are invariably stigmatised by gender and ethnic identity (Worsley 1990: 60–1), the interaction of gender and division of labour cannot be ignored.

In *The Origin of the Family, Private Property and the State* (1884), Engels argued that only the release of women from the confinement of the home – the private sphere – would create the conditions to alter power arrangements (1986: 102). There is no denying that this proposed strategy has provided the means for women's struggle to be carried out, but as socialist feminists like Iris Young contend (in Sargent, 1981: 58), the ideology of male dominance has continued into this century even though large numbers of women have entered the labour force. Field studies have led Judi Marshall (1984: 55–7) to argue that a common feature characterising most women's jobs is that they provide *support* rather than competition for male organisation members.[3] This said, from a liberal stance, perhaps the greatest single achievement of the feminist movement, when it reappeared in the 1970s, has been the opening up of formerly male professions to women (Ehrenreich 1990: 54). What occurred, however, was that the chief beneficiaries of women's campaign for access to male-dominated occupations were women who already had the advantages of good schools, an encouraging home life, and the money and leisure for higher education, which means that entrance to the top professions has been sharply limited by, yet again, 'class'. Katharine Parker represents the type of woman who would have been allowed to drift into the male preserve on the strength of her charm or of her class credentials. On the other hand, through Tess, the film seemingly questions not only the core assumptions of the patriarchal infrastructure – the elitist exclusivity of the professions – but also the egalitarian ideology of liberal feminism: surely, the story appears to suggest, the aim of the feminist struggle was not to propel a few women to the top of a fundamentally unjust and biased hierarchy in which most women count for little more than cheap, supportive labour!

A partial resolution of the conflict comes in Jack Trainer's sudden change of attitude. In their short *tête-à-tête* outside the lift, Tess confesses to him that she has 'bluffed' her way into the fortress of big business because: 'If I'd told you I was just some secretary you would never have taken the meeting. I mean, think about it. Maybe you would have fed me a few drinks and tried to get me into the sack! End of story!' – a stinging comment that points to the ongoing interaction of capitalism and patriarchy, despite all the advances brought about by the women's movement. The result is that Tess is no longer excluded by Jack Trainer as an 'intruder' from the lower classes. More importantly, it is again the combination of class and gender that brings about Tess's final triumph. By nature and by circumstance, Tess is an adept of a typical 'low' form of literature. It turns out that it is by means of magazine chit-chat rather than through dry, specialised and technical information that she has managed to put together the idea of Trask investing in a radio station. In this way, the much denigrated 'womanly knowledge' is simultaneously glamorised and vindicated for it is shown to be both the key that debunks power games and a more humane and necessary dimension in the high world of finance.

The denouement comes with Tess taking up her new post as manager and establishing a language of exchange with her secretary. The end of the film therefore, highlighting as it does the female manager's capacity for blending assertiveness with a style of co-operation and concern for others, reasserts how personal growth can be achieved by the individual coming to know and respect her own female grounding. In other words, *Working Girl* underlines how, both ideologically and practically, women's way forward is to develop and respect their own womanhood even while engaging in the world of patriarchy and capitalism. Only then, it seems, will they be able to escape from oppression without seeking to oppress in their turn. Tess is a model of what women can hope to achieve by balancing personal and interpersonal energy. She appears as a type of individual through whom equal and comradely relationship between woman and man could eventually become possible. In this sense, even the 'morning scene', showing Jack Trainer offering Tess a lunch-pack as the couple are having a hasty breakfast, is significant in that it totally erases the older notion of man as a reliable breadwinner and woman as a dependant. Although there are signs of old-fashioned or traditional romantic values in Jack's caring concern for his companion's well-being, the film does circumvent obsolete and restrictive sex roles by presenting 'a professional couple' – the romantic aura of equal partnership demonstrating, by the same token, that women are more likely to attain effective equality within their unions or marriages as economic partners and helpmates. Hence, both in the public and private realms, the character of Tess heralds the possibility of social transformation as conjectured by Betty Friedan in 1982, when she suggested that society was moving on to a 'Second Stage' of dialogue and joint development with men.

This said, close attention to the last shot reveals an unequivocal 'twist' in this reverberating message of hope. Against the background melody of the hymn: 'Come the new Jerusalem', the camera starts receding and never stops tracking backwards until the site of the heroine's triumph dwindles into a mere spot in the distance – a spot which then loses itself completely amidst the panoramic view of the town's sky-scrapers. Could this ending imply that Tess's achievement is so insignificant as to mean nothing?

Considering that stories like *Working Girl* seldom happen, the film could also be viewed as a barely disguised form of fairy tale. As occurs in romantic comedy (Neale and Krutnik 1990: 141), much of the appeal of fairy tales usually derives from all the complications and obstacles that keep the heroine away from Prince Charming, and from the certainty that, in the end, all will be resolved. From this perspective, the character of Jack Trainer becomes more than relevant in the story for he embodies all in one a stepping stone to success for Tess, the assistant unconsciously helping her tread dangerous ground and, more importantly, the one who offers her the potential to recognise that a stable heterosexual relationship is the necessary, complementary dimension in the life of a successful career woman. Seen in this light, the film seems to suggest, as screwball comedies did in their time, that Tess's desire for professional success is not necessarily an obstacle to finding 'Mr Right-Man'.[4] On the contrary, as opposed to the self-seeking, narcissistic careerist Katharine, it is Tess's heavy reliance on Jack as guide or mentor that removes any trace in her of peril to men or to eventual union (Krutnik 1990: 67). Nor is it surprising that Katharine Parker should be *punished* for her deceit through uncorresponded desire and ridicule – the way Jack slides out of her embrace when visiting her on the day of her return home. What makes the character especially vulnerable is that it is not her person but her physique, rendered grotesque by the plaster – a 'form of ugliness or deformity that is painless and has no harmful effects' (Aristotle quoted by Neale and Krutnik 1990: 66) – which is used as a source of derision. Thus, Katharine Parker's elaborately constructed image of herself as the super-feminine, super-woman exuding dignity and authority is marred by the ridiculousness of her enforced hobble, and totally pulverised when she is finally told by Trask to get 'her bony ass out of sight'.

The formulaic closing of the tale marks the final triumph of Good over Evil as the all-powerful, kingly or paternalistic figure of Oren Trask (representing ethical and benevolent patriarchy) sanctions the union between the heroine and Prince Charming. Hence, by pushing forward the idea of the romantic couple as the source of all happiness, *Working Girl* discreetly preserves the notion of male potency while reinscribing Tess within traditional concepts of (vulnerable) femininity.

The ambivalence towards women executives I have detected in the film could therefore be summarised in the following way: *Working Girl* dramatises how, given the right qualities, even a working-class girl (a person affected by the double stigma of class and gender) can 'make it' in the corporate world. The film also discreetly underlines how men are still the audience for any proposed activities, and consequently, what is possible for a woman is still dependent on their guidance and approval – approval in the sense of conforming to *male* dictates regarding femininity.

By way of conclusion, I would like to suggest that these two simultaneous (and yet contradictory) readings of *Working Girl* are more related than separate, especially if the film is considered as an allegory of the Reagan era. During the 1980s, the destiny of the USA was steered by an ex-cowboy-movie actor who had risen to the presidency of the United States. After the confusion, frustrations and compromises of the Carter years, the nation experienced, for the first time, signs of economic distress and, consequently, lacked the optimism that had

dominated the immediate post-war period. To an important extent, the
essence of Reagan's success seems to have rested on two fundamentals:
on the one hand, the new president symbolised the American dream –
America was indeed 'the new Jerusalem' where *anyone*, should she or
he be shrewd, resourceful and ambitious, could succeed. On the other
hand, Reagan was an elderly man when he reached the White House –
an elderly man who wanted to keep things settled in the old certainties
with which he had grown up. This simple delineation should help
explain why, for some, the advent of Reaganism heralded a new phase
of hope and activity. The average citizen – women gave him 57 per cent
of their vote (Chafe 1995: 481) – saw Reagan as personifying the next-
door neighbour whose talent, dedication and enterprise would make
the nation stand tall once again.

Once in power, the new president moved quickly to implement his
credo for a new America. While performing radical surgery on the
welfare system of the nation, he proceeded, as the surest guarantee of
sustained prosperity and growth, to give full economic power to the
private sector. By leaving economics on automatic pilot, the American
spirit of individualism, competition and personal pride would once
again be restored and, in no time, America's renewed vitality would,
Reagan promised his voters in 1984 (Chafe 1995: 482), match the
Olympic triumphs of American athletes in Los Angeles. In this way, the
Reagan credo succeeded in inspiring millions of people with a new
faith in themselves and in their country. It is apparently this new era of
good feelings that *Working Girl*, as a cinematic allegory, is celebrating.
Tess is 'the girl next door' whose natural aptitudes (she is bright, talented and ambitious) spell out for her a life of unparalleled opportunity.
The fact that the heroine manages to rise from the secretarial pool into
the upper-class world of executive management also serves as ideological legitimation of the moment in showing corporate capitalism
wiping out the rigid class demarcations of the past. However, if the
film can be read symbolically as an exaltation of the affluent 'classless'
community boosted by Reaganomics, it is at the cost of ignoring the
text's otherwise too obvious conservatism – not to say sexism. One of
the major political developments of the 1970s had been the increased
mobilisation of conservative voters by the 'New Right' around volatile
social issues. Feminism, for example, was seized upon by this 'new
faith' as the cause of myriad social problems (illegitimacy, divorce,

abortion). By 1980, the New Right had embraced the candidacy of
Ronald Reagan and with him they hoped to 'take control of the culture'
(Chafe 1995: 465), that is, to impose a return to and a reassertion of
what were conceived of as traditional familial and sexual standards
(Weeks 1992: 292–4). With this in mind, the film *Working Girl* can also
be viewed as a barely disguised form of fairy tale that contributes to
'cultural control' by the pressure it exerts upon women to emulate fairy
tale prototypes. Under the guise of a conventional tale, the story makes
'finding Mr Right-Man' not simply an ideal but the one state towards
which even working women should aspire. Thus, by means of this
romantic cover-up, the film avoids dealing directly with the problem of
how to define equality between the sexes in the public sphere by substituting in its place the looser concept of 'equal opportunity'.

NOTES

1 Genuine 'sisterhood' does appear in the film when it foregrounds, in a
   somewhat schematic manner, the friendship between Tess and Cyn (Joan
   Cusack). This relationship is treated, especially by Cyn, in terms not of
   personal advancement but of genuine co-operative acts and sincere
   woman-bonding (even Tess's continual demands on Cyn can be rated as
   fairly utilitarian).
2 Tess's reiterated efforts at finding the right pitch or tone of voice can also
   be viewed in the light of those feminist critics whose work is directed at
   enabling women to 'find a voice'. In feminist theory, the silence of
   women stands for their repression in patriarchy as well as for their situation of 'absence' in relation to language. In other words, in the symbolic
   order, women are forced to use a discourse that is imposed on them and
   therefore inadequate to express their reality (Moi 1985: 150–61).
3 The six female-dominated occupations in the 1980s are, according to
   Dorothy Sue Cobble: secretary, clerk-typist, saleswoman, private household worker, waitress and teacher (James and Berg 1996: 265).
4 The film is clearly balancing out two different worlds. By having Tess and
   Jack simply come together or 'make it' as a couple, the film is acknowledging the breakdown or disintegration of the marriage institution in
   the modern world. On the other hand, in Frank Krutnik's words, 'there
   is a return to the priorities of the screwball films' in that the coupling is
   presented 'as necessary for, rather than incompatible with, individual
   emotional and sexual security' (1990: 69).

WORKS CITED

Chafe, William H. 1995. *The Unfinished Journey*. Oxford: Oxford University Press

Conroy, Marianne 1996. 'No Sin in Lookin' Prosperous'. In James and Berg, eds, 114–37

Daly, Mary 1991. *Beyond God the Father*. London: The Women's Press

Duchen, Claire 1988. *Feminism in France*. London: Routledge & Kegan Paul

Eagleton, Mary 1986. *Feminist Literary Theory*. Oxford: Basil Blackwell

Ehrenreich, Barbara 1990. 'Feminism and Class Consolidation', *Dialogue*, 90, 4: 52–6

Engels, Friedrich 1986 (1884). *The Origin of the Family: Private Property and the State*. Harmondsworth: Penguin

French, Marilyn 1985. *Beyond Power: On Women, Men and Morals*. New York: Summit Books

French, Marilyn 1991. *Beyond God the Father*. London: The Women's Press

Harker, Andrew 1987. 'Women and Work', *Dialogue*, 77, 3: 2–7

Irons, Glenwood 1992. *Gender Language and Myth*. Toronto and London: University of Toronto Press

James, David E. and Rick Berg, eds, 1996. *The Hidden Foundation: Cinema and the Question of Class*. Minnesota and London: University of Minnesota Press

Jordan, G. and C. Weedon 1995. *Cultural Politics*. Oxford: Basil Blackwell

Kleinhans, Chuck 1996. 'Class in Action'. In James and Berg, eds, 240–63

Krutnik, Frank 1990. 'The Faint Aroma of Performing Seals: The "Nervous" Romance and the Comedy of the Sexes', *The Velvet Light Trap*, no. 26 (Fall): 57–70

Marshall, Judi 1984. *Women Managers: Travellers in a Male World*. Chichester: John Wiley & Sons

Marx, Karl and Friedrich Engels 1986 (1888). *The Communist Manifesto*. London: Penguin Books

Moi, Toril 1988. *Sexual/Textual Politics*. London: Methuen

Neale, Steve 1992. 'The Big Romance or Something Wild?: Romantic Comedy Today', *Screen*, 33 (Autumn): 284–99

Neale, Steve and Frank Krutnik 1990. *Popular Film and Television Comedy*. London: Routledge

Rowe, Kathleen 1995. *The Unruly Woman*. Austin: University of Texas Press

Sargent, Lydia, ed., 1981. *Women and Revolution: A Discussion of the Unhappy Marriage of Marxism and Feminism*. Boston: South End Press

Walters, Danuta Suzanna 1995. *Material Girls*. Berkeley and London: University of California Press

Weeks, Jeffrey 1992. *Sex, Politics and Society*. Harlow: Longman

Worsley, Peter 1990. *Marx and Marxism*. London: Routledge

Chapter 8

LOVE AND OTHER TRIANGLES:
ALICE AND THE CONVENTIONS OF
ROMANTIC COMEDY

Celestino Deleyto

Alice: *Affluence as hysteria: Alice (Mia Farrow) longs for change on her way out of a Fifth Avenue boutique*

Comedy in Woody Allen's films has traditionally been associated with his comic persona, the *shlemiel* 'Heywood Allen' (Wernblad 1992: 16), a persona which was first constructed in his stand-up live acts and, later on, definitively established in his writings, plays and films of the 1970s. Critics as diverse as Babington and Evans (1989), McCann (1990),

129

Hirsch (1991), Wernblad (1992), Krutnik (1995) and, to a lesser extent, Girgus (1993), all analyse the films as 'comedian comedies' (Seidman 1981, Krutnik 1995: 17) and, whenever they consider the films of the 1980s, their main focus tends to be on the developments experienced by the original persona in the later films. This excessive emphasis on Allen the comedian has obscured the importance of the increasingly sophisticated narrative structures of his films since *Annie Hall* (1977) (Deleyto 1994/95) and their consideration as romantic comedies.

An indirect consequence of this critical bias has been the overwhelming concentration on the films' representations of masculinity and new forms of male control. For Babington and Evans, Allen is 'the confused prototype of the new "feminised" man' and 'the product of a heterosexuality . . . anxious about the ideals of masculinity it feels it has to live up to' (1989: 152 and 165). Neale and Krutnik include *Annie Hall* and *Manhattan* (1979) among the group of 'nervous romances' of the late 1970s and early 1980s and argue that in these films 'the contemporary breakdown of monogamy represents a particular challenge to the male, and . . . it is the "post-feminist" woman who is largely to blame' (1990: 171–2). Finally, for Rowe, the apparent feminisation of the Allen characters is only a strategy to 'prop up their own authority, which they then invoke to "instruct" women about relationships, romance, and femininity itself' (1995: 197).[1] While these authors are surely correct in their analysis of the films' representation of post-feminist beleaguered masculinity and its rearguard attempts to construct new patterns of patriarchal supremacy, their views hardly account for the construction of gender relationships in films like *Hannah and her Sisters* (1986), *Husbands and Wives* (1992), and, especially, *The Purple Rose of Cairo* (1985), *September* (1987), *Another Woman* (1988) or *Alice* (1991). All of these share a focus on their female characters which cannot be solely explained through a male perspective. In this chapter, I wish to start filling some of the existing gaps in Allen criticism by concentrating on *Alice*, a film which contains instances of all the most interesting developments in the director's career: its increasingly complex representation of women, its sophisticated use of narrative and formal strategies for the filmic rendering of subjectivity and, especially, its exploration of the conventions of romantic comedy and their relation to fantasy and social criticism.

THE COMIC BALANCE: FANTASY AND REALITY
IN ALLEN'S FILMS

Whereas, as is known, Aristotelian comedy is realistic and its function corrective, romantic comedy is a comedy of wish-fulfilment and is based on what Frye calls 'imaginative faith' on the part of the spectator (1965: 19). It is a type of comedy that abounds in unexpected turns, unforeseen changes and coincidences and, in Frye's words, its 'drive toward a comic conclusion is so powerful that it breaks all the chains of probability in the plot' (1965: 123). For Rowe, the reason why romantic comedy persists as a narrative genre is that 'it speaks to powerful needs to believe in the utopian possibilities condensed on the image of the couple' (1995: 212). Yet, as Frye himself argues, these two types of comedy are just two ways of developing one single comic structure and, although, as Nelson points out, fantasy is often perceived as anti-thetical to reality, both fantasy and reality ultimately coexist in the comic text (1990: 144–9).

Allen's comedies seem to confirm this theory. Whereas his early parodies belong to an openly fantastic pre-Oedipal mode (Horton 1991: 10–12), his most popular romantic comedies – *Annie Hall*, *Manhattan* or *Hannah and her Sisters* – are firmly placed within the context of a very recognisable reality of white intellectual middle-class New York society. Yet, even these films combine their apparent concern with a 'post-feminist, post-Vietnam culture' (Babington and Evans 1989: 152) with a romantic drive towards wish-fulfilment, unrealistic turns of the plot and comic visualisations of the protagonists' flights into fantasy. *The Purple Rose of Cairo* is, perhaps, the clearest example: its heroine's escape from patriarchal and economic oppression in a 1930s' US small town consists in a fantastic romantic involvement with the fictional hero of one of the Hollywood films she loves and repeatedly goes to see. According to McCann, Allen's films show, in general, his delight in the power of the cinema to transgress conventions of reality and fantasy (1990: 179). For Wernblad, however, although many of Allen's characters show an interest in magic, fantasy and dreams, the films are critical of those characters who cannot distinguish between dream and reality (1992: 28–9). Talking about *The Purple Rose of Cairo* Allen himself said that the film is about 'the difference between fantasy and reality and how seductive fantasy is and how, unfortunately, we must live with reality, and how painful that can be' (quoted in Girgus 1993: 70).

In any case, both *The Purple Rose of Cairo* and *Alice*, along with other Allen films, would seem part of a more general trend in contemporary romantic comedy: the 'return to fantasy' in the genre noted by some critics. For Rowe, *Moonstruck* (1987) is representative of a tendency to include 'allusions to some external frame of reference, whether "magic" and "signs" or opera and old movies, to make believable its claims for the fantasy of romantic love' (1995: 205).[2] It would seem that, in the face of the long-lasting and seemingly irreversible crisis of romantic love and the social institutions of marriage and the family (Lasch 1979: 169), these films are aware that 'love is perceived to be a much-craved but easily denied commodity for contemporary audiences' (Comino 1995: 49), and opt for a frank acknowledgement of the Shakespearean wish-fulfilment drive of romantic comedy. Like *The Purple Rose of Cairo*, *Peggy Sue Got Married* (1986), *Big* (1988), *Pretty Woman* (1989), *Ghost* (1990), *Groundhog Day* (1992) and other 'new romances' (Neale 1992), the comic plot of *Alice* features a supernatural event that places the heterosexual romance between its protagonists beyond the reach of the everyday. Yet, as I will try to prove in this chapter, *Alice* is ultimately different from all the other films in that in it reality is never totally displaced by the dream. On the contrary, it is constantly lurking throughout the story and reappears at the end of the film to problematise and even to disavow the credibility of its own fantasy and its attendant conventions.

DREAMS AND BACKACHES: THE SPACE OF ROMANTIC COMEDY

From *Annie Hall* to *Crimes and Misdemeanors* (1989), Allen has experimented with ways of breaking narrative chronology in order to represent a character's subjective world: dreams, memories, reveries, obsessive anticipations of the future, visualised accounts of past events and open distortions of reality are all part of what Girgus calls 'interior space' in Allen's films, an interior space whose constant presence makes the narratives progress in 'unconventional ways' (1993: 118–19). Although other Allen films use various formal techniques to represent this interior space, those that carry stylistic experimentation in this field furthest are those that feature female protagonists. *The Purple Rose of Cairo* can be said to take place entirely within Cecilia's mind through the conceit of the film screen that can be crossed by the power of her imagination. *Another Woman* and *Alice*, on the other hand, display a rich variety of ways of visualising what is happening in the characters' minds, including memories, dreams, reveries, imagined conversations with characters in the past, and other scenes that spring directly from the protagonists' psyche. The beginning of *Alice* heralds later developments. After the credit sequence, Alice Tait and Joe Ruffalo (Joe Mantegna) are seen walking together inside the penguin house at the zoo. A lateral pan to the left finds the same two characters in close-up kissing tenderly (which suggests that either the beginning or the end of the shot is a reflection in a mirror *or* that the space of the shot is not realistic). There follows a cut to the present of the narration: Alice, still in close-up, sits at the breakfast table of her luxurious Manhattan apartment, obviously reminiscing about the kiss, while her husband Doug (William Hurt) is getting ready to leave for his office. The non-diegetic tune that we have heard over the credit sequence and the first shot – 'Limehouse Blues', one of the main songs of the film – is still heard for a few seconds in the present, reinforcing the impression that she is indeed thinking about the penguin house. The first shot, therefore, is apparently a flashback which narrates the protagonist's betrayal of her husband with another man. This, however, is a false impression: the event portrayed in the first shot has not occurred in reality, only in Alice's mind. She has indeed seen Joe briefly at their children's school but they have only crossed a few words. In fact, a few minutes later the opening shot may look like an anticipation, since Alice and Joe eventually do arrange to meet at the penguin house, but this assumption is wrong again: Alice changes her mind in the last minute and decides not to go. The film has gently manipulated the spectator in order to suggest that, when it comes to Alice Tait, the differences between memories and imagination are unclear and indeed irrelevant. Later on, Alice, under hypnosis, tells Dr Yang that, like Catholics (Alice is a Catholic), penguins mate for life and so they become a comic reminder of the sin she is about to commit.[3] On the other hand, this and other instances of Alice's 'Catholic' guilt will undercut the pull of the romantic fantasy in two ways: by suggesting that an extra-marital affair, in the moral universe of the film, is not the solution to her problems, and by indirectly helping the protagonist to recuperate the positive aspects of her childhood religious beliefs. To sum up, in this first scene, the exuberant fantasy that is going to be all-important in Alice's development is both powerful enough to dictate the film's structure *and* undercut in crucial ways by the force of the protagonist's moral universe, a moral universe which will eventually lead her to the rejection of the fantasy.

The opening shot is the first (and briefest) of many scenes that take place in Alice's interior space. In pointed contrast, the rest of the first scene introduces her exterior space. After the cut mentioned above, the rest of the scene is a long take which, in just under two minutes, describes the protagonist's everyday life.[4] In this shot, the frame follows her around her flat, focusing on the excessive superfluities in the life of the wealthy middle-class housewife. The absence of classical editing and the obsessive follow-focus suggest, on the one hand, the pointlessness of Alice's present endeavours and, on the other, her as yet unrecognised but urgent need to escape from her suffocating existence. The formal strategy becomes, therefore, a symptom of the protagonist's psyche and is, in this sense, a stylistic correlative of the diegetic symptom: her persistent backache.

The spectator learns from the beginning that the backache is a hysterical somatisation of her problems with her husband and their life together. In romantic comedy, the convention of the 'wrong partner' is usually connected with the protagonist's process of learning (Neale 1992: 288–94): the wrong partner embodies all the negative values with which the hero or heroine is initially associated and that the film seeks to overturn. In *Alice*, Doug is clearly the wrong partner and he, along with Alice's friends, represents the loss of profound values brought about by excessive wealth. It is through her/his romantic involvement with the right partner that the protagonist learns to endorse those values defended by the film. The process of liberation from repression involves, therefore, a change of partner and a rediscovery of the sexual instinct (Frye 1965: 82). The convention, therefore, dictates that Alice's liberation from the repressive social structures will come from her romantic involvement with a new partner.[5] Yet, even though she does get involved with Joe Ruffalo, who initially looks like the right partner, the film, frustrating the spectator's expectations once again, will prove that he is not the right choice either. For the time being, however, what seems obvious is that Alice must undergo an internal change. As Frye suggests, although repression always has an external component, it is internalised repression that the protagonists have to learn to defeat through a change of identity (1965: 78). At bottom, romantic comedy maps an internal process of change, what Salingar, following the pattern – and the words – of Shakespearean comedy, has termed 'losing in order to find': the temporary loss of identity in the middle section of the plot becomes a phase in the characters' knowledge of themselves (1974: 24). In order to embark on this interior journey, Alice enlists the help of Dr Yang.

In a film in which the characters never move out of Manhattan 'physically', the 'other' space of romantic comedy – the forest or foreign city of Shakespearean comedy in which inhibitions are lifted and a new identity is found – is represented, on the one hand, by Alice's interior space and, on the other, by Dr Yang's apartment in Chinatown.[6] The camera follows Alice closely as the limousine drops her in this 'exotic' space and as she goes up the stairs and through the threshold of the apartment, symbolically moving into a different world. It must be pointed out that the 'otherness' of this space is limited and, as in the case of Alice's first fantasy (the only one, by the way, which is not induced by Dr Yang), it is openly colonised by the repressive world from which she is instinctively trying to escape. Chinatown is not exactly the Far East but the result of several centuries of difficult adaptation of Chinese people to life in the centre of Western civilisation, preserving part of their cultural identity but in a way that has become acceptable for the dominant culture. 'Limehouse Blues', the song with which Alice's visits to Dr Yang are associated throughout the film, is an American appropriation of stereotyped Eastern musical motifs. Dr Yang himself is played by Keye Luke, best remembered for his role as Charlie Chan's 'Number One Son' in many films of that detective series, and, consequently, associated with Hollywood's frequently trivialised version of exoticism.[7] This is, therefore, an otherness that Alice can cope with and an illustration of her initial reluctance to drastic change. In any case, Dr Yang does help her to embark on her journey of self-discovery.

Her resistance to change is comically rendered when she doubts Dr Yang's power to hypnotise her, which he does without difficulty. Hypnosis, one of the most direct roads to the unconscious in films, immediately draws a confession from Alice: 'I'm at a crossroads. I'm

lost', explicitly associating her with romantic comedy as described by
Frye, Salingar and others. So Dr Yang will make it his job to help her
find herself, to discard her present superficial values and learn to know
her true self.[8] During her last visit, Dr Yang will summarise the success
of his mission with the following words: 'Mrs Tait has better idea who
she is, who her friends are, or are not, who is husband, lover, sister,
mother. What are her needs, her limits, her gifts, what are her innermost feelings. Now must decide which road her life will take.' In the
meantime, Dr Yang's herbs will bring Alice in contact with the most
important people in her past: her old boyfriend, her mother, her sister
and, of course, her husband when they first met. Her successive revis-
itations of the important moments in her life make her gradually aware
of all the wrong decisions she has made and the 'proper' values she has
lost. While Freudian accounts of comedy emphasise the importance of
regression to a pre-Oedipal world previous to repression in comic
structures (Horton 1991: 10–12), Alice's various fantasised returns to
her past are not to a childhood utopia of limitless potency but consist
of often painful rediscoveries, through the lens of her new awareness,
of the different stages through which her present social identity has
been formed. Dr Yang is immediately drawn to his patient's love life
and, sensing her dissatisfaction with her married life, directs her first
'confession' to her relationship with her husband. In this second stage
of Alice's journey into her interior space, the film deploys a set of
stylistic strategies, which will be repeated in the rest of the film, in
order to blend Alice's interior and exterior worlds. The moment of
introspection begins with a close-up of the back of Alice's head, signalling that her interior space is about to be projected outside on to
the film's *mise- en-scène*. She then conjures up Doug, starts speaking to
him and is transported to their first meeting and their decision to get
married. All this takes place without physically moving from Dr Yang's
apartment and it is only through the changes in the lighting and the
dialogues that the flashback is represented. There is no break of narrative frame, and indeed no change of frame, since the shot is, after
Doug's first appearance, another long take. After what is perceived by
the spectator as the symbolic moment in which Alice destroyed her
hopes for the future and agreed to become the submissive wife of
Doug's dreams, Dr Yang summons her back to the present. In the rest
of the film, the same blend of interior and exterior spaces is used to

convey Alice's comic progress. Sometimes, Dr Yang's magic herbs produce an analogous effect to that of her first visit and take Alice on similar excursions to the past. At other times, the herb's magic properties allow her to see her present reality differently, either by making her invisible or by lifting her inhibitions in her relationship with Joe. In general, the film enlists all its stylistic strategies to convey the protagonist's subjectivity and to explore the causes of her present dissatisfied self. Like *The Purple Rose of Cairo* and *Another Woman,* the film becomes an indictment of the sometimes devastating effects of patriarchal culture on women's lives.

ENTER MOTHER TERESA: WOMEN IN ROMANTIC COMEDY

There is nothing new in placing a woman in a patriarchal society at the centre of the structure of romantic comedy. In their analysis of the differences between romantic comedy and melodrama, Neale and Krutnik argue that, whereas romantic melodrama focuses on the female protagonist's desires, romantic comedy focuses equally on men and women (1990: 139). Yet, although the emphasis in the genre is on – generally heterosexual – romantic love and, consequently, at least two characters are needed at the centre of the narrative, in practice most romantic comedies tend to focus on either the male or the female protagonist as the main subject of the process of learning, in such a way that Mulvey's classification of 1950s' melodramas as male or female could, with obvious adjustments, also be applied to this genre (1989: 40). Neale and Krutnik, in fact, argue that what is most at stake in romantic comedy is the '*conversion* of the woman, her progression towards the position occupied by the hero' (1990: 145). The films defend an 'ideology of love' in which heterosexual love is the '"natural" channelling of female desire' (Neale and Krutnik 1990: 146). Whereas these critics relate the narrative centrality of women in the genre to their progression towards normative patriarchal femininity, Rowe focuses on the genre's potential for transgression. Even though, like all mainstream cinema, the genre is ultimately conservative, it *does* manage to give 'expression to the contradictory nature of women's desires concerning romantic love and the relations between the sexes, reminding us of the doubleness of all cultural forms, the intermingling of the ideological and the utopian within them' (1995: 211–12). *Alice* illustrates the contradictory nature of women's desires by placing its heroine at the centre of a love triangle which includes her husband together with the social stability and personal security he embodies, and her lover, who represents the utopian possibilities of a more egalitarian and, at the same time, passionate relationship. When she visits Dr Yang for the last time, she is still trying to decide between the two men, afraid now that she could lose both. Yet the film has been dropping hints that this is not the only triangle that Alice has been involved in and that the genre's normative progression towards self-discovery has been threatened all along by the pull of reality and unexpectedly – for a film which devotes so much space and technical and narrative ingenuity to the representation of the mind and romantic fantasy – by a form of social commitment which will exclude the bond of romantic love. If, as Neale and Krutnik argue, romantic comedy always ends with the conversion of the woman to normative femininity, the liberation of Alice, like that of Marion (Gena Rowlands) in *Another Woman*, can only exist through a transgression of the conventions of the genre, even if her new role as the nurturing woman hardly signifies a rupture with the norm of femininity in patriarchy.

Dr Yang is, throughout the film, the representative of fantasy and, with his love herbs, which openly parody the magic powder of *A Midsummer Night's Dream* and other classical romantic fantasies, of the conventions of romantic love. For him, love brings about suffering but, in leading Alice through a careful re-evaluation of her love life and helping her to consummate her love affair with Joe, he does not seem ready to envisage a different kind of ending for his patient. Even though he has access to some of Alice's innermost thoughts, he never seems to question the patriarchal dominance that she has been subjected to through her endorsement of the *ethos* of romantic love and the dreams and hopes that she has had to abandon for its sake. For him, as Rowe argues for the genre in general, romantic love 'absorb[s] all other needs, desires, and contradictions' and promises the 'fulfillment not only of sexual desire, but of *all* desire' (1995: 129). Yet there has been another character hovering over the narrative: Mother Teresa, who represents the pull of reality and social commitment within the film. Although she does not feature as centrally as Dr Yang, her influence on Alice proves to be decisive. The fact that Dr Yang and Mother Teresa are more powerful rivals to win Alice to their cause than either Doug or Joe can be observed in the scene in which Joe and Alice make love in his apartment, possibly the first climactic scene of the film. In a more conventional contemporary romantic comedy, this scene would have been presented as the culmination, or at least a crucial stage in the protagonist's development.[9] However, here the film clearly parodies convention: Alice is nervous, keeps talking, appears exaggeratedly self-conscious about her sexual allure and promises to go on a diet. After they have made love, the long aftermath is dominated by the repetition of two well-known thematic motifs of Allen's films: the classical concern of the characters with sexual performance (Babington and Evans 1989: 162) and a more recent anxiety about the gradual disappearance of sexual desire in married couples (a concern that also appears in *Another Woman, Husbands and Wives* and others). As a result, the atmosphere produced by the pseudoromantic *mise-en-scène*, the soft Thelonius Monk music and the rain beating against the huge window is 'fatally' counteracted by the distancing, parodic presentation.[10] However, the most decisive aspect of the scene is, ironically, the brief and intense episode that has preceded it: Alice's attendance at an evening in Mother Teresa's honour. Her incessant talk about the impression caused in her by this experience before she makes love with Joe means much more than just a way to voice her embarrassment at the situation. Even though, from Alice's viewpoint, their sexual encounter seems satisfactory, it is easy to see that her experience of the previous day was emotionally much more fulfilling and was pointing the way out of her personal and emotional crisis in a direction romantic comedy cannot contain.

The successive presentation of these two climactic moments clarifies the nature of the struggle between romantic fantasy and social commitment that defines the thematic structure of the film and it also anticipates the final outcome of the struggle. But there is an earlier scene which shows this perhaps more clearly: following an argument with Joe and a frustrated first evening together, Alice decides on a surprise visit to Dr Yang to ask him for something to relax her nerves. His apartment has been transformed into an opium den and, after some but not too much hesitation, Alice joins in. The drug launches her into what is stylistically and narratively her most complex hallucination and, unexpectedly, one that does not have to do with her love life but with her relationship with her sister. Here she conjures up Dorothy

(Blythe Danner) and discusses her differences with her, their childhood together and their Catholic upbringing. She then remembers how, when she was a child at Catholic school, she always wanted to help other people and devote her life to social work. Dorothy's criticism of Alice's frivolous life and the objectionable way in which she is bringing up her children was the cause of their falling out and what now joins them again. Dorothy's narrative function is to recuperate the social dimensions of Alice's old faith and, at the same time, help her to reject its empty rituals and repressive norms. Through her intervention, it is suggested that in taking Mother Teresa as its ultimate role model, the film is not interested in the protagonist's religious faith but her social conscience. It is significant that the temporary crisis in her relationship with Joe is alleviated by this hallucination. This works as an anticipation of the ending, in which Alice's romantic predicament is permanently resolved by her decision to abandon everything and join Mother Teresa in Calcutta. Dorothy is, then, narratively responsible for Alice's final conviction that, in our society, narcissistic romantic infatuation ultimately brings about betrayal and moral degradation (it is at Dorothy's party that Dr Yang's magic herb is misused and all the men in the party fall 'madly' in love with her).

The film, therefore, in spite of its exuberant use of old romantic melodies in the soundtrack (Neale 1992: 296), and in spite of its apparent adherence to the structure and to most of the traditional elements of romantic comedy, gradually and almost imperceptibly moves away from the genre's basic ideology to end up openly confronting it. The spectator, who had been led to believe that Alice's comic choice between Doug and Joe would have brought about the happy ending, sees its expectations frustrated when the traditional love triangle is replaced by the other triangle and Mother Teresa finally defeats Dr Yang in Alice's devotion. This is the final triumph of reality over fantasy and, more specifically, of social commitment over romantic escapism.[11] The final scene is made up of documentary images of Calcutta (borrowed from Louis Malle's *Calcutta* (1969)) and pseudo-documentary shots of Alice back in New York, having left her husband and abandoned her old way of life and doing volunteer work. The soundtrack is occupied by her two friends' voice-over gossip about her and the 'Limehouse Blues' tune, heard for the last time in the film. Whereas in most films voice-over commentary tends to control the spectator's perception of the images, here the terms seem reversed: the contrast between Alice and her friends underlines the worthlessness of the latter's values while reinforcing Alice's moral position. On the other hand, the song both cues the spectator to read this scene as a comic ending and, since image is generally dominant over sound, it undercuts the ideological discourse of romantic fantasy with which it had been associated.

ECHOES OF TRANSCENDENCE: SEX, MARRIAGE AND OTHER UTOPIAS

Marriage or some promise of a permanent relationship between the protagonists has traditionally constituted the happy ending of romantic comedy. For Frye, marriage is the most common form of identity, 'in which two souls become one' and it marks the triumph of the new society, underlining the theme of social identity (1965: 82 and 87). Gardner, likewise, considers marriage the great symbol of what she calls 'pure comedy' (1970: 193). This glorification of marriage as the symbol of 'natural vitality' (Purdie 1993: 154) has been denounced by feminist critics. For Purdie, Frye's and Gardner's theories can be included within the 'mythical' accounts of comedy, which emphasise the triumph of life over death and the unchanging structures of human existence, thus masking the relationship between the individual and her/his historical and social context. They produce as 'normal, natural and unchangeably given what is in fact one particular social construct, whose unreflective celebration ignores the disadvantage it entails for many "abnormal" individuals' (Purdie 1993: 155). In a similar vein, Neupert argues, in his discussion of film endings, that, in many Hollywood films, the problems raised by the female characters are resolved by marriage or death (1995: 106). In romantic comedy it is marriage, 'the comic equivalent of apocalypse', that acts 'as an ideological end point, the restriction of woman, and the end of feminine "spunk" and independence, guaranteeing the desiring male's success' (Neupert 1995: 73).

After the rather awkward endings of his early parodies, Allen's films have been characterised by a bittersweet quality at the moment of closure, tending towards the bitter in *Annie Hall* or *Stardust Memories* (1980) and towards the sweet in later films like *Broadway Danny Rose*

(1984) and *The Purple Rose of Cairo* (Wernblad 1992: 106–7). Yet, none
of them ends in a wedding celebration. Contemporary uncertainties
about the institution of marriage and durable heterosexual relationships seem to have affected the traditional convention of the happy
ending in the genre, and the open endings of *Manhattan* and *Broadway
Danny Rose* – with the two prospective partners interrogating their
own desires and the difficulties of a future together – are more representative of recent romantic comedies than the celebratory commitment
of the classical period.

Of all Allen films, the only one to date that ends in a wedding celebration is *Crimes and Misdemeanors*, paradoxically, his most pessimistic
film. In this film, the wedding of Ben's daughter is used as a bitterly
ironic counterpoint to Clifford's (Woody Allen) and Judah's (Martin
Landau) devastating moral experiences and, perhaps more ironically,
to Ben's predicament. Ben (Sam Waterston) is a rabbi and the film's
most fervent believer in a moral order for the universe. By the final
scene, he has gone completely blind – blindness and the eyes of God
are a running metaphor in the film, which for some critics is too obvious
and heavy-handed (Girgus 1993: 110) – and we see him dancing with
his daughter, naively smiling in the confidence given him by his faith
in a moral structure, while, all around him, the spectator notices that
this structure has totally collapsed. More than a celebration of life, the
wedding becomes a bitter counterpoint to the 'end of the world' that
the film pessimistically forecasts. The ending of *Husbands and Wives*
once again uses Allen's fake documentary style in an attempt to escape
from the realm of fantasy and portray the complex and extremely difficult romantic relationships of five couples with a clearly realistic,
almost *cinéma-vérité* vocation. Thematic realism goes hand in hand
with cinematic techniques and the final snatches of interviews with the
characters suggest that, in our modern world, any utopian search for
happy stable relationships is, even in a romantic comedy, just not
possible. Both these films engage with the tradition of a genre that they
use but to which they do not fully belong. By using the convention of
marriage and the happy ending ironically, *Crimes and Misdemeanors*
radically recontextualises it in a historical moment in which the moral
crisis of the individual is 'legible' in terms of the crisis of modern social
institutions (Lasch 1979: 188–9, 248–9). By replacing the happy ending,
whether closed or open, by an acknowledgement of the inconclusive

nature of marital crises in 'real life', thus altering the structure of the 'comedy of remarriage', *Husbands and Wives* indirectly underlines the wish-fulfilment nature of the genre, at least, as it is perceived in our time.

The ending of *Alice* must be seen within the context of the exploration of the happy ending carried out in these two films, but, in contrast to these, from within the genre. Both marriage and remarriage are perceived as threats to the heroine's individuality and proper socialisation. Alice's comic development proves to be incompatible with the sexuality which has been the central element in the definition of women in patriarchy (Foucault 1981: 104) and also with Allen's reputation as the chronicler of contemporary sexual relationships (Babington and Evans 1989: 156–66). Yet, unlike the other two films, *Alice* remains a comedy and substitutes an ending in which the heroine is both in control of her own life (like Marion in *Another Woman*) and an active member of her new community, thus replacing the new society symbolised by marriage by one in which the woman is the centre. In this way, the film departs from Rowe's description of romantic love absorbing all forms of desire in comedy and responds to Dyer's complaint that 'modern discussion of cultural pleasures tends to take sexuality as the founding form of all enjoyment, as the appetite *par excellence*' (1994: 10). Alice's rejection of sexual involvements is a way to regain her own identity and an indictment of those forms of socialisation of female sexuality in modern culture that the 'unchanging' structures of romantic comedy constantly reinforce.

In his analysis of sexuality and love in our century, Giddens argues that when sexuality was tied to reproduction, it was a symbol of a transcendental order. The emergence of 'plastic sexuality', a sexuality freed from the needs of reproduction, has not managed to deprive it of an 'echo of the transcendent', yet one which is surrounded by nostalgia and disillusion. In this sense, sexuality has become 'not the antithesis of a civilisation dedicated to economic growth and technical control, but the embodiment of its failure' (Giddens 1992: 203). It could be argued that romantic comedy has either undergone the same drastic transformation as sexuality, progressing from a culture in which sex was linked with reproduction, regeneration and transcendence to one in which it is bound up with the concept of the self *or* remained as a nostalgic structure that takes the spectator back to an era of fantasised greater satisfaction with the place of the human being in the universe. In its origins, comedy was bound up with fertility and the natural cycles. Sexuality figured centrally in it as a means to obtain integration in the cosmic order. This feeling of integration is still present in Shakespearean comedy but now a sense of a search for self-identity is added, one which is still bound up with nature. Sex is harnessed within marriage as the 'proper' culmination of a love which will guarantee a stable social order. Foucault's theory of the putting of the erotic into discourse (1981: 19–23) explores the same process of regularisation of sexual practices as a means to control individuals and social groups. In this sense, plastic sexuality came to pose a threat to a normative view of sexuality on which much depended ideologically. Contemporary romantic comedy can be seen as an attempt to represent and contain these changes. Allen's films and other 'nervous romances' explore the tensions between a narrative structure still based on erotic love leading to regeneration and transcendence and a modern experience of sexuality as a culturally prestigious channel of access to the contemporary project of self-identity. These texts attempt to explore relationships as they are in our society, including the ever growing centrality of plastic sexuality and consequent anxiety about transcendence. Therefore, the classical structure must suffer in various ways. Some films clearly betray a nostalgia for the past – *Annie Hall, Manhattan, A Midsummer Night's Sex Comedy* (1982) – others are dominated by the hesitancy of postmodernist self-consciousness – *The Purple Rose of Cairo, Hannah and her Sisters* – while yet others suggest in various ways the precarious feasibility of romantic comedy – *Crimes and Misdemeanors, Alice, Husbands and Wives*. While other contemporary examples of the genre attempt to uphold an uneasy alliance between the modern experience of sexuality and a utopian return to a transcendence denied by, among other things, the emancipation of women and the democratisation of gender relationships, *Alice* reveals the impossibility of this alliance and replaces the romantic utopia of the traditional love triangle by a different, more urgent, social utopia, subverting without abandoning the boundaries of the genre.

NOTES

1 Of Allen's critics, McCann is the most interested in defending Allen's 'feminism' (1990: 94–104); even Wernblad, who is generally sympathetic

towards Allen's representations of women, notes the negative evolution of the central female character in *Annie Hall* (1992: 67).

2 See also Babington's chapter in this book and Neale (1992: 294–9).

3 Connoisseurs of Allen's films will recognise the connection between penguins and Catholics from *Manhattan*. In this film, Isaac Davis (Woody Allen) supports permanent relationships (even though he himself has been married and divorced twice and moves between two girl-friends in the course of the film) and openly criticises his friend Yale for betraying his wife (and him) with Mary (Diane Keaton). Betrayal is a general symptom in Allen of the contemporary decline of moral standards.

4 Since *Hannah and her Sisters*, Woody Allen has consistently used the long take as an alternative to classical continuity editing, a formal choice which has not been sufficiently noticed by critics and one that affects, among other things, the way his films present gender relationships.

5 Or with an old partner in the 'comedy of remarriage' (Cavell 1981, Musser 1995).

6 Calcutta turns out to be the definitive 'other' space signifying Alice's change of identity, but we will return to that in due course.

7 Keye Luke was 86 when he made *Alice* and died the following year. His presence in the film is parodic in the sense that in the Charlie Chan films he plays the impulsive son of the wise oriental detective. Here he is himself the experienced 'detective of the mind' who will assist Alice in her quest to find the truth about herself.

8 Confession is, according to Foucault, the central mechanism in our culture's relentless search for true identity in sex (1981: 35, 64–7).

9 See Henderson for the absence or postponement of sex as the central structural principle of classical romantic film comedy (1978: 21–2).

10 *When Harry Met Sally* (1990) is another recent example of a film in which the long-protracted love-making scene involving the romantic couple produces an unexpected anticlimax in terms of generic conventions, but, in this film, the ending allows the characters to overcome their difficulties and confirms their sexual compatibility, finally endorsing the values of the genre. More recently, *Romy and Michele's High School Reunion* (1997) openly parodies the convention of the romantic or sexual encounter and replaces it by a renewed friendship between the two women. Like Alice, Romy and Michele are two heroines of romantic comedy who do not need romantic involvements with men to achieve emotional maturity.

11 Even though it could be said that the ending also shows Alice's new 'vocation' as utopian and, in its own way, a different kind of wish-fulfilment.

WORKS CITED

Babington, Bruce and Peter William Evans 1989. *Affairs to Remember: The Hollywood Comedy of the Sexes*. Manchester: Manchester UP

Cavell, Stanley 1981. *Pursuits of Happiness: The Hollywood Comedy of Remarriage*. Cambridge, MA: Harvard UP

Comino, Jo 1995. 'Only You', *Sight and Sound*, 5, 2 (October): 48

Deleyto, Celestino 1994/95. 'The Narrator and the Narrative: The Evolution of Woody Allen's Film Comedies', *Film Criticism*, XIX, 2 (Winter): 40–54

Dyer, Richard 1994. 'Action!', *Sight and Sound*, 4, 10 (October): 7–10

Foucault, Michel 1981 (1976). *The History of Sexuality, Vol. 1: An Introduction*. Trans. Robert Hurley. Harmondsworth: Penguin

Frye, Northrop 1957. *Anatomy of Criticism: Four Essays*. Princeton, NJ: Princeton UP

Frye, Northrop 1965. *A Natural Perspective: The Development of Shakespearean Comedy and Romance*. San Diego, New York and London: Harcourt Brace Jovanovich

Gardner, Helen 1970 (1959). '*As You Like It*'. In *Modern Shakespearean Criticism: Essays on Style, Dramaturgy, and the Major Plays*, Alvin B. Kernan. New York: Harcourt Brace Jovanovich

Giddens, Anthony 1992. *The Transformation of Intimacy: Sexuality, Love and Eroticism in Modern Societies*. Cambridge: Polity Press

Girgus, Sam B. 1993. *The Films of Woody Allen*. Cambridge: Cambridge UP

Henderson, Brian 1978. 'Romantic Comedy Today: Semi-Tough or Impossible?', *Film Quarterly*, 31, 4 (Summer): 11–23

Hirsch, Foster 1991 (1981). *Love, Sex, Death and the Meaning of Life: The Films of Woody Allen*. New York: Limelight Editions

Horton, Andrew S., ed. and intro., 1991. *Comedy/Cinema/Theory*. Berkeley, Los Angeles and Oxford: University of California Press

Karnick, Kristine Brunovska and Henry Jenkins, eds, 1995. *Classical Hollywood Comedy*. New York and London: Routledge

Krutnik, Frank 1995. 'A Spanner in the Works? Genre, Narrative and the Hollywood Comedian'. In Karnick and Jenkins, eds, 17–38

Lasch, Christopher 1991 (1979). *The Culture of Narcissism: American Life in an Age of Diminishing Expectations*. New York and London: W. W. Norton

McCann, Graham 1990. *Woody Allen: New Yorker*. Cambridge: Polity Press

Mulvey, Laura 1989 (1977). 'Notes on Sirk and Melodrama'. In *Visual and Other Pleasures*, L. Mulvey. Bloomington and Indianapolis: Indiana UP, 39–44

Musser, Charles 1995. 'Divorce, DeMille and the Comedy of Remarriage'. In Karnick and Jenkins, eds, 282–313

Neale, Steve 1992. 'The Big Romance or Something Wild?: Romantic Comedy Today', *Screen*, 33, 3 (Autumn): 284–99

Neale, Steve and Frank Krutnik 1990. *Popular Film and Television Comedy.* London and New York: Routledge

Nelson, T. G. A. 1990. *Comedy: The Theory of Comedy in Literature, Drama, and Cinema.* Oxford and New York: Oxford UP

Neupert, Richard 1995. *The End: Narration and Closure in the Cinema.* Detroit: Wayne State UP

Purdie, Susan 1993. *Comedy: The Mastery of Discourse.* London: Harvester Wheatsheaf

Rowe, Kathleen 1995. *The Unruly Woman: Gender and the Genres of Laughter.* Austin: University of Texas Press

Salingar, Leo 1974. *Shakespeare and the Traditions of Comedy.* Cambridge: Cambridge UP

Seidman, Steve 1981. *Comedian Comedy: A Tradition in Hollywood Film.* Ann Arbor: UMU Research Press

Wernblad, Annette 1992. *Brooklyn Is Not Expanding: Woody Allen's Comic Universe.* London and Toronto: Associated University Presses

Chapter 9

THE FEVER AND THE ITCH:
MATCHING PLOTS IN SPIKE LEE'S
JUNGLE FEVER

Isabel C. Santaolalla

Jungle Fever: *The interracial romance between Flipper (Wesley Snipes) and Angie (Annabella Sciorra)*

The more contact I have with humans, the more I learn.
                                        (*Terminator 2: Judgement Day*, 1991)

When Spike Lee's *Jungle Fever* was released in 1991, it was hailed by many as a turning point in the narrativisation of interracial romance in

the American cinema. The marketing of the film itself made every effort
to foreground the romance between the African-American architect
Flipper (Wesley Snipes) and his Italian-American temp secretary Angie
(Annabella Sciorra) at the expense of the various other pairings and
issues explored by the film. The shocking colour clash of intertwined
black and white hands on the film's promotional poster carried with it
the promise of transgression of an enduring sexual taboo – interracial
sex on the screen – and the blunt two-word title branded in black and
white on white and black fingers respectively intensified the effect by
suggesting primitiveness and sexual heat.

Unquestionably, the scene in which Flipper's dark athletic body
makes love to the virginal light-skinned Angela on the office drafting
table was meant to shock audiences. No romantic music or filtered soft
lighting tempers the physicality of the scene. Instead, white and black
vertical and diagonal lines cut the frame into pieces, isolating and
entrapping the couple in sheets of chromatic polarity, all bathed in a
cold, stark light.

Lee's explicit, unabashed representation of interracial sexual desire
on screen touched a hypersensitive fibre in American consciousness –
the unresolved ambivalence between the nation's foundational myths
of equality and its distressing realities of racism, ghettoisation and
miscegenation. It had an irresistible appeal for audiences accustomed
to a long history of prudish and oblique treatments of the subject by
a film industry which, from the outset – for example, Griffith's *Broken
Blossoms* (1919) – has inexorably subjected interracial lovers to its
unwritten codes of miscegenation. Despite contemporary audiences'
greater expectations of sexual explicitness on the screen, scriptwriters
remain too nervous of visually frank interracial sex, preferring a more
censored treatment of the subject. Films as recent as *Fatal Beauty*
(1987), *Love Field* (1991), *The Bodyguard* (1992), *The Pelican Brief* (1993)
or *Corrina, Corrina* (1994), among others, have resorted to a variety of
strategies in order to keep the interracial couple's sexual encounter at
bay. Regardless of the fact that, according to Stephens, census figures
show that about 2.5 million United States citizens are currently partners in an interracial marriage (1995: 67), the industry has not yet been
able to accommodate this reality into its frames of representation.

But Spike Lee is not one to flinch from overt treatment of the subject:
the industry's fear of white audience prejudice has little, if any, impact

Jungle Fever: *The African-American family under threat*

on his directorial decisions. Admittedly, Lee emerged from the independent sector but, by the time *Jungle Fever* was released, the unexpected
box office success of his previous low-budget films – particularly *Do the
Right Thing* (1989) – had already guaranteed him access to mainstream
audiences (without totally wiping out his aura of controversial free
auteur largely untouched by market pressures). Lee had become a
cross-over director popular with both black and white audiences, his
success earning him financial backing for *Jungle Fever* from Universal,
by now aware that much of his box office appeal lay in his capacity to
shock, a view exemplified by a remark from the studios: 'Lee's films
usually create controversy. We don't expect this one to be any different'
(in Goodman 1991: 21).

And controversy it created. Flipper Purify and Angela Tucci – the
surname of the former and the first name of the latter providing through
their holy aura ironic commentary, perhaps, on the nation's Puritan
and racist heritage – became much more than the latest incarnation of
hundreds of transgressive lovers with which romantic comedies and
melodramas have populated film screens: stepping out of movie theatres,
their affair acquired a sociological dimension and became a catalyst of

real-life racial and sexual politics in 1990s' America. Given the scarcity of mainstream black directors Spike Lee was regarded by many as the mouthpiece of the African-American community, his *Jungle Fever* deemed to be the latest statement of black America on race relations.

My aim here, however, is to argue that, although exploration of the pleasures and pains raised by race-related sexual myths and stereotypes was definitely high on the director's agenda, the relevance of the interracial love/sexual affair between Flipper and Angie does not reside in itself but in the consequences it has literally for Flipper's marriage and, more widely, for the African-American family of the 1990s. Thus, for all the visual and dramatic intensity of Flipper and Angie's affair, the film's real concern lies not so much in this apparent *breaking free* from ethnic and racial prejudices but in their certain *breaking up* of an African-American marriage and family which the film's opening sequence depicts as ideal. When seen in this light, Flipper's affair with Angie becomes a secondary concern and, at one level, can be seen as a simple device to unsettle the initial equilibrium, the complication that prompts narrative development. The melodramatic collapse and eventual failure of the interracial affair becomes narratively relevant precisely because it facilitates the restoration of Flipper and Drew's (Lonette McKee) marriage. When this double romantic plot is considered, *Jungle Fever* can be seen not only as an interracial romantic melodrama but also as an example within the tradition of film romantic comedy, more particularly of the marriage plot variety concentrating on the temporary crisis and eventual reunification of the married couple.

The centrality of the African-American married couple is established from the start through a circular framing device, opening and closing the film at Strivers' Row, a fashionable section of Harlem where upwardly mobile Flipper lives with his wife Drew – a buyer at Bloomingdale's – and their 10-year-old daughter Ming (Veronica Timbers). A conspicuously high-angled camera shot reveals a bucolic neighbourhood blissfully bathed in a soft, warm early-morning light, kindled back to life by melodic music. As the newspaper-boy throws the *New York Times* on to a front garden, the camera glides its way towards and through the upper floor window of the house, there pausing and unashamedly recording a couple's love-making before moving on to another room where their little daughter lies awake in her own bed, her face beaming as she hears them reach sexual climax. The highly idyllic mood governing this sequence and its only slightly modified recurrence at the end of the film insinuates that what comes *in between* acquires relevance in as much as it affects this very special partnership and their little daughter. The plausibility of this family-scene, however, is simultaneously affirmed and undermined by an excess of rhetorical artifice. Although the initial establishing shots convey the recognisable image of a typical New York street, the *mise-en-scène* constructs a cardboard, fairy-tale ambience of unreality and fantasy. The film's opening, then, situates the spectator in a space simultaneously real and unreal, as if the gap between fact and fantasy had not yet been bridged by the reality-principle, as if things were being looked at through a child's (Ming's) eyes. In fact, all along, Ming is granted unusual narrative and symbolic relevance: not only is she an occasional focalising agent but also the barometer by which the adults' actions and attitudes are measured. In recording Ming's reaction here, the child's carefree, light-hearted optimism is foregrounded: Ming's vicarious enjoyment of her parents' apparently highly satisfactory sexual life suggests that her pleasures – shared voyeuristically by the spectator – construct them as a privileged, well-adjusted family who deserve preservation.

The next two scenes continue to reinforce Ming's importance as focalising agent and arbiter of adult behaviour: in a naive, charming way, the flaws of the surrounding world reveal themselves through her. First, as Flipper, Drew and Ming sit at the breakfast table – suspiciously resembling the exemplary Cosbyesque family – Ming manages to embarrass her father through her enquiries about her mother's bedroom screams in the mornings. Unable to formulate an answer, Flipper instructs her: 'eat your oatmeal'. When Drew begins to explain 'the sexual thing' to her, Ming, amused, confesses: 'I know. I was only testing you to see if you'd tell me the truth'. At one level, of course, the light tone of the scene provides an opportunity for the comedy of paternal embarrassment, but in view of later developments it could also be argued that the moment already reveals a minor flaw in Flipper's disposition: unlike Drew, he has failed to deal convincingly with his growing daughter's sexual curiosity.

Later, as Flipper walks Ming to school (in the first of three similar but significantly differentiated sequences), a trivial comment made by the girl reveals that there are further flaws in the family. Ming's complaint about boredom with the routine of having oatmeal for breakfast is eagerly endorsed by Flipper, whose comment 'yes, I am also tired of oatmeal myself' perhaps anticipates the seven-year-itchish 'danger' of married-life tedium. Besides, Flipper's final remark – 'we should ask mummy to fix something different' – clearly indicates that Drew is being blamed for this little 'something' that both Flipper and Ming are missing. By the time Flipper drops Ming off at school, kissing her tenderly and reassuring her that he loves her, enough clues have pointed towards the imminent destruction of family harmony. If the formation of the home and the family is courtship comedy's typical ending, the disturbance of that ideal usually marks the opening of the comedy of remarriage.

The term 'comedy of remarriage' as coined by Stanley Cavell in *Pursuits of Happiness* was meant to account for a sub-genre of romantic comedy whose basis is 'the classical problem of comedy and that of marriage, namely, the problem and the concept of identity . . . Comic resolutions depend upon an acquisition in time of self-knowledge; say this is a matter of learning who you are' (1981: 54–5). Although, according to Cavell, 'the genre places special stress on the female rather than on the male protagonist' (1981: 56), more recent work on comedy contends that a 'melodramatised man' has now replaced romantic comedy's traditional emphasis on women in many narratives (Rowe 1995: 192–200). This is certainly the case of Spike Lee's *Jungle Fever*. Although the film apparently engages with the dynamics of race, gender, sexuality and class, its ultimate interest lies in the narrativisation of *black masculinity*. From the start, as the camera follows Flipper on his journey away from the safeness and warmth of the home, across the bleakness of the ghetto, into the inhospitable surroundings of the white-owned architectural firm where he works, the film signals him both as the narrative's main object of interest and as the prospective *agent* of change – a change triggered by the imminent encounter which will disturb the sanctity of the couple.

In the cold and glaring atmosphere of a shared, soulless office, Flipper and Angie meet for the first time. When she is introduced to him as the new temp secretary, they both stand out against the colour-less background, their maroon clothes providing the only flicker of warmth, their matching colour patterns metaphorically linking them at the outset, anticipating mutual attraction – like the two posters hanging behind them: a photo of a phallic sculpture and the equally phallic name of the firm: MAST. By the time the boss tells Flipper 'She's all yours', the future course of events has been unambiguously heralded through the *mise-en-scène*. Regardless of Flipper's initial animosity towards Angie – a conventional ploy of romantic comedy – the film's visual rhetoric *has* united them, the emphatic use of colour and light already prefiguring their future difficulties. The next time we see Flipper and Angie together is an elliptically linked sequence of late work evenings at the office, as they share a series of Chinese take-away dinners. The sequence is highly reminiscent of the succession of linked breakfast-scenes in *Citizen Kane* (1941) tracing the progressive alienation of the couple. Here, however, the effect is the opposite: as they eat these meaningfully 'ethnic' meals together, Flipper and Angie become more and more intimate. There is only one appropriate culmination for their 'racial' banquet: for each of them to 'eat the other'. Although the ellipsis suggests that at least some days have passed, the narration's compression of the story time has the effect of showing Flipper and Angie making love after only five minutes of previously shared time on the screen.

Thus begins a story of transgressive love, the stuff of which romantic comedy – and melodrama – is made. For an audience accustomed to a long tradition of such romances, a whole set of familiar motifs and situations is immediately conjured up, and a series of expectations built upon them. However, it soon becomes obvious that Lee's romantic plot will not abide by the rules. All the ingredients of romantic comedy – classical as well as more contemporary – appear in an either exaggerated or distorted manner: practically everybody is a blocking character, the lovers' confidants (Cyrus (Spike Lee) and Angie's girlfriends) are totally untrustworthy, the bystanders are unhelpful, sex takes place too early in the narrative, and the couple's harmless playfulness is mistaken for aggression. Whatever expectations are created by the film's adoption of the familiar motifs of romantic comedy are mercilessly shattered, sooner rather than later.

Yet *Jungle Fever*'s real target is not the genre's formal and thematic traditions, but rather its uncontested reliance on love as the narrative's primary driving force. In his treatment of the interracial affair, Spike Lee seems determined to subvert Hollywood's assumptions about the relations between the sexes, as well as against myths and conventions traditionally used to represent them in popular culture. Through the main characters – Flipper in particular – the narrative sets out to invalidate not only the myth about the all-conquering power of love, but also the presumption itself that love – rather than sex – is what has brought the couple together in the first place.

In the pressbook, as elsewhere, Spike Lee has explained that the motivation behind Flipper and Angie's affair is curiosity. According to him, *Jungle Fever* is a film about 'two people who are attracted to each other because of sexual mythology' (in Shore 1996: 62). His original idea – shot but not included in the film's final version – was to foreword the film with a prologue in which he himself would descend from the sky on a camera crane and directly address the audience:

> All I have is questions. . . .
> Is a person a racist if he or she doesn't approve of interracial marriages or relationships? . . . Is the epitome of beauty in this world always gonna be the WHITE ANGLO-SAXON FEMALE? Is the BLACK MALE the SUPERHUMAN SEXUAL STUD and that's all? . . . (in Patterson 1992: 171)

Dispensing with this rather crude, didactic prologue was probably one of Lee's wisest editorial decisions. However, if the film was spared this breach of narrative distance, various other features were left that reveal its self-conscious dialogue with traditional narrativisations of romance. Lee insisted during shooting that the affair between Flipper and Angie had to exude physical attraction exclusively – in fact, Bogle records that, during shooting, the crew rechristened the film as *Fear of the Big Black Dick* (1994: 350). However, against Lee's wishes, Annabella Sciorra insisted on performing her role as if Angie were really in love with Flipper, an attitude that led to persistent friction with the director (Patterson 1992: 166–7). But although Sciorra did her best to infuse her character with greater emotional depth, Lee's more unromantic tendency elsewhere prevailed. The film's unsentimental foundations are dramatically exposed above all when, wishing to terminate their affair, Flipper tells Angie: 'I give up. It's not worth it. It's over. I don't love you. And I doubt seriously if you've ever loved me.' As Flipper utters these brutal words the whole tradition of Western love-centred narratives is shattered. Not only do we realise that the lovers will have to part, but more sadly, that the cause for the romance's failure is not only external but also internal. It is not only that the twentieth-century Capulets and Montagues are opposed to the lovers, but that Romeo himself admits he never really cared for Juliet. As for her, not even a dignified, romantic death is at hand: only the shameful return to her Italian (even if not Veronese) background.

Ultimately, then, the film never allows the interracial affair to be lyricised by romance, aiming, instead, for emotional detachment. This has caused much consternation among critics and moviegoers alike, who have sometimes complained that the sketchy account of their relationship turns the film into an incomplete exploration of interracial romance, regretting that the affair between Flipper and Angie is unexpectedly relegated to the margins, suddenly losing all its narrative prominence. 'It's difficult not to feel' – a *New Yorker* reviewer writes – 'that Lee has really missed a chance in *Jungle Fever* to reveal, through his character's sexuality, the subtle, day-to-day emotional consequences of racial misunderstanding . . .' (Skin Deep 1991: 100). My argument here, however, is that this is neither an accident nor a directorial flaw: it is, rather, a structural necessity, a sought-for effect because, as in all comedies of remarriage, the partnership which the film emotionally endorses is the one characterised by the marital knot, and not the extra-marital affair. It is also a mechanism that both prioritises the African-American milieu and allows an African-American the opportunity, for a change, to reject the white alternative.

The interest of Flipper's affair with Angie lies in its revelations about himself and his own marriage to Drew. What really matters is, to use Cavell's terms, the 'acquisition of self-knowledge', and this is what the affair with this Italian-American female Other will help Flipper to reach. In Flipper's case, this entails recognition of his identity as an African-American male, husband and father; because, although *Jungle Fever* shares romantic comedy's wider preoccupation with the relations between the sexes, it also displays a more culturally and ethnically specific interest in gender and sexual issues *as lived by* the 1990s' African-American community. It also concerns itself very deeply with inter-generational relationships, especially with fatherhood, thus departing from the typical structure of romantic comedy which has tended, in view of its avoidance of interest in reproduction, to neglect the subject of children even in the more family-centred 'marriage plots' (there are, of course, exceptions like *A Hole in the Head* (1959), *The*

Courtship of Eddie's Father (1963) or *Sleepless in Seattle* (1993)). Yet inter-generational relationships are often explored in Spike Lee's films: as in *Jungle Fever*, the narratives of *Do the Right Thing, Mo' Better Blues* (1990) and *Crooklyn* (1994) touch delicately on the relations between parents, offspring and siblings. This is an aspect of Lee's work which, as Silverberg remarks (1996: 66), has not yet been given enough attention and which interestingly links in with analyses elsewhere carried out by critics and cultural analysts concerned about what hooks calls the 'crisis of communal living' among African-Americans (1990: 206).

In *Representing Black Men*, Blount and Cunningham voice similar anxieties, drawing attention to the connection between 'the increasingly bleak statistics on the black family and the status of African-American men' (1996: xii). In fact, the plight of the contemporary black man in America has become the object of sociological as well as artistic interest during the 1990s. Commenting on his own film *Boyz N' the Hood* (1991), the African-American director John Singleton remarked 'there's a certain schism between black men and black women right now . . . things have been made easier for black women but not for black men . . .' (in Brunette 1991: 13). After the enormous success of this film, the American film industry realised that 'black ghetto' narratives could become popular among black and white audiences alike. Since then, countless films – *New Jack City* (1991), *South Central* (1992), *Juice* (1992), *Fresh* (1994) and Lee's own *Clockers* (1995) to mention only a few – have placed the urban African-American (young) man at the centre of their narratives of dispossession and violence. Spike Lee himself has often expressed his belief that the high incidence of fatherless families is one of the greatest threats to the contemporary African-American community. *Jungle Fever* engages with the anxieties of the contemporary black man, aware that the gap between African-American men and women has somehow affected the structural position of the former in marriage, family and society as a whole. In this respect, the film diverges from the more general pattern of romantic comedy in that it does not attempt to gloss over those aspects from the surrounding culture that threaten the romance. Instead, it highlights and incorporates them, which explains its more than ambivalent ending.

However, although the African-American dimension is unquestionably important, *Jungle Fever* would benefit from readings made in the light of wider (American) cultural and psychoanalytical theories.

Interest in the plight of the contemporary male relates Spike Lee's narrative – even within the relatively restricted field of film marriage plots – to comedies like Blake Edwards' *Ten* or dramas like *Leave of Absence* (1994). But in its sweet and sour concoction of sexual, ethnic and ideological masculinity-related issues, the film perhaps resembles, above all, some of Woody Allen's films. This is not only because both Allen and Lee tend to appear in their own films, or because *Jungle Fever* sometimes recalls the tone of Allen's typical 'comedy of analysis' – for example, the women's reflections on the complexities of the relations between the sexes at the 'council' held in Drew's apartment. The similarity lies, above all, in the fact that Flipper's predicament very much resembles that of the Allen persona, which, as Rowe says, 'taps into broader cultural anxieties about romance and masculinity itself' (1995: 195–6). This is a 'nervousness' which partly originates in the 'acute experience of feminism and women's new assertiveness' which feminist psychologist Wendy Hollway has seen as one of the historically specific causes of the present-day heterosexual male's infidelity (in Rutherford 1992: 44). When, in *Jungle Fever*, Drew and her all-female group of friends complain that most black men are incapable of coping with a professionally successful woman – thereby indirectly suggesting that Flipper's choice of a secretary as a lover reveals his 'dread' of the emancipated woman – they are voicing a conflict which has inspired films as diverse as *Adam's Rib* (1949), *Kramer vs Kramer* (1979) and *Annie Hall* (1977).

Even *Jungle Fever*'s concern with 'the paternal' forms part of a wider move which, in mainstream American cinema is now allowing expression of a more sensitive kind of masculinity. Susan Jeffords (1993) has shown that films of the 1990s have begun to project a more introspective form of masculinity, unafraid to voice its traumas, burdens and other preoccupations. She bases her analysis on the male-action film genre, but it can be argued that the 'fatherly' side of the male is now on display in a wider variety of films – for example, *Three Men and a Baby* (1991), *Look Who's Talking* (1991), the two *Father of the Bride* remakes (1991 and 1995) or *Mighty Aphrodite* (1996).

Like many other films of the 1990s, then, *Jungle Fever* is concerned with the many complexities and anxieties of the contemporary male, of which the racial/ethnic dimension forms only a single, though essential, element. In relation to Drew and Ming, Flipper is defined as an

African-American husband and father, but in the architectural firm where he works he is a black employee subjected to white racial prejudice; he is also explained through interaction with his mate Cyrus, constructed as a son through strained emotional exchanges with his fanatically religious father the Good Doctor Reverend Purify (Ossie Davies) and his well-intentioned but ultimately powerless mother Lucinda (Ruby Dee), and further portrayed as a brother through interaction with his dispossessed crackhead sibling Gator (Samuel L. Jackson). Flipper's identity is as intricate and complex as the New York web of streets and the myriad of sign-posts with contradictory directions, warnings and prohibitions in the opening credit sequence. Among disconcerting, paradoxical signs Flipper embarks on a journey of self-discovery and self-definition. He will re-enact the archetypal quest of the male who leaves the familiar space to head for the unknown in search of self-knowledge. But the archetype, Jung claimed, always manifests itself within a specific cultural and psychological context, and this is why Flipper's quest in *Jungle Fever* is both an allegorical tale of male physical and spiritual testing and a realistic portrayal of a late twentieth-century New York buppy. Flipper crosses geographical and racial as well as psychological frontiers, and the affair with Angie is only one step on this journey, although an important one because it puts his identity to test. His is a journey from unquestioned black masculinity to a wiser individual and communal self, obtained through temporary exposure to and exploration of the Other. Spike Lee himself defined Flipper and Angie's affair as a metaphorical journey of transgression: 'Sometimes when the boundaries of Race, Class and SEX are crossed, you are headed into that region called *JUNGLE FEVER*' (1991: 1). When Patterson criticised Spike Lee's style in this piece – regretting the fact that he should 'mistake a fever for a region' (1992: 173) – he was clearly overlooking the fact that love and space have formed a metaphorical unity from the codified *locus amoenus* of medieval tradition to Foucault's meditations on love and sex *as a space* of multiple interrogations. Fictionalised interracial romance itself has been theorised through the metaphorical concept of the 'racial frontier', its participants portrayed as 'inhabiting or crossing a "no man's land" between one group and another, between civilization and savagery' (Stephens 1995: 62).

And in truth, Angie's space couldn't be more Other and 'savage' for

Flipper. The blue-collar working-class Italian-American Bensonhurst section of Brooklyn where Angie lives with her widowed father and two brothers is clearly set apart from Flipper's familiar space, not only literally (geographically, ethnically and socially) but also metaphorically. Flipper and Angie's search for an alternative neutral space of love in the Village only leads them to an inhospitable wasteland. The *mise-en-scène* of their 'love-nest' – a flat almost devoid of furniture and persistently bathed in cold colours – visualises the emptiness and sterility of their romance, thereby anticipating its failure. In this hostile space, they are never seen engaged in romantic conversation, but rather looking in opposite directions, always sitting or lying on the floor, the level of their emotional – and for the film, perhaps, even moral – stature. They are never seen having satisfying sex here either, and the emphatic barrenness of their physical and emotional 'space' is more dramatically highlighted when Flipper bluntly refuses even to consider the possibility of ever having children with Angie. As a number of depressing scenes in the Village apartment follow one another, the spectator is inevitably made to ponder how much Flipper's situation has degenerated since the film's opening scene.

Although the film insistently poses colour as the main difference between them, Angie's gender and class are clearly also significantly alien to Flipper. The motivations behind Flipper's affair with Angie therefore arguably go beyond the colour question. At one level, Flipper's justifications first to Angie ('I've never cheated on my wife before') and then to Cyrus ('I have to admit that I've always been curious about Caucasian women') point at two of the possible reasons for Flipper's infidelity: the ten-, not seven-, year 'itch' of faithful marriage to Drew, and the 'fever' of the attraction for Angie, the complaisant Other. However, these two explanations are only partially satisfactory: first, there is evidence that Flipper and Drew's marriage is emotionally and sexually fulfilling; and secondly, Angie herself cannot be considered as the 'epitome of white beauty' (Spike Lee's intended prologue to the film defined her as 'white *Anglo-Saxon* female'). After all, she is herself an ethnically marked character, her Italianness systematically emphasised by the narrative. Moreover, as Angie herself makes Flipper notice, 'her [Drew's] skin is whiter than mine'. Furthermore, after the all-female heated debate on racially related male and female desires, Drew tells her girlfriends: 'It don't even matter what colour she is. My man is gone.' All this suggests that, regardless of Lee's declared intentions, 'race' alone cannot account for Flipper's emotional and psychological complexities.

In fact, Flipper's infidelity can be better explained through Freud's essays on the psychology of love, according to which the adult hetero-sexual male's search for a love-object is inextricably linked to the search for the mother. In his essays on adultery Freud maintains, first, that the adulterous man looks 'for a debased sexual object' (1981b: 254) who 'should not be unattached' (1981a: 236). Angie fulfills all these conditions: not only is she Flipper's inferior economically, socially and professionally, but she is also attached to a third party, her long-term boyfriend Paulie (John Turturro).[1] Freud further claims (1984) that the adulterer's choice of object is simultaneously despised (so that no emotional input is required) and admired (because closely related to the mother figure, the child's first ever object of desire). This is a pattern also followed by Angie, who actively performs the role of mother in her household, feeding and taking care of her father and brothers. Significantly, when she tells Flipper that she will bring a container of home-cooked spaghetti for him to the office, he is deeply amused and touched, his reaction revealing that he has hitherto been denied such care and attention. Flipper inevitably falls for this mother-figure, this nurturer missing in his marriage to a professional woman. Flipper's affair is marked by the ambiguity that psychoanalysis sees as the basis of the desire for the mother, always represented as an object of simul-taneous love and hate. After all, as in any process of identity-formation, contact with the Other should only be a temporary, transitory phase that can help the individual acquire self-knowledge. Once Angie has served that purpose, she becomes dispensable and Flipper can conclude his circular odyssey of self-discovery.

Confirmation that Flipper's engagement with Angie should never become permanent is given by Ming again, who once more serves as moral barometer of adult behaviour – of her father's, now. Flipper's alienation is highlighted when for a second time he is shown walking Ming to school in the morning. The pattern is similar to that of the first sequence, but there is a major difference: Flipper's grave countenance, his failure to converse with Ming and to kiss her goodbye when he carelessly drops her off by the school's gate is a mark of his estrange-ment. When, for the third time, Flipper is seen walking his daughter to school, the narrative introduces a further variation in the pattern. As the crackhead Vivian (Halle Berry) accosts Flipper and Ming in the street, her explicit offer of cheap sex, to a certain extent, replicates Flipper and Angie's 'immorality'. Through her, too, the lure of drugs and illicit sex which so bedevil African-American neighbourhoods is crudely exposed. Interestingly, Flipper's immediate reaction is to rebuke his startled daughter thereby establishing a symbolic link between the still clean – even though precocious – Ming and the debased Vivian. The film has thus pointed at the two types of dangers – internal and external – which threaten the integrity and well-being of the African-American family.

And if this scene with Ming signals Flipper's 'fall from grace', the last stage of this fall is dramatically represented by his visit to the Taj Mahal, a crack-factory supposedly located in Harlem. Interestingly, Flipper goes there at his mother's request, in search of his brother Gator, who has stolen his parents' colour TV set to pay for his addiction. This complication of the plot conceals, of course, deeper metaphorical meanings. When Flipper enters the unreal, nightmarish world, the 'vision' of Gator and Vivian fighting over a crack-smoking-pipe in the squalor of this temple of death makes him confront the Other existing *within* his own self and community. In Gator, Flipper visualises his 'other self, the self that he escaped becoming' (Gates 1991: 166); in Vivian – his symbolic daughter – the bleak future of the African-American urban youth. The nature of Flipper's process of learning is at least as paradoxical as the meanings summoned up by the name of the place where his *anagnorisis* takes place: the Taj Mahal, the emblematic palace that an Indian Moghul emperor built in pure white marble – facing his own black marble palace – as a tomb for his late beloved wife and as a token of the eternal battle between love and death. In its pairs of opposites – white/black, love/death, female/male – the mythical temple perfectly symbolises the tensions within Flipper's own subjectivity. With masterly compression, the whole narrative is thus replicated in this *mise-en-abîme* micronarrative which suggests that Flipper's – perhaps the African-American male's – search for self-definition entails recognition of his own internal divisions and, above all, identification with his own communal – rather than individual(istic) – self. After his visit to this macabre death-den – after his symbolic descent into the Inferno – Flipper emerges a more enlightened man. In his long journey of initiation, he has learnt not only about his own inner frailties but also about the vulnerability and precariousness of heterosexual partnerships. Even apparently perfect marriages and families contain the seed of their own destruction, for to be human is to be imperfect. But whereas in James Cameron's 1991 sci-fi film, the Terminator (Arnold Schwarzenegger) has to kill himself because, for all his cybernetically programmed parental perfection, he cannot learn to love and cry, Flipper here is allowed a second chance: he is neither the perfect father nor the perfect husband, but, in his humanity, he can and does learn to love through suffering. And this is what makes the film's closure – Flipper resuming his double role as husband and father – if not an unambiguously happy ending, at least a hopeful new beginning.

Although the circularity of the plot – its return to the opening sequence's setting and lyricism – at first seems to point towards a happy conclusion, Drew's silent cry after sex – a deviation from its earlier twinned scene – introduces a note of bitterness. This, however, is only witnessed by Flipper and the spectator for, as the camera repeats the opening-sequence flight to their daughter's room, it once again delights in the giggling of a child, Ming, unaware of the sadness behind her parents' love-making. Like Maisie's in James's narrative of divorce, *What Maisie Knew* (1897), Ming's grasp of her parents' behaviour is only partial and therefore highly naive but, by recuperating the child's point of view the narrative sanctions the reunion of the couple. If wholly untroubled bliss is no longer a plausible ending, here, as in *Peggy Sue Got Married* (1986), the presence of the daughter – grown up in the Coppola film, still a child in Lee's – at least 'consecrates' the remarriage and signals reunion as the right moral choice.

Jungle Fever shows that real-life hardships can be counterbalanced – if not subsumed – by idealistic fictions, but it also acknowledges awareness of the gap. If even classical instances of the genre resorted to narrative self-consciousness to playfully 'indulge in wish-fulfilment' without ignoring the 'laws of reality' (Babington and Evans 1989: 9), exposure of filmic and generic conventions has become even more noticeable in later examples of the genre. Films with backgrounds as different as *Pretty Woman* (1990), a star-studded Hollywood superproduction, and *I Like It Like That* (1994), an African-American woman director's consciousness-raising story of an oppressed New York

Chicano housewife, use illusion-breaking techniques which slightly undermine the conventional happy ending without completely erasing the emotional pleasure derived from the couple's reunion. Likewise, *Jungle Fever* delights in frame-breaking strategies. The artificiality of the settings, the clear-cut use of colours, the conspicuousness of the camera movements and angles, the overt stereotyping of ethnic groups and individuals, the director's self-referentiality, and perhaps above all, the prioritisation of Ming's infantile, fantasy-laden perspective, turn the film into an ambiguous text, and its director into a tightrope-walker hanging between Harlem and Never-Never Land.

Unsurprisingly, an unqualified happy ending is inconceivable for a film like *Jungle Fever* which, despite its widespread distribution, still claims to have an oppositional agenda.[2] As an epilogue, Flipper walks away from home in a scene reminiscent of those previous three occasions on which he had been shown accompanied by his daughter. But when, as in the preceding scene, a prostitute offers to 'suck his big black dick', Flipper's very different reaction heralds narrative conclusion. When he embraces her and shouts 'Noooo!', he proves that he is 'recuperated' and knows how to be a good African-American husband and father: his 'no!' now being a refusal of extra-marital sex, his embrace a sign of protection rather than rejection – as in the former scene – of the symbolic daughter, a sign of his commitment to the future of his community.

Spike Lee's unromantic abandonment of the warmth of the family home in favour of a return to the external squalor of the ghetto at the film's closure obviously strikes a sad chord which again compromises the happiness of the ending. As a result of Lee's refusal to offer cinematic pleasure at the expense of social and political blindness, bleak readings of the film have outnumbered optimistic ones. Even here, an unqualified positive reading of *Jungle Fever* is not possible because, whereas the film's commitment to the representation of social hardships does not necessarily invalidate its greater optimism in and defence of the partnership between African-Americans – within the couple, the family or the community as a whole – it can be claimed that its more than noticeable disregard for the role of women in that enterprise certainly undermines its achievement. Lee's films – even those whose action and point of view seem to be governed by a female character, like *Crooklyn* and *Girl 6* (1996) – have often been criticised for their failure to account for the black *female* experience, and *Jungle Fever* is no different in this respect.[3] Considering the varied treatment of Flipper's subjectivity, Drew's and Angie's, the two other vertices of the triangle, lack serious analysis. Drew is one-dimensionally portrayed as a typical 1990s' middle-class professional African-American wife, and the very little that is mentioned of her family background only serves to endorse her imaging as the stereotypical 'tragic mulatta'. Angie, for her part, was largely conceived by Spike Lee as a token of 'white womanhood' – perhaps in much the same way as Marilyn was projected as a 'male fantasy of an idealised female sexual otherness' in Wilder's *The Seven Year Itch* (Babington and Evans 1989: 229) – and if she partly escapes the stereotype it is only thanks to Annabella Sciorra's refusal to accept Lee's simplistic project. When Angie/Sciorra tells Flipper/Lee 'don't tell me what I felt', the film's total lack of interest in – white or black – female subjectivity is stridently brought home. Arguably, these sketchy portrayals of femininity – where the women become types, rather than full-bodied counterparts – serve strategically to alleviate the threat to black male heterosexual identity. If, as Michele Wallace contends, Flipper is 'deeply threatened by the prospect of dominant female sexuality' (1992: 129) and the film is really about 'the threat of a female or aberrant sexuality to traditional family values' (1992: 127), both the simplistic depiction of women and the recourse to Ming as a focalising agent are readable as co-ordinated strategies which serve to remove from the film the most menacing aspects of present-day gender and sex-related conflicts.

And yet through all the bleakness, bigotry and incomprehension, Ming's exhilarating smile lingers on and prompts the trusting, even childish instincts of the audience. Her use in *Jungle Fever*, then, inspires innocence and hope and, together with Lee's formal and thematic self-consciousness, reveals a utopian belief in the desirability – even the ideological necessity – of bringing to life many a happy-ending African-American romantic comedy and/or family romance.

NOTES

1 Paulie (practically the only likeable male character in Bensonhurst) is a sensitive young man. He, too, feels the attraction of the Other in the shape of Orin (Tyra Ferrell), a smart black woman who, although not particularly

interested in him, tactfully accepts his approaches. The excessive length of the original cut of the film forced Lee to suppress the planned unromantic outcome of this other bourgeoning interracial heterosexual relation, its open-endedness providing it, in fact, with greater complexity and suggestiveness.

2 Lee's dual engagement with both independent and mainstream film production has sometimes been harshly criticised as a sign of *duality*. See, for instance, Baraka (1993), Baker (1993) and Lubiano (1996).

3 For a critique of specific aspects of Lee's fictional treatment of women see, for instance, hooks (1990 and 1994), Gilroy (1993) and Wallace (1992).

WORKS CITED

Babington, Bruce and Peter W. Evans 1989. *Affairs to Remember: The Hollywood Comedy of the Sexes*. Manchester and New York: Manchester University Press

Baker, Houston A., Jr., 1993. 'Spike Lee and the Commerce of Culture'. In Diawara, ed., 154–76

Baraka, Amiri 1993. 'Spike Lee at the Movies'. In Diawara, ed., 145–53

Blount, Marcellus and George P. Cunningham, eds, 1996. *Representing Black Men*. New York and London: Routledge

Bogle, Donald. 1994 (1973). *Toms, Coons, Mulattoes, Mammies, and Bucks: An Interpretive History of Blacks in American Films*. Oxford: Roundhouse

Brunette, Peter 1991. 'Singleton's Street Noises', *Sight and Sound*, August: 13

Cavell, Stanley 1981. *Pursuits of Happiness: The Hollywood Comedy of Remarriage*. Cambridge, MA: Harvard University Press

Diawara, Manthia, ed., 1993. *Black American Cinema*. New York and London: Routledge

Freud, Sigmund 1981 (1910). 'A Special Type of Choice of Object Made by Men (Contributions to the Psychology of Love I)', *On Sexuality*. Harmondsworth: Penguin, 227–42

Freud, Sigmund 1981 (1912). 'On the Universal Tendency to Debasement in the Sphere of Love (Contributions to the Psychology of Love II)', *On Sexuality*. Harmondsworth: Penguin, 243–60

Freud, Sigmund 1984 (1915). 'Instincts and Their Vicissitudes', *On Metapsychology: The Theory of Psychoanalysis*. Harmondsworth: Penguin, 105–38

Gates, Henry Louis Jr, 1991. '*Jungle Fever*; or, Guess Who's Not Coming to Dinner?'. In *Five for Five: The Films of Spike Lee*, Spike Lee and David Lee, eds. New York: Stewart, Tabory & Chang, 162–9

Gilroy, Paul 1993. 'Spiking the Argument: Spike Lee and the Limits of Racial Community'. In *Small Acts: Thoughts on the Politics of Black Cultures*. London and New York: Serpent's Tail

Goodman, Joan 1991. 'Breaking the Last Taboo', *Evening Standard*, 11 April: 21 and 24

hooks, bell 1990. *Yearning: Race, Gender and Cultural Politics*. Boston, MA: South End Press

hooks, bell 1994. *Outlaw Culture: Resisting Representations*. London and New York: Routledge

Jeffords, Susan 1993. 'Can Masculinity Be Terminated?' In *Screening the Male: Exploring Masculinities in Hollywood Cinema*, Steven Cohan and Ina Rae Hark, eds. London and New York: Routledge, 245–62

Lee, Spike 1991. *Jungle Fever*. Production Notes

Lubiano, Wahneema 1996. '"But Compared to What?" Reading Realism, Representation, and Essentialism in *School Daze*, *Do the Right Thing*, and the Spike Lee Discourse'. In Blount and Cunningham, eds, 173–204

Patterson, Alex 1992. *Spike Lee*. New York: Avon Books

Rowe, Kathleen 1995. *The Unruly Woman: Gender and the Genres of Laughter*. Austin: University of Texas Press

Rutherford, Jonathan 1992. *Men's Silences: Predicaments in Masculinity*. London and New York: Routledge

Shore, Mitchell 1996. 'Multiculturalism and Spike Lee's Mixed Messages', *Cineaction*, May: 57–65

Silverberg, Cory 1996. 'More than the Violence: A Reading of Intergenerational Relationships in *Do the Right Thing* and *Jungle Fever*', *Cineaction*, May: 66–72

Skin Deep 1991. 'The Current Cinema', *New Yorker*, 17 June: 100–1

Stephens, Gregory 1995. 'Romancing the Racial Frontier: Mediating Symbols in Cinematic Interracial Representation', *Spectator*, 16, 1 (Fall/Winter): 58–73

Wallace, Michele 1992. '*Boyz N the Hood* and *Jungle Fever*'. In *Black Popular Culture*, Gina Dent, ed. Seattle: Bay Press, 123–31

Chapter 10

ALLISON ANDERS'S *GAS FOOD LODGING*: INDEPENDENT CINEMA AND THE NEW ROMANCE

Kathleen Rowe Karlyn

Gas Food Lodging: *In the modern romance, love is rarely here to stay*

What do you do with yourself if you can't imagine the future the way you want it to be?

(Shade in *Gas Food Lodging*, 1992)

One of the most significant influences on US popular culture and cinema in the 1990s has been the independent film. The existence of an independent cinema in the USA first became widely known in 1989, when Steven Soderberg's *Sex Lies and Videotape* won the grand prize at the Cannes Film Festival. Less than a decade later, not only 'Sundance' but 'Slamdance' have become familiar enough to the general public to appear without definition or explanation in mainstream magazines, and in 1997 the Academy Awards were dominated as never before by films originating outside Hollywood.[1]

The 'independent' in independent cinema is relational, according to Chuck Kleinhans, indicating a practice that is independent 'in relation to the dominant system' rather than 'totally free-standing and autonomous' (1997: 3). However, it is safe to say that the independent film is produced and distributed outside mainstream channels, often articulating a self-conscious, irreverent and funky countervoice to mainstream filmmaking. Typically it has fed off Hollywood traditions and genres in order to rewrite them for the smaller and more particularised audiences it targets. At the same time, Hollywood itself – in the wake of such surprise money-makers as *Roger and Me, El Mariachi* and others – has begun to feed off this cinema, stepping up its efforts to recruit directors who will bring it not only cachet but cash. For Hollywood executives, Kleinhans writes, independent cinema has become 'a kind of minor league training ground for new talent who, if they succeed, will then be brought into the majors'; and for some independent directors, a successful fiction feature is primarily a 'calling card' that guarantees an entry into the dominant industry (1997: 14 and 3).

This breakdown of boundaries between mainstream and independent filmmaking is perhaps inevitable given the ever-increasing power of megacorporations linking film, television, video, and other media and consumer products. The textual effects of this flow of talent and capital among related industries may be hard to pinpoint but they can surely be seen in the intertextuality, pastiche and pop sensibility – qualities associated with postmodernism – that characterise so much contemporary culture, both high and low. Some critics, writing from an auteur perspective, note the pressure of mainstream thematics and aesthetics on the work of independent directors who migrate from 'Sundance to Sunset'. Decrying the inevitable loss of idiosyncracy and bite in the work of directors as they begin to incorporate bigger budgets and stars into their work, they unfavourably compare Spike Lee's *She's Gotta Have It* (1986) with *Jungle Fever* (1991); or Richard Linklater's *Slackers* (1991) with *Dazed and Confused* (1993); or Robert Rodriguez's *El Mariachi* (1992) with *Desperado* (1995).

However, just as Hollywood has compromised independent films, it is also likely that the thematic and aesthetic innovations created in the independent cinema will begin to exert pressure on the mainstream. One area in which that pressure is likely to register is genre. Examining these films from a theoretical perspective that emphasises genre over auteur shifts critical attention away from questions of artistic quality and the development of an individual's vision towards the more encompassing issues of ideology and its manifestation in form. Romantic comedy, an enduring and adaptable film genre, has proven particularly well suited to the independent cinema of the 1980s and 1990s. If in recent years Hollywood has given us *When Harry Met Sally* (1989), *Sleepless in Seattle* (1993), and *While You Were Sleeping* (1995), the independent cinema has given us *True Love* (1989), *Trust* (1991), *I Like It Like That* (1994), *The Incredibly True Adventures of Two Girls in Love* (1995) and *Waiting to Exhale* (1995), engaging and often quirky films that make use of independent cinema's affinity for genre play to provide alternative perspectives on gender, love and sex in the 1980s and 1990s.

Structurally and thematically, romantic comedy depends on the concept of romantic love, and as film scholars long have noted, the genre's continued viability past its Golden Age in the 1930s and 1940s has been tested by the social and cultural changes that have altered the relations between the sexes in the post-war era and the decades that followed.[2] Most recently, Hollywood has attempted to revive romantic comedy by evoking that Golden Age with references to Hollywood films, genres and stars from that period (*Sleepless in Seattle*, *Pretty Woman* 1990), 'oldies' music (*When Harry Met Sally*, *Sleepless in Seattle*), and even opera (*Moonstruck* 1987 and *Pretty Woman*). These references create a comforting nostalgia for a time of greater certainty about the relations between the sexes and about what it meant to be a man or a woman, often using melodrama to elicit sympathy for the suffering post-feminist man.[3]

Along with the apparent utopianism of the classical romantic comedy, however, was an engagement with the crucial social issues of its time. Narratively built on the conflict between the sexes, it used that conflict as a site on which to displace other compelling social conflicts, most notably the divisions among social classes heightened by the Depression. This layering of conflicts in such films as *It Happened One*

Night (1934) *The Lady Eve* (1941) and *Bringing up Baby* (1938) contributed to the genre's characteristic tension in tone, a scepticism that
countered its sentimentalism about the possibilites of romantic love to
resolve all issues of individual desire and social difference. In contrast,
the recent Hollywood romantic comedy, with a few exceptions, has
tended to retreat from contemporary historical realities and the social
tensions of an increasingly fragmented and multicultural world. As a
result, despite an awareness of their generic history, these films have
tended to reproduce the letter but not necessarily the edgy spirit of the
most interesting of the classics. They replay the most obvious narrative
formulas, cinematic conventions, and thematic concerns of the earlier
films but without the subtexts of social critique.

Those formulae and conventions from the past are also appealing to
independent filmmakers. When they use them, however, it is more
often with an eye towards the important issues of the present. This
practice, as evident in the 1992 film *Gas Food Lodging*, provides Hollywood a provocative model of how to enhance the vitality and popular
appeal of the genre by engaging it more directly with the social realities
of the present.

With *Gas Food Lodging*, her first feature-length film, Anders established herself as one of the 1990s' most promising directors, and her
work has been supported by the Sundance Film Institute and the
famous MacArthur 'Genius' Fellowship. She was born in Kentucky in
1954 and many of the events of her life – poverty, rape, single-mother-
hood – found their way into the film.[4] The film is set in a bleak and
isolated truckstop in the New Mexico desert, an environment of natural
beauty that is eclipsed by the poverty of the characters' lives and their
struggles against racism and sexism. The plot centres on teenage Shade
(Fairuza Balk), her promiscuous and unhappy older sister Trudi (Ione
Skye), and their mother Nora (Brooke Adams), a waitress who has
brought up her daughters alone after their father left them years ago.
Shade spends many of her afternoons at the local cinema where the
Mexican melodramas she loves give her the idea that she could solve
her problems – her longing for a 'real family' – by finding a new man
for her mother. The man she wants most to find, however, is her
missing father. Her quest for him coincides with her discovery of her
love for Javier, the young Mexican-American projectionist at the cinema.
This discovery occurs after her comical attempt to seduce Darius, a

friend who is probably gay unbeknownst to Shade. Trudi, meanwhile, falls in love with Dank, a geologist who is passing through town and who leaves her pregnant. When Dank fails to return from a trip as promised, Trudi leaves town to have her baby, and gives the infant girl up for adoption. By the end of the film, Nora has settled into a loving relationship with Hamlet, the owner of a satellite dish company. Shade has found her father. She has also learned that Dank didn't return because he had been killed in an accident. Shade carries the knowledge of Dank's fidelity with her as she sets out into the next phase of her life.

The film warrants careful study for several reasons. It is part of an emerging body of work by female directors and media makers, for and about girls and women.[5] Moving deftly between melodrama and romantic comedy, home movie and road movie, Western and coming-of-age story, it also suggests how Hollywood genres can be hybridised towards explicitly feminist ends. In particular, it gives a distinctly feminist cast to romantic comedy by playing it off against melodrama. Moreover, unlike the contemporary Hollywood romantic comedy, *Gas Food Lodging* considers not only the relations between the sexes in the 1990s but the social divisions of a multicultural world characterised by downward economic mobility. While recalling the classical romantic comedy in its accessibility, utopianism and social subtext, however, it remains distinctly contemporary in its outlook. The film does not back away from the consequences of poverty and dead-end jobs, but shifts its attention from class, which underlay the classical romantic comedy, to race, the primary obstacle between the lovers, Shade and her Mexican-American admirer Javier. Thus it provides an opportunity not only to reflect on the endurance of romantic comedy as a genre, but to explore how that genre is being rewritten and revitalized by independent filmmakers to incorporate new social concerns about class, gender and race.

Finally the film is built around the point of view and voice of Shade, a teenage girl with a passion for Mexican melodrama. For Shade, cinema becomes a means not only to solve the problems of her life but to narrate them and in so doing to alter history. Fusing the emotional intensity of melodrama with the utopian vision of comedy, *Gas Food Lodging* provides an intriguing study not only of feminist genre-play but female cinephilia, insisting on women's capacities as film viewers and artists to define themselves, to imagine a different world and to create the new stories necessary to bring that new world about. As a result, it encourages a fresh look not only at the genres it explores but at women's relation to them and to cinema in general.

CINEPHILIA AND GENDER

The film introduces its teenage heroine Shade by showing her alone in a darkened theatre, her gaze riveted to the screen, her face streaked with tears, while we hear a woman's impassioned voice speaking in Spanish to the sounds of swelling 'movie music'. It is a striking image of cinematic suture, and in a voice-over, Shade tells us what film – and her identification with a particular film star – means to her: in a word, everything. 'If it weren't for Elvia Rivero, this story wouldn't be worth telling. She made me laugh when I needed to, she made me cry when no one was looking, she made me put into words . . .'

Shade has a serious case of movie love, and Anders uses her to invite us to reconsider the relation between women and cinema. First, the film poses the question of female spectatorship, for the suture so powerfully evoked in the opening scene is also interrupted from the outset by the rare sound of a female voice-over, which continues throughout the film. In what can be seen as an allegory of feminist film theory and practice, the film tracks Shade's metamorphosis from enthralled spectator into the storyteller of the film's final moments, when she marches away from the camera into the natural world, lyrically laying claim to her power to carry and tell a tale that has 'changed the paths of daughters not yet heard from, not yet born'.

Cinephilia is a familiar trope in film history but one that assumes a very different shape for women than it does for men. The male cinephiliac has most often been represented both behind the camera and on the screen, and indeed the onscreen versions – in the films of Truffaut, Godard and Woody Allen, for example – are often openly acknowledged projections of their director-creators. That is because for men, cinephilia is tied to their presumed ability to manipulate the language of cinema, not merely consume it.

For women, film love has been quite another matter, thinkable primarily in terms of women's position on the screen or in the audience, not behind the camera. This position is consistent with the notion of women as passive consumers of culture, rather than active creators of it – and even more, as consumers who are weak, over-emotional, uncritical. In 1973, Molly Haskell first wrote of women's surrender to the 'wet, wasted afternoons' of the weepies. The idea of women's passive and pre-linguistic identification with the image has formed the foundation of most feminist theories of female spectatorship and remains quite alive in the cultural imagination. As the possibilities for women behind the camera have expanded, however, so has our cultural capacity to think about and represent women's relation to cinema *on screen*. Anders shows us another dimension to those 'wet, wasted afternoons' Haskell describes. Shade weeps, but then marches resolutely out into the world to change it.

Anders destabilises other structures through Shade's attachment to Elvia Rivero. Her same-sex identification with a female star indicates the film's interest in relationships among women, while her cross-cultural identification with a *Mexican* star in an environment of extreme prejudice indicates its interest in race.[6] Shade recalls the female fans of Valentino, who became the site of a powerful fantasy of interracial passion and female desire for millions of women in the 1920s. In Miriam Hansen's words, the female cinephilia aroused by Valentino may be read 'as a kind of rebellion, a desperate protest against the passivity and one-sidedness with which patriarchal cinema supports the subordinate position of women in the gender hierarchy' (1986: 25). Both forms of identification challenge the notion of the passive female spectator that has informed so much classical feminist film theory.

GENERIC TENSION AND TONE

Gas Food Lodging's focus on the point of view of a teengirl cinephiliac produces considerable tension and unpredictability of tone, and the film repeatedly surprises the viewer with shifts from pathos to comedy, ugliness to beauty, irony to lyricism. Recalling the tension the classical romantic comedy created from its interest in social class and gender conflict, *Gas Food Lodging* expands the range of social conflicts it explores, building tension through startling uses of *mise-en-scène* and genre.

The film places its characters in a world that is confined, oppressive and often ugly, creating through *mise-en-scène* a visual correlative of the social confinement of its characters' experience because of sexism, racism and poverty. Domestic life for Shade, Trudi and Nora takes place in a trailer where they are photographed in tight compositions, hemmed in by internal frames, shot at a medium to close distance against cluttered backgrounds. This environment is filmed respectfully and affectionately, with a warm palette and careful attention to the details that define the characters. The trailer is a place of bickering and lonely silences, rare moments of intimacy and laughter, and outbursts of pent-up anger. Not surprisingly, cars play an important role in this film about 'gas food lodging'. However, here the automobile is not the means to adventure mythologised in US popular culture but yet another claustrophic setting for painful emotional events: Nora kissing her old lover goodbye, or sobbing alone after a fight with Trudi; Shade's tense drives with her father; the ride back from Dallas, when Hamlet, Nora and Shade appear physically close but emotionally distant and lost in their own thoughts. The film captures the town's social claustrophobia in the similarly oppressive settings of the truckstop and laundromat, where if the images are composed with greater depth, the backgrounds are bleak and washed out, devoid of movement.

The film does not abandon its characters in this setting, however, but offers brief glimpses of a different reality available to them if they only learn how to perceive it. The desert surrounding the truckstop becomes a site of transformation for Trudi and Shade, and Anders depicts this natural world in vibrant contrast to the oppressive social environment of their everyday lives. Trudi literally sees the world differently through Dank's 'magic light' or mineral lamp. Her discovery takes place against a brilliantly coloured sunset and sunrise, and in a cave glowing with phosphorescent light. Shade also learns an important lesson about the power to create and experience beauty when she visits Javier's house on the edge of town and watches his deaf mother shift from silence and stillness into a graceful and animated dance to music she *feels* rather than hears. The film sets the sequence apart from the rest of the film with a shift in colour towards clear and luminous whites. Later, after a montage of shots of desert flowers, Shade and Javier appear in the desert against an intensely blue sky, photographed in a low-angle, extreme long shot. Visually these shots link the openness and beauty of the setting with Shade's sense of both exhilaration and peace.

In addition to this use of *mise-en-scène*, the film creates tension by contrasting two traditions of cinematic genre: the genres of classical

Hollywood and the newer, hybridised genres of postmodern culture. With important exceptions, the classical genres assumed a relatively unchanging social world, where social class and gender difference – while open to challenge – remained fairly stable structures. Anders draws on these genres, especially the female melodrama, to capture the boredom and frustration of the Evans' women's lives. At the same time, she evokes the more open culture of contemporary times by combining these genres in unusual ways, towards new ends.

THE WESTERN: A MAN'S WORLD

At one point in the film, Javier says to a dejected Shade, 'Hey, it's the Movie Lady . . . What's the matter, no movies today? Just real life.' The 'real life' of *Gas Food Lodging* unfolds within the tradition of two great American film genres – the Western and the road movie – but retold from a female perspective, and it is within these genres that Anders embeds her strongest feminist critique. Both the Western and the road movie romanticise movement, freedom, the open road, the quest for the new, and both make important use of landscape and open space. *Gas Food Lodging* evokes this iconography in its introductory shots of an open road taken from a moving camera. Within moments, however, the film moves to the increasingly confined spaces where most of its drama will unfold: the truckstop, the theatre, and finally the tiny trailer that is home for Nora and her girls.

This opposition between open and closed, outside and inside, corresponds to the ideological tensions the film explores: the fact that the freedom and movement of the road are available only to men and are possible for them only because women, especially mothers, have little choice but to stay put, to tend to the material necessities of life ('gas food lodging') for those who depend on them. The motif of men leaving women runs throughout the film, and its ever-present consequences range from abandonment to sexual violence. Although men's freedom to walk away has maimed all three women to varying degrees, Trudi has suffered the most dramatically, having been abandoned by her father, gang-raped, and finally left without explanation by the first man she loves. She speaks the film's hardest-hitting words when she tells Dank, 'Men always walk away. Their emotions walk away, their minds walk away, their promises, they all walk away.' Through her the film dramatises the social origins of the category 'whore' (or the virgin-whore dichotomy), suggesting that Trudi's promiscuity has resulted from her longing for a father's love combined with her experience of female powerlessness during her initiation into sex. A shot of Trudi waiting for Dank's return, standing with her arms outstretched in a position of longing, hemmed in by trucking whizzing behind her, visually conveys the consequences to women of the ethos celebrated by the Western.

Trudi's final experience with 'walking away' occurs when she walks away, herself, from her newborn daughter and gives her up for adoption. This moment in the film is a pivotal one. On the one hand, by giving up her baby she gives her into another story, freeing the infant into a life that will presumably be easier than her own has been. Trudi also secures for herself the freedom men enjoy, moving herself into the male space of the Western. However, the film allows us to experience Trudi's act only through the melancholy and grief of melodrama by showing us Nora, Hamlet and Shade gazing wistfully at the baby in a lingering shot, Shade's anguish, and Trudi's private tears. Trudi's emancipation has come at a great cost, rupturing the tenuous bonds not only between Trudi and her mother but between Trudi and Shade and causing the matrilineal line in this female-centred movie to disappear into off-screen time and space.

The film refuses to take an overly simplistic feminist position, however, on the issues of women's waiting, sexual desire and abandonment. Instead, it shows women's implication in their own suffering. Shade is not only spirited but at times excessively romantic. Trudi is not only a passive victim but foolish in her promiscuity and desperate, or at least unreflective, in her decision to give up her baby even though the other family members would have loved and accepted the child. The film also treats the issue of race with great sensitivity, showing the complex interrelationship between structures of gender and race. Javier – the character who has the most to teach the other characters – is the first male charged with 'walking away' when he abandons his work station to Nora. But he does so only after Trudi has made a racist remark to him.

MELODRAMA: A WOMAN'S WORLD

The genre most overtly referred to in *Gas Food Lodging* is melodrama, which exists both as a series of clips within the film and in the narrative itself. Anders's use of 'Mexican' melodramas for the clips (Anders shot them herself when she couldn't get rights to existing ones) is appropriate given the setting of the film in the Southwest. It also serves as a quiet reminder of film traditions outside Hollywood. Throughout the film, Anders valorises melodrama and what it offers the female spectator while at the same time gently contextualising its values by placing the clips within a narrative defined by the more utopian vision of comedy.

The Elvia Rivero clips, which are beautifully conventionalised in *mise-en-scène*, dialogue and soundtrack, provide a running commentary on the events of the story that frames them as well as a catalogue of the feminine virtues and situations which Shade tries on and discards. The first clip establishes the melodramatic trope of female martyrdom by introducing Elvia in a dramatic low-angle shot on a stairway, as she identifies herself with her heroic willingness to sacrifice herself for a man who remains offscreen: 'I am the one who feeds your soul. My giving comes from my strength, not my weakness . . .' Later, at her parents' urging, Elvia picks a suitor from a pile of photographs, teaching Shade that a woman must have a man, and that romantic love – the possibility of falling in love at first sight, with a picture, no less – exists. Another clip, intercut with scenes of Shade sizing up a local man as a possible match for her mother, makes a sly commentary on masculinity as a masquerade by showing machismo as a pose built out of gestures of manly bravado. The last clip depicts a story of 'forbidden love' – a nun's love for a man – which parallels Shade's struggle with her own feelings not only for Javier, off-limits because of his race, but for her father as she uncovers the truth about him.

Gas Food Lodging uses melodrama in the frame story as well, to convey the need for emotional intensity and the costs of its absence. The opening montage depicts Laramie as a place that is static, surreally bright but unmoving. Laramie is dead to those who are stranded there without some vision or capacity to transform it, or some of the 'magic' that becomes a leitmotif in the film, from the Olivia Newton-John song ('You Have to Believe in Magic') to the desert rock that becomes a totem, passed from character to character. The images of pop culture icons plastered on the walls, the sounds of bickering, giggling, silences and tears, the shot of Nora on the toilet asking who didn't replace the tampons – all convey the ambivalence and uneasy intimacy of female lives shared in cramped quarters. Anders uses a series of melodramatic misunderstandings and mistimings to heighten the film's pathos and dramatic irony: Just as Trudi comes out of her depression, an unknowing Nora gives her an ultimatum to leave. Just as Nora hums with happiness after having sex with Hamlet, Shade accuses her of ruining their lives because she 'hates men'. The most dramatic of these is Dank's death, which Trudi interprets, true to her own history but wrong, as yet another betrayal.

THE HOME MOVIE, OR 'REAL LIFE'

The last film Shade watches at the Sunn Cinema is not a fictional melodrama but in important ways it stands as a melodrama nonetheless, at least in Shade's mind. Shade finally watches a fragment of a home movie from her early childhood that has become a fetish for her, the basis of a fantasy she has fabricated about her own family and built around an image of her father that would make him like the men in Elvia Rivero's films – as faithful as the repentant husband, as dashing as the macho 'Marlboro Man'. Yet that fabrication is just that, a fiction. Moreover, it has caused a rift between her and her mother, whom she wrongly blames for his absence. And finally, it has prevented her from coming to terms with the relation between the fantasy derived from her cinephilia and 'gas food lodging', or the material realities of life.

In this sequence, Shade finally sees the two kinds of films – fictional melodrama, factual documentary – in each other's lights. Just as she had always known the 'reality' of the fictional melodrama – its power to keep alive her imagination – she now sees the fiction within the home movie, which she discovers is not 'reality' but a genre in its own right, produced within the same ideology that informs melodrama and employing its own conventions (the father smiling at the camera, hoisting children, a dog wandering into the frame). These images anchor the myth of the 'real' family Shade has longed for, and it is not until they are projected – literally illuminated, held up to the light – that Shade is able to see through them to what they are: a fantasy that has prevented her from seeing the realities of her existing family. The happy image of her young father is only that, a spectre, frozen in time, only a small part of the identity of the kind-hearted but weak man she discovers him to be.

ROMANTIC COMEDY

Shade makes this discovery with Javier by her side, not in the projection booth, and it is no accident that each of the three women in the film finds a man whom we are led to believe will be 'faithful to the end' as Shade will finally say about Dank. The film asks about the possibilities of romantic and enduring attachments between men and women and answers affirmatively, drawing on a revised version of the utopian narrative of the couple, or romantic comedy, as the basis for its optimism. Moreover, *Gas Food Lodging* uses the narrative structure of romantic comedy as a means of mediation or translation not only between men and women, but between ethnic groups, at the same time it accommodates a shift of social and creative power towards women.

Some classical theories of comedy emphasise its use of irony, wit and satire to deflate the pretentious, expose the hypocritical, and eliminate abstractions and false ideals. Others emphasise comedy's movement towards social renewal through the use of structures and motifs of community and festivity, such as weddings, dances and feasts. While these impulses may seem at odds, they are not, and most comedy usually includes elements of both. *Gas Food Lodging* uses laughter to expose its primary target, the persistence of patriarchal power and the notions of gender on which it is based. This exposure occurs not only in the Elvia Rivero clips about female martyrdom and male machismo, but in the frame narrative itself, most comically when Trudi teaches Shade how to masquerade as a woman in order to seduce Darius, her sexually ambiguous friend. The sequence was set up by an earlier one in which Darius instructed a wide-eyed Shade on what women want ('to go over the edge', to do 'that weird scarey feminine shit'), drawing attention to the degree to which femininity is something created in the imagination of men, including men who may not be entirely certain about their own sexual identity.

At the same time Shade is learning to discard these fantasies, the film moves towards overcoming the obstacles that keep the two young lovers apart. In the classical period, these obstacles were most often associated with social class, and class continues to function similarly in such recent romantic comedies as *Pretty Woman* and *While You Were Sleeping*. In contrast, *Gas Food Lodging* creates a uniformly poor or working-class world in which the upward mobility promised by *Pretty*

Woman is no longer viable, or even visible. The film adapts romantic comedy for a multilingual, multiracial world, in which economic difference has become displaced on to racial difference. In this world, the comedic values of connection, community and communication become literally issues of translation – of learning, as Shade does, to approach difference on its own terms and to seek out new grounds for connection, as Javier's home and the desert eventually become for the young couple.

Each of the men who ultimately proves faithful – the touchstone male virtue of this film – is tied to ethnic groups or nations the truck-stop culture defines itself against: Dank is from England, and Hamlet – whose name evokes traditional high culture – sells satellite dishes, the means of creating a global village via popular culture. It is not Javier's poverty that stands between him and Shade, but the fact that his roots are Mexican. These men figure the possibilities of crossing linguistic and cultural boundaries just as Shade does in her love of Mexican film and in her ability to respond to Javier's deaf mother through touch and dance. The mother–daughter connection represented by Javier's mother and Shade provides a glimpse of a sensuous and extra-linguistic means of communication across the barriers of race and generation. Javier speaks his words of love to Shade in Spanish and they are not translated in subtitles for the viewer, implying that emotional truths can be communicated in ways that transcend symbolic differences. In the context of a film about men who walk away, his promise to love her 'por vida' (for life) may well seem suspect and in fact we never learn if he keeps it. The film is more concerned with Shade's maturation, whether she can sort out the place of fantasy and imagination in her life. When her dreams are tested after her failed tragicomic seduction of Darius and she takes down his pictures from her walls, she asks, 'What do you do with yourself if you can't imagine the world the way you want it to be?' This capacity to dream about a different world, the film suggests, is the first step towards bringing that new world about. In insisting on Shade's need to hold on to her capacity to dream, the film also insists on the necessity and integrity of the comic vision.

At one point, when reluctantly dumping her married lover, Nora admits, 'Women are lonely in the 90s, it's our new phase, I've been lonelier. We'll live.' This 'long view' of the lot of women anchors Shade's dreams in a tougher vision of reality, but one that does not rule out the possibilities for loving relationships between men and women, and it is a measure of the film's generosity that it exposes the consequences of a patriarchal social order while granting individuals the ability to position themselves in differing ways within that order. Even the father is shown to be less a villain from melodrama than a figure of weakness unable to find his way in the economic wasteland of Laramie. Just as it refuses to show women only as victims, the film refuses to show men only as victimisers.

The film's triumvirate of faithful men holds out the possibilities of genuine love between the sexes, and of sexuality itself as a means of ecstatic transcendence from not only the deadening confinements of the town but from the gender inequities represented by the 'male' genres. If for Nora sex takes place in the prosaic confines of her small bed, sex itself for a mother – sex that doesn't lead to disaster – departs from the conventions of the traditional melodrama. For Trudi and Shade, love takes them outside the limits of Laramie into an outside world which they learn to see as magical and alive and which makes them come alive too, as melodrama has done for Shade.

A GIRL'S-COMING-OF-AGE FILM
AND FEMINIST FILM THEORY

The final genre *Gas Food Lodging* brings to mind is the coming-of-age movie, for if nothing else, the film depicts the maturation of its female protagonist. Overwhelmingly, the coming-of-age film, like cinephilia, is a 'guy thing', whether in art cinema or in popular film, and Shade's quest for identity like that of the conventional male hero hinges on the familiar quest for a father. She desires to know who she is and believes the answer lies in learning who her father is. The fact that only a handful of films about girls' coming-of-age exists bears out the conventional belief that femininity simply 'is', it doesn't grow or change. *Gas Food Lodging*, in contrast, concludes with its heroine in a very different place from where she was in the beginning, weeping at the Sunn Cinema. Now she strides away from the camera towards the mountains or the open space of the Western.

This movement of the girl into open space recalls similar moments in film history but with important differences. The Gamin in Chaplin's *Modern Times* (1936) walks towards a similar landscape but on the arm of the Tramp. While we suspect that Javier will be 'in the picture' with Shade, literally he is not and the film closes on her alone, a radical rewriting of the couple-centred ending of romantic comedy. Dorothy of the *Wizard of Oz* (1939) ends her quest over the rainbow by returning to the little farmhouse. The heroines of *Thelma and Louise* (1991) escape domesticity only to be frozen in time and space at the end of their road. In contrast, *Gas Food Lodging* brings Shade to a point where she is poised to enter a larger world, and on her own terms. Through her evolving understanding of the role of cinema in her own life, she has bridged the gap between nature and culture. She can now walk away from the cinema-driven fantasies of the Elvia Rivero films and the home movie, having found in the 'real world' the intensity she had previously found only in cinema. She has learned to discard some of her dreams without losing her capacity to dream, just as she has learned to be independent without losing her capacity to love.

Gas Food Lodging might finally be seen as a coming-of-age story about feminist film theory and the female spectator. Shade insists at the beginning of the film that none of this would have been 'worth telling' without Elvia Rivero, and Elvia is linked not only with Shade but with her mother, who resembles her in Hamlet's eyes. These links point to a woman-to-woman bond that is explicitly cinematic, the bond of spectator to screen. Consistent with recent developments in feminist film theory, such as Jackie Stacey's work on stars, this cinematic sisterhood does not swallow up the subjectivity of the female spectator but suggests the productive power of women's relationships with female film stars, with melodrama and with film overall.

This treatment of Hollywood genres departs significantly from what has occurred in much recent Hollywood romantic comedy. Nora Ephron's *Sleepless in Seattle*, for example, overtly cites melodrama with references to *An Affair to Remember* (1957) as well as more recent media genres such as the call-in confessional radio show, in order to poke fun at the women who weep at them. Yet when it appropriates the conventions of the despised weepie to evoke sympathy for the suffering Tom Hanks character, it does so with little or no irony. Moreover, while laughing at the female tears triggered by the weepie, it does nothing to call into question the ideologies that bring those tears about: women's suffering for love, their self-sacrifice for men and children, the many instances of female martyrdom made so visible in *Gas Food Lodging*'s

Elvia Rivero clips. In fact, the film reaffirms those values when Meg Ryan, at the end, walks away from a life and career 3,000 miles away and into an instant family. With a gesture as simple as taking a child's hand, she assumes the role of wife and mother, a role that appears inseparable from the fantasy of romantic love so crucial to the film. Like the classical romantic comedy, the film assures us that love conquers all. But unlike the classical comedy, it provides little challenge to conventional thinking about gender and the relations between the sexes.

In contrast, *Gas Food Lodging* doesn't reject Hollywood conventions outright but finds new uses for them, providing a model for a kind of filmmaking that does not offer a stark alternative to mainstream filmmaking but something more complicated and diverse. By recombining and hybridising mainstream genres, films such as *Gas Food Lodging* retain what's most valuable about mainstream filmmaking – its power to move audiences and give them pleasure, for example – but also puts the beliefs it embodies under scrutiny. Not surprisingly, some of the most innovative of this work is happening in experimental cinema, short films that explore women's relations to the fantasies produced by popular culture (Jane Campion's *A Girl's Own Story*, Sadie Benning's videos *It Wasn't Love*). Other filmmakers, such as Nancy Savoca (*True Love* 1989), Mira Nair (*Mississippi Masala* 1992), Rose Troche (*Go Fish* 1994), Ang Lee (*The Wedding Banquet*) and Leslie Harris (*Just Another Girl on the IRT* 1993) are rewriting the conventions of romantic comedy and melodrama in interesting, independently produced feature-length films.

An invisible Nora held the camera for the home movies in *Gas Food Lodging*, and for my purposes it would be ideal if Shade were carrying a Camcorder or better yet a Bolex camera as she marches resolutely into the hills. She does not. And the film ends with her extravagantly romantic observation about Dank being true to Trudi 'till the end' – which happened only a day or two after he left her. We might ask here, what has Shade done to earn that romanticism? The answer lies in the gap between Shade and Anders, and in all that has preceded this ending, all that remains offscreen in the new fragments of cinematic memory the film has implanted in us; for the film has given us not only Trudi and Shade in the Technicolor desert, but Nora in her cramped bed. Anders refuses a film-centred utopia like the one Shade built around the home movie, just as Shade learns to refuse the martyrdom of the Mexican melodramas she once escaped into. But Anders also allows Shade to keep the optimism her love of cinema has nurtured. And so, along with her voice, Shade now carries a vision or story, an awareness of her power, and as such she can be seen as a 'shade' or image of the feminist filmmakers of the 1980s, 1990s and beyond who, like Anders, are using old genres in new ways and in so doing change the paths of their own cinematic sisters and daughters 'not yet heard from, not yet born'.

NOTES

Thanks to Karen Ford, Julia Lesage and Chuck Kleinhans for their helpful comments on this chapter.

1 See Chuck Kleinhans's 'Independent Features: Hopes and Dreams' for an overview of the recent history of US independent cinema (1997). Kleinhans cites the April 1996 special issue of *Vanity Fair*, headlined on its cover with 'Hollywood '96, From Sundance to Sunset' as evidence of the mainstreaming of independent cinema. More recently, the 21 July 1997 issue of the popular US news magazine *Newsweek*, in an article on cultural trends, mentioned Sundance Film Festival under the category of 'mainstream (post-cool)', and Slamdance Film Festival under 'mutation (neo-cool)' (Kleinhans 1997: 59). Slamdance is a festival that began in 1994 as a venue for films that weren't accepted at Sundance. At the Academy Awards of 1997, the only Hollywood film to be nominated for Best Picture was *Jerry McGuire*. According to film historian Robert Sklar, the others (*Shine, Secrets and Lies, Fargo* and the winner, *The English Patient*) were neither financed nor distributed by a major Hollywood studio.

2 As David Bordwell, Janet Staiger and Kristin Thompson have noted in *Classical Hollywood Cinema* (1985), a romantic plot line occurs in most (95 per cent) classical Hollywood films, where it serves not only ideological but formal purposes, signalling the closure that defines the classical Hollywood film. While in most genres the romantic plot line is secondary to the main line of action, in romantic comedy it is primary.

3 See Frank Krutnik (1990), Steve Neale (1992) and the contributions of Peter William Evans and Celestino Deleyto in this volume for more on recent romantic comedy. I have addressed similar issues in 'Melodrama and Men in Post-Classical Comedy' (1995) and 'Comedy, Melodrama and Gender: Theorizing the Genres of Laughter' (1995), where I argue that in the 1980s and 1990s, melodrama has increasingly been appropriated for

mainstream 'male backlash' films about suffering, victimised men (a new mini-genre almost single-handedly built by Michael Douglas), or in small independent films (*The Brothers McMullen*, 1995). I might also mention a spate of romances and other recent films that feature men who are impotent, wounded, and weak – *Edward Scissorhands* (1991) and other Johnny Depp films, *Forrest Gump* (1994), *Untamed Heart* (1993), *Scent of a Woman* (1992), *Leaving Las Vegas* (1995).

4 According to Rich's profile in *Sight and Sound* (1995), Anders presents herself as an outspoken middle-aged mother with a working-class background. This persona resonates with the one Roseanne has brought to network TV, suggesting (along with newer sitcoms such as *Grace under Fire*) a greater interest in more varied representations of motherhood, age and class. In 1993 Anders directed *Mi Vida Loca* about girl gangs in East LA. In 1995 she directed a segment of *Four Rooms* along with Alexandre Rockwell, Robert Rodriguez and Quentin Tarantino, among the most sought-after indie directors. *Grace of My Heart*, a film about a female songwriter based on the life of Carole King, followed in 1996.

5 In its 1996–7 season, ABC built its highly successful Friday night line-up around a spin off of *Clueless*, a romantic comedy directed by Amy Heckerling. Girls have become an audience to be reckoned with and they like romantic comedy, but not necessarily on the old terms.

6 One of the most provocative challenges to the idea of the passive female spectator is Jackie Stacey's *Star-Gazing: Hollywood Cinema and Female Spectatorship* (1994), an exploration of the connection among female fans and female stars. Stacey argues that female fans during World War II used their attraction to and identification with female stars in productive ways.

WORKS CITED

Bordwell, David, Janet Staiger and Kristin Thompson 1985. *The Classical Hollywood Cinema*. New York: Columbia University Press

Hamilton, Kendall 1997. 'Blowing Smoke', *Newsweek*, 80, 3 (21 July): 54–61

Hansen, Miriam 1986. 'Pleasure, Ambivalence, Identification: Valentino and Female Spectatorship', *Cinema Journal*, 25, 4 (Summer): 6–32

Haskell, Molly 1973 (1987). *From Reverence to Rape: The Treatment of Women in the Movies*. Chicago and London: University of Chicago Press

Kleinhans, Chuck 1997. 'Independent Features: Hopes and Dreams'. In *Independent Features: Hopes and Dreams*, Jon Lewis, ed. Durham: Duke University Press

Krutnik, Frank 1990. 'The Faint Aroma of Performing Seals: The "Nervous" Romance and the Comedy of the Sexes', *The Velvet Light Trap*, no. 26 (Fall): 56–72

Neale, Steve 1992.'The Big Romance or Something Wild?: Romantic Comedy Today', *Screen*, 33, 3 (Autumn): 284–99

Rich, B. Ruby 1995.'Slugging It out for Survival', *Sight and Sound*, 5, 4: 14–17

Rowe, Kathleen 1995.'Melodrama and Men in Post-Classical Comedy'. In *Me Jane: Masculinity, Movies and Women*, Pat Kirkham and Janet Thumim, eds. New York: Lawrence & Wishart, 184–93

Rowe, Kathleen 1995.'Comedy, Melodrama and Gender: Theorizing the Genres of Laughter'. In *Classical Hollywood Comedy*, Kristine Brunovska Karnick and Henry Jenkins, eds. New York: Routledge

Sklar, Robert 1997.'Taking Hollywood by Storm: Behind the Triumph of Independent Films', *The Chronicle of Higher Education*, 43 (14 March): B7

Stacey, Jackie 1994. *Star-Gazing: Hollywood Cinema and Female Spectatorship*. London: Routledge

Chapter 11

MEG RYAN, MEGASTAR

Peter William Evans

Meg Ryan: The reaffirmation of romance

Isn't it romantic?

(*Love Me Tonight*, 1932)

INTRODUCTION: RYAN'S DAUGHTER

Meg Ryan is the quintessential 1980s/1990s' female Hollywood romantic comedy heroine. Her major vehicles, all courtship comedies, *When
Harry Met Sally* (1989), *Sleepless in Seattle* (1993) and *French Kiss* (1995),
are some of the genre's most characteristic films. As well as featuring
in these, and in a few other somewhat less convincing examples, such

as *Joe Versus the Volcano* (1990), *IQ* (1994) and *Addicted to Love* (1997), she has also starred in various other types of film playing, for instance, an alcoholic in *When a Man Loves a Woman* (1994), a groupie drug addict in *The Doors* (1991), and a military officer in *Courage under Fire* (1996), where attributes ideal for romantic comedy survive even in roles that call on other resources. *Mutatis mutandis* the connotations of these films, as will later become clear, also play into her romantic roles in significant ways.

In the three key romantic comedies mentioned above the Meg Ryan roles to some extent reprise those immortalised by her illustrious pre-decessors, especially Katharine Hepburn and Barbara Stanwyck, in classic screwball comedies like *Bringing up Baby* (1938) and *The Lady Eve* (1941). Although increasingly weary of her American sweetheart roles – hence the radical make-over from Wendy House doll to fake druggy tank-girl in *Addicted to Love* – Meg Ryan has nevertheless also sought in interview to identify herself with that tradition (Thompson 1989: 88, 90). Her romantic comedies cover much the same territory as screwball, exploring the meanings of romantic love, the arts of courtship, the social implications, fulfilments and limitations of marriage, as well as the pursuit of identity through the pathways of desire.

Yet while many elements of form remain constant in the genre from screwball to the present day, the pressures and constraints under which romantic comedies are made have naturally varied from one generation to another, offering a temporal framework to their timeless theme of love. These questions are all given a woman's perspective in Meg Ryan films where even in the 1990s despite the greater trend towards male-centred comedy, the genre's traditional female-dominated allegiances continue to flourish. Much has been written about the rise of screwball comedies – and their prioritisation of 'the woman ques-tion' – against the background of the first wave of feminism in Europe and America (Rowe 1995, Babington and Evans 1989). Relating these films to their social contexts reveals the extent to which Katharine Hepburn's 1930s' meanings are considerably informed by the achieve-ments in public life of women like Amelia Earhart, Frances Perkins and Eleanor Roosevelt. In screwball comedies, too, the *éducation sentimentale* forced upon the male not only repeats a seemingly eternal ploy but also registers the triumph of the assertive woman in times more conducive to recognition of female achievements. Even so, for all the ambiguity and veiled radicalism of screwball, other pressures ensured that certain codes – for instance the taboo on sexual explicitness – now commonplace, could not be broken then.

The products of a much more body-conscious society – although still somewhat quaintly, like their antecedents, governed by an aesthetics of decorum – the Meg Ryan 'new romances' remain subject to the distortions of a durable ideology, one that demonises women, and is given here its specious exorcism through the presence of the star herself, for to look at Meg Ryan is to contemplate a world free of demons and terror. One of the most hysterical formulations in recent times of the 'monstrous feminine', Glenn Close's nightmarish Freudian fall-guy in *Fatal Attraction* (1987), even earns a direct mention in *Sleepless in Seattle* through Sam's (Tom Hanks) warning to his son Jonah about the perils of dating unknown women.

And yet, of course, for all their nervousness about post-Aids sex and deadly designing women, the Meg Ryan films, undeniably shaped by social and ideological pressures, are also driven by more enlightened impulses. Meg Ryan belongs, after all, to what Molly Haskell has termed an 'age of ambivalence', where after the early 1970s, a period in which plausible women all but disappeared from Hollywood screens, the climate improved sufficiently to allow the emergence of a new generation including Sissy Spacek, Sigourney Weaver, Jessica Lange, Meryl Streep and others, women stars appearing in different genres to become the symbols of 'defiance, of a refusal – or inability – to live by the old rules, accompanied by the doubt and confusion that any such shift must necessarily bring' (Haskell 1987: 373).

For Haskell, these stars and their films challenge the somehwat restricted view of Hollywood as first outlined in Laura Mulvey's theorisation of spectacle and pleasure as irredeemably patriarchalised.[1] Since Mulvey's first seminal article on the topic many theorists of spectatorship – Gledhill (1991), Stacey (1994), Cowie (1997) and so on – have echoed Haskell's reservations concerning not only the limited view of the interaction between role and female star, but also the passivity and complicity of spectators, especially female spectators who must, on this reading, view the spectacle tied to the fixed perspectives of patriarchal discourse. Although to some extent the commercial success of these films (*Sleepless in Seattle* made $17.3 million in its first week of release in the USA) is inseparable from dominant assumptions about identity, gender and the relations between the sexes, the appeal of the Meg Ryan romantic comedies is at least as much attributable to their engagement with the changing needs and desires of their 1980s/1990s' female audiences as the Hepburn and Stanwyck films were to the treatment for 1930s' and 1940s' women of issues relevant to their day. And like the screwball films, her romantic comedies both endorse and occasionally problematise in surprising ways the ideology of romantic love in a fashion that clearly connects with the contradictory tastes of modern audiences.

Nevertheless, the Meg Ryan films overwhelmingly hold fast to many of the genre's traditions, especially its idealisation of the couple. Even in the 1990s when the relations between the sexes have been more than ever undermined by mutual suspicion, fears of commitment and the equivocal effects of serial monogamy, the irrational instinct that propels men and women towards one another to form loving couples remains the pivotal subject of romantic comedy. The firm embrace by the Meg Ryan comedies of these consoling values in uncertain times remains of durable appeal.

As Virginia Wright Wexman has remarked, since first taking hold in the nineteenth century in line with Romanticism's cult of the individual, the meanings of the romantic couple have undergone constant processes of evolution. Patriarchal forms of marriage have largely given way to an ideal of partnership based on companionship, a trend leading, moreover, in recent times to relationships not limited to heterosexual norms. Furthermore, of course, the notion, during this period, of sexual pleasure as 'a means of self-expression and mainstay of identity rather than as simply a means of forging stable heterosexual bonds using romantic love as glue' (Wright Wexman 1993: 13), has been echoed in films that both welcome as well as resist this development. Even though they remain to some degree compromised by the dominant ideology of the day, 1980s' and 1990s' romantic comedies are made against a postmodern background of greater self-consciousness and public debates around such issues. The 1980s and 1990s have not invented discussion of sex and gender, but the explosion of mass circulation popular media interest in these subjects means that Meg Ryan comedies are much more integrally a part of open public debate on such matters than were, say, the Katharine Hepburn prototypes of the 1930s and 1940s.

ROMANCE: ONLY YOU

Which comes first, the narrative or the star? 'To suit the action to the word, or the word to the action?' Are these films 'vehicles' for their stars, or do they demand a certain kind of performer to fulfil their narrative aims? Nora Ephron's post-production remarks on *When Harry Met Sally* seem to prioritise role and narrative over performer:

> though I had a great experience with Rob Reiner on *When Harry Met Sally*, it was a big shock to him that the movie was as much Sally's as Harry's. Harry had more jokes but he was a less complex character. I knew this when I wrote it but he (Reiner) didn't know it, so when Meg began to work in the movie they were all stunned since she kept stealing scenes. But those scenes were all there in the script ready to be stolen by the right actress. (Francke 1994: 110)

While most romantic comedies conform to basic patterns of courtship – lovers meet, separate, endure ordeals, pair up with other lovers or become reunited – it is clear that the choice of a star, say Julia Roberts, over another, say Goldie Hawn, inevitably pushes the meanings of the role and narrative in different directions. While Julia Roberts usually connotes openness and an affectionate heart, Goldie Hawn – the memories of her *Laugh-In* days still vibrant – conveys a limitless potential for anarchy. The complementary dual process of interaction and creativity between star, role and narrative underpins the strategies of the narrative as it maps out its own version of social and psychological realities, while the star places these in tension through the play of meanings already developed, as Dyer (1979) and others have claimed, through semiotics and intertextuality both on and offscreen. Meg Ryan's romantic comedies all conform to the traditional conventions of courtship, loss and fulfilment (although in modern romances closures are typically caught between tensions both affirming romantic love and marriage and by reservations about any union's durability) but they all also mediate 1980s/1990s' inflections of these conventions. Furthermore, although the structural meanings of these narratives varies little through the casting of different stars, having Meg Ryan at their centre gives them an even more upbeat tone than would have been the case had Melanie Griffith, Marisa Tomei, Debra Winger or any other contemporary romantic comedy star been preferred.

The endorsement in all her romantic comedies of the genre's formal conventions as well as of changing attitudes towards gender and subjectivity is not radically affected by the choice of Meg Ryan – as distinct from any of her rivals – for one of the key roles. But her presence does serve to modify their emphasis. While, as Barbara Creed (1993) and others have argued, other genres, especially horror and modern *film noir*, project male-directed cautionary images of the monstrous feminine, the vast majority of romantic comedies relay for all audiences reassurances about heterosexual love and marriage. Although sometimes revealing signs of edginess, even in early films like *When Harry Met Sally*, Meg Ryan more than most epitomises the genre's safe-sex alternative to some of her rivals in romantic comedy, never mind the murderous vamps of modern Gothic. Above all, Meg Ryan does not toy with men's feelings. The very essence of loyalty, trustworthiness and all things natural, she is the approachable safe harbour for all those negotiating the Scylla and Charybdis of modern sexuality. For every siren lying in wait 'out there', as Sam puts it in *Sleepless in Seattle*, there is a Meg Ryan character offering wholesome relief with a friendly grin. Unlike, say, Kathleen Turner, ever poised in *Peggy Sue Got Married* (1986) to activate her *noir*-related potential – as in *The War of the Roses* (1989) – Meg Ryan promotes love as a refuge from modern alienation and solitude. A stranger to the perverse, she often plays a career girl, but not in a way that seems overbearingly ambitious or competitive. In *Sleeples in Seattle*, for instance, she is a journalist on the *Baltimore Sun*, in *French Kiss* a teacher, but these films neglect the potential for drama related to her professional life – in a way that is welcomed, say, by *Broadcast News* (1987) or *Working Girl* (1988) – in order to concentrate on romance.

Highly artificial in construction, Meg Ryan is projected as the antithesis of artifice; even the abbreviation of her Christian name (her real name is Margaret Hyra) stresses the evasion of pretence and the promotion of next-door neighbourliness in its preference for the informal 'Meg' over the more stately nuances of the completed form 'Margaret'. Her offscreen comments on sex and relationships reinforce these onscreen meanings: 'Today people are more careful about dating and beginning relationships. Yes, it's because of AIDS, but I think there's also been a general rethinking of values – maybe we've grown up a little' (Thompson 1989: 88–90).

In some respects this appeal to maturity deviates from the tone of screwball with which she has claimed affinity, echoing more the conservative tendencies of 1950s' America, when directors like Billy Wilder made romantic comedies tracing the quest of beleaguered males for relief from the moral securities of the Eisenhower era. In *The Hearts of Men* (1983) Barbara Ehrenreich argues that even the phenomenal success of *Playboy* magazine could be read as the cry of the prematurely mature male revisiting the playing fields of a pre-Oedipal paradise. Since then, and especially in the post-AIDS climate, as Ryan herself remarks, America continues to be trapped between the conflicting drives both of an ever-increasing explicitness of subject treatment and of a roaring permissiveness, and the counter claims of reactionary lobbyists, at one extreme the shrill sobriety of the moral majority, at another the radical feminist anti-pornography crusaders. Meg Ryan's appearances in her non-comic films emphasise the point even more forcefully. In, for instance, *When a Man Loves a Woman* and *The Doors* she exemplifies the all-American girl's ruin not only by weakness of character but also by the fatal *Zeitgeist* of the times. Both films imbue the Ryan character's destruction by external forces with an almost elegiac pathos. In *When a Man Loves a Woman* the flower of her natural beauty is crushed by alcoholism; in *The Doors* it is annihilated by the sex, drugs and rock and roll milieu of 1960s' America, both films, of course, aiming their fire at modern decadence and corruption. Ryan's clear forget-me-not blue eyes, flaxen hair and slender, slightly scrawny build, which can slip from almost Tom Sawyerish boyishness to senior prom virginal prettiness, perfectly match the obligatory ornamental, wispy, fern-like shape of 1960s' rock band Marianne Faithfull groupie clones. Driven to distraction by Jim Morrison's infidelities and other forms of wild behaviour, she does explode with anger from time to time. The unexpected and slightly shocking demotic register on which she occasionally relies, such as 'You put your dick in this woman?', also serves, like the outbursts of rage, not to reveal a temperament by nature monstrous or perverse, but to highlight with even more pathos, as in the scenes of her sexual humiliation, the defeat of innocence by experience. *The Doors* is also the only film where she is disrobed beyond the limits allowed by the conventions of romantic comedy, though even here the modesty of her exposure stresses the identification of the star with girlish sweetness and innocence.

Though there are some exceptions, such as *Something Wild* (1986) and *Gas Food Lodging* (1991) – where nudity belongs to these films' knowing violations of various generic codes – the usual taboo on the body's exposure, and thus on the realities of genital sexuality, falls in line, as Neale and Krutnik (1990) have noted, with the genre's idealisation of heterosexual romance. It is not that the Meg Ryan comedies ignore genital sexuality – indeed *When Harry Met Sally* is largely concerned with its often troublesome intervention in the life of the couple – but that they are intent on negotiating a complex pact between, on the one hand, the films' tendency to treat the lovers' baser appetites with the decorum ingrained in a genre affirming more the lyrical than the prosaic elements of human desire and, on the other, the Meg Ryan persona's frequent identifications with innocence (even childishness), and the affirmation of dependency associated with home and family life.

The childish features of the persona are often stressed, as in the opening sequence of *French Kiss*, where she is seen learning to overcome her fear of flying (in aeroplanes) in the flight simulator, or when in *Prelude to a Kiss* (1993) she jumps up into the air to touch tree branches on her way home. Her casual clothes (white shirt over jeans in *French Kiss*) and unkempt hair, her baby teeth, her barefoot shots in publicity photos, and preference for cotton nightgowns over decadent lingerie worn by her fetishised rivals, maintain the childish aura. In *Seattle* this is even further developed through the identification between Annie (Meg Ryan) and Jonah, the child desperately seeking a suitable bride for the father. The narrative is driven by the conspiracy between Jonah and Annie to create not only a romantic couple but also a nuclear family. Both characters are addicted to the same radio talk-in programme; both scream at unsuitable partners: Jonah at the opportunist threatening to usurp the place of his dead mother and thus to destroy the family romance fantasy of his mother-ideal; Annie at the man whose utter conventionality and unromantic air make him ultimately ineligible for romantic love.

When Walter discovers her hidden in the kitchen broom cupboard in the middle of the night, tuned into the talk-in programme where Jonah (significant name) is mother/wife fishing on his own and his father's behalf, she screams at him, 'Walter, you scared me. Don't ever do that again!' The remark is as significant as Walter's own *Cluedo*-inspired accusation: 'Miss Scarlett, in the broom closet, with the radio!' Both the accusation and the reaction it provokes are given a comic mode and setting, but their aim is higher than farce. There is an unconscious level at which the remark belongs to a pattern of dramatised frustrations and tensions surrounding the Meg Ryan persona which sometimes seems in spite of itself to wish to free it of its American sweetheart packaging. Read deconstructively, the remark represents an unconscious desire for the cynical, darker, more sexualised Meg Ryan to come out, if not from the closet, then from the domestic broom cupboard of ideological fantasy. But, of course, at straighter, conscious levels, Walter's joke has a far more benign meaning. He identifies himself with detection and Annie with guilty sex, but the film is arguing that while the former may be a partially accurate representation of Walter's possessive interest in Annie, the latter carries no conviction, since rather than seek liberation from it, the Meg Ryan character desires deep confinement in the closet of family life. Even though an early view of Meg Ryan sees her draped in a red dressing gown and nightie, in none of her romantic comedies, not even the supposedly more *risqué Addicted to Love*, could Meg Ryan ever conceivably be considered a 'Miss Scarlet' or *femme fatale*. The inappropriateness of Walter's weak joke is therefore also his failure as a lover, a blindness to the essence of the woman he loves, a misjudgement underlying his ineligibility for creating with her the specialness of the couple. In this context her shriek registers not just the fright of a woman caught unawares by an intruder, but also a primal scream arising from an increasingly turbulent unconscious against a lover failing to match up to the romantic comedy ideal. Moreover, the prohibition on the successful conclusion of Walter's courtship of Annie places in even greater relief the eventual appreciation of her qualities by her true partner, Sam.

His first glimpse of her, at the airport, follows significant remarks made by Sam to Jonah in which he refers to his dating of the woman considered unsuitable by Jonah – and by the audience – but the implications of which are only properly grasped when Annie comes into view: 'This is what single people do. They try other people on and see how they fit. But everybody needs an adjustment. Nobody's perfect. There is no such thing as perfection . . .' Throughout this scene Sam is the audience's surrogate in a *mise-en-abîme* of desire, giving shape to our fantasies in the pursuit of a socially constructed feminine ideal. The first part of the remark rings true of modern life, as aspiring lovers in the freer climate of serial monogamy, divorce and experimental co-habitation try one another on for size before commitment, however short-lived the fate of any final arrangements. Later on in the film, with just a hint of edginess, Annie herself recoils at the thought of 'forever' in the timetables of future lives: 'Don't you get nervous about "forever"?' she asks Walter. But romantic comedy refuses to be exclusively sustained by reality principles – however much it is regulated by them – and, for all modernity's anxieties about commitment and the vicissitudes of desire, still seeks perfection. His words still hanging in the air, Sam turns to see the very image of perfection summoned up by the sorcery of romantic comedy in its magical settings of desire. If, like Jane Greer in *Out of the Past* (1947), *noir* heroines are creatures of night, making their entrances out of the moonlight, their romantic comedy sisters are the handmaidens of the sun, the golden-glow girls whose captivating radiance is nowhere more luminous in the modern variants of the genre than in Meg Ryan. Often photographed in close-up (as in the plane conversation sequence with Kevin Kline in *French Kiss*), the image of perfection is here introduced to her admirer in medium-shot dressed informally in pastel hues, her beige full-length coat covering cream-coloured dress combining to set off the loosely tied haloed aura of hair and softly bright, health-and-beauty freshness of the face. And yet, of course, as Sam – and, through him, the real spectators in the cinema – look at this image of perfection, an image that serves both as ego-ideal and as object of desire (Morin 1957), the apparition before him, like Lacan's child's reflection in the mirror, is only a mirage of truth, an imaginary domain where absence becomes confused for presence. However, as Elizabeth Cowie argues, 'The imaginary . . . is not characterised simply by a making present what is absent, but rather the imaginary arises when the relation of desire set in play is the demand for presence, for plenitude, in the face of its absence – a desire, that is, to fill the gap' (1997: 99).

What matters here, as in responses to all screen imagery, is the way in which a complex process involving both identification and desire becomes in a public space a site for the revelation of interactive personal and social determinants or fantasies. As Elizabeth Cowie further argues, 'Fantasy is first and foremost not a wish for x, but a scenario, a structure of positions and relationships for the subject, and the "apparent" wishes may tell us little or nothing about this scenario and its relationships' (1997: 163). Put another way, rather than looking through Sam at Annie as if she were a real person, we look in reality, as Norman Holland (1968) remarks *vis-à-vis* literary and dramatic characters, into ourselves because, expressed through a variety of different formal strategies, fictional characters satisfy needs in us. The dynamics of identification are even more complicated in film, of course, because as has been repeatedly noted in the history of star theory, audience awareness of the real persons – the stars behind the character – is inalienably linked to knowledge about their fictive lives. Inspired, like Cowie, by Freud's remarks on identification in 'Group Psychology and the Analysis of the Ego' (1957), Holland argues that so-called identification with literary characters is 'actually a complicated projection and introjection, of taking in from the character certain drives and defences that are really objectively "out there" and of putting into him [sic] feelings that are really our own, "in here"' (1968: 278). As we respond to characters we absorb both their drives and defences: our own drives will be engaged by the romance-inspired pursuit of Sam by Annie, our defences by the muted caveats about idealised love made by the secondary characters. As Holland further comments in a discussion of *Romeo and Juliet* that could in its generalisations apply equally well to *Sleepless in Seattle*, 'we use the drives and defences of a Mercutio to manage tensions within ourselves, not only the tensions the tragedy creates, but also the tensions from our own lives that we bring to the play because they are close to the emotional themes of the play' (1968: 280). The characters of the play *Romeo and Juliet* or of the film *Sleepless in Seattle* become more than just screens on which we project the history of our own fulfilled or repressed desires. They are the very catalysts that call them into being.

Meg Ryan, then, becomes in this representative scene both an object of desire (potentially for all sexual orientations, though her appeal seems primarily aimed at heterosexual audiences), as well as the mirror of our drives and defences. In an unmistakeable allusion to *Some Like It Hot* (1959), one of Hollywood's greatest romantic comedies, Sam remarks that 'nobody's perfect'. But just as Marilyn Monroe – if not Jack Lemmon as Daphne – belied the truth of the remark for 1950s' audiences, so in the 1990s, if Sam's judgement is to be trusted, Meg Ryan continues to place in question the prejudiced opinion of Osgood Fielding the third (Joe E. Brown). She is the creature of changing attitudes towards romantic relationships, yet someone also through whom modern lovers are made to yearn for the securities of the past, the back-to-the-future star brought up on experiment and change who brings back the promised future of monogamous marriages and fidelities.

The image plays on realities and fantasies, but what is especially interesting here is how under the influence of negative publicity related to her mother's indifference and through the transparent commodification of her trade-mark virginal adolescence, the Meg Ryan persona is onscreen significantly affected. As Dyer and others have argued, a star's persona emerges as a result of the complex processes between on and offscreen interactivity. The star is, additionally, a mixture of ordinary and extraordinary components held in tension in order to keep the audience at once reassured by the former and overawed by the latter. In Ryan's case there is sometimes a slight disparity between the onscreen persona of the romantic comedies and offscreen difficulties – so fully documented (Bernal 1995: 66) – which contribute to the ultimate sense of the performativity of the 'good girl' onscreen persona, a contradiction that in the view of some critics all too clearly accounts for the self-protective exaggerations of that image in offscreen public appearances: 'The hair is a cropped wheat bob. The skin's all made up. The lips fleshier than flesh. And that nose – it screws itself up, rabbity twitch, rabbity twitch, hello aren't I cuter than cute, safer than safe' (Iley 1993: 6–7).

The histrionics of the offscreen persona – mirroring the often slightly exaggerated onscreen performance style of high-pitched, looping cadences of voice, and over-animated facial kinetics – seem to bear out the Foucault-inspired remarks by Judith Butler on performativity of gender (1990). Judith Butler's concern is with essentialist social constructions of gender and their bearing on the cultural marginalisation of gay and especially lesbian sexualities, but her discussion of the fabricated nature of all sexualities is relevant in this context:

> acts, gestures, enactments, and desire produce the effect of an internal core or substance, but produce this on the surface of the body, through the play of signifying absences that suggest, but never reveal, the organizing principle of identity as a cause. Such

acts, gestures, enactments, generally construed, are performative in the sense that the essence or identity that they otherwise purport to express are fabrications manufactured and sustained through corporeal signs and other discursive means. That the gendered body is performative suggests that it has no ontological status apart from the various acts which constitute its reality. (1990: 136)

Despite the attempts in her other genre films to vary the semantics of her romantic comedy persona, Meg Ryan comes across as a star of fixed meaning, the essentialist work of artifice signifying virginal good daughterliness, with the potential for good wife and motherliness. Her persona is constructed by hegemonic discourse, not left free to explore the full range of subjectivity and sexuality. Despite the multiple roles she plays in *Joe Versus the Volcano*, and despite the cosmetic and costume changes in *Addicted to Love* – where Karen Foster is even used as a sort of throwback to Meg Ryan past, all the better to contrast her with Meg Ryan future – the performance, to use Butler's term, of the persona is inhibited both on and offscreen by an essentialist script. She is the antithesis of Irigaray's notion of the 'Sex which is not one'.

COMEDY: NOBODY'S PERFECT

The clearest indications of the Meg Ryan character's hesitations between modernity and tradition, between fixity and fluidity of subjectivity, occur in *Addicted to Love* and *When Harry Met Sally*. In the former, the girl with attitude fails to obliterate the hidden small-town sweetheart; in the latter, the tensions are treated with greater subtlety because the inner conflicts of the character are reflected in the overall aesthetic patterns of the film. Sally lives in a world fragmented by modernity, a point further stressed by the episodic formal structures of the film. The mission of the film, though such are the vicissitudes of modern relations between the sexes that it takes twelve years of fictive time to achieve this, is to restore wholeness and harmony – the eventual union of Harry and Sally – attempting through its rhetoric of romance to allay the audience's secret feelings of modern distress about modernity. As in all her other romantic comedies, *When Harry Met Sally* transports its heroine to comedy's magical 'green world' of romance: France in *French*

Kiss and Seattle in *Sleepless in Seattle*, or, as in *When Harry Met Sally* and *Addicted*, the unlikely urban pastoral of New York. The setting of *Addicted* is not simply designed to show that love blooms in the strangest of settings, but that the city itself can act as a spur to mutual desires. Kelly Foster, like some modern female Quixote, is in flight here from the tedium of Nebraska; Meg Ryan, though, once nurtured on the decadent ambrosia of the city paradise, is eventually weaned off her urban fixes by the prospect of healthier nourishment, sharing a life with the star-gazing country boy from Nebraska. As the jilted lovers (Ryan and Matthew Broderick) spy on their former partners' idyllic courtship in their downtown sanctuary of love, they begin to discover in each other the reflection of their shared desires in a condemned building from which their voyeuristic espionage is carried out, its dereliction serving as a potent correlative for broken relationships and identities awaiting repair. In this context these settings are identical to the 'green world' milieux of films like *Bringing up Baby* (1938) or *Midnight* (1939), rescuing their lovers – the latter in the city, the former in the country – from slavery to convention. In the settings of her films, New York, France, Seattle, Ryan's role follows comic tradition both in her clownish antics and in the genre's prosecution of the thematics of identity through the pursuit of idealised partners.

Like Katharine Hepburn's pratfalls in *Bringing up Baby*, Meg Ryan's bout of accidental mayhem in the hotel restaurant in *French Kiss*, or the notorious fake-orgasm scene in *When Harry Met Sally*, conform to romantic comedy's release of regressive, instinctual behaviour. These irrational moments belong to the genre's pattern of lovers released from learned, socialised models of conduct. In *French Kiss* the awkwardness of the Meg Ryan character's behaviour, as she crashes into waiters, plates, tables and cordon bleu dishes at the luxury French hotel where her ex-fiancé is courting his new girlfriend, registers both her incompatibility with the values of the conventional society epitomised by the hotel milieu, as well as an onslaught – albeit a mild one – upon it by the girl who stands for ordinariness, freshness, sincerity and naturalness, unfazed by the exotic glamour to which her ex-fiancé is now so unwisely drawn. The scene in *When Harry Met Sally* of the fake-orgasm joke performs a similar function in its transgression of the codes of decorum – orgasm in a public space – but its potential for real anxiety is defused because of its attribution to an unthreatening star. In itself, as a satire of male sexual prowess, the joke recalls the stock of castration-anxiety jokes so characteristic of the humour of Mae West (Babington and Evans 1989: 138). Handled by Mae West the scene would have truly wounded male self-esteem; given to Meg Ryan, her laughing, wide-mouthed face easily slipping into the clownish irrascibility of a Daffy Duck, the joke is really only a joke.

The wariness of the exotic and the pursuit of sincerity and tenderness in a lover are reflected in her choice of partners and their mirroring of her comic identity. 'It Had to Be You', the key song in *When Harry Met Sally* points to the Neo-Platonic search for the romantic comedy lover's ideal other half or self-reflection. Sally's quest for the famous song's 'You' (or, 'Only You', to quote another song-alluding title of another recent romantic comedy), is readable in psychoanalytical terms as narcissistic. Where anaclitic object-choices are outwardly focused, narcissistic object-choices are inwardly directed. In general, according to Freud, men follow the former course and women the latter, though post-Freudians have problematised the gender-specific divisions further. Here it does seem that the film follows unproblematised Freud, though not in the historically limited terms outlined in his discussion of female drives (Cowie 1997: 79), in delivering a female persona whose object-choices are prompted by narcissistic motivation.

In each film what Neale and Krutnik define as the 'specialness' of the couple is affirmed in a variety of ways, one of the most significant being the choice of partner who eventually proves worthy of her love. Couples in romantic comedy are mirrors of mutual ideals, and one may discover almost as much, in this instance, about Meg Ryan the star by studying her partners, their star meanings and the impact these have on the roles they play, as by focusing on her. Where others merely serve as the staging posts of conformism or mediocrity through which the heroine must pass, the male leads, Billy Crystal, Tom Hanks, Kevin Kline and Matthew Broderick all emerge – in keeping with the traditions of classical romantic comedy – as the true partners for Meg Ryan. The secondary wooers, Timothy Hutton (*French Kiss*), Bill Pullman (*Sleepless in Seattle*), and their equivalents in other films – the Ralph Bellamies of their day (but denied his pathos) – are too colonised by the consumerist ethos to earn the favour of a modern heroine, admittedly one who in some ways herself emerges from the production lines of a consumerist art. In 1930s' romantic comedy the heroine's demand for equality in relationships drove her away from the conformist securities of a Ralph Bellamy and into the arms of anarchy of a Cary Grant or a Herbert Marshall. The Meg Ryan films, to a certain extent weary of – though not, of course, hostile to – significant advances in social attitudes towards sex and gender prefer to celebrate some of the traditional values sometimes undervalued or ignored by a changing society. In *French Kiss*, for instance, Timothy Hutton forfeits the film's true prize, Meg Ryan, not simply because he is seduced by the exotic (since, after all, Meg Ryan also falls for a foreigner), but because he fails to see in her the more natural, fresher qualities of the all-American sweetheart type, the good-daughter innocent of any fashionably glossy lifestyle of temporary gratification and permanent regret. For her part, the Meg Ryan character is ultimately attracted less than Katharine Hepburn's to men whose dormant pre-Oedipal potential for transgression only required the spark of a kindred spirit, and more to someone whose embrace of tradition awaits its sympathetic response in shared desires. Kevin Kline is ultimately suitable for Meg Ryan because he is close to nature – the vineyard motif – and to family – the sprawling, rural, bread-eating and wine-imbibing French family of Hollywood imagination. The subversiveness of the Kline character – much in evidence early on in the film – is initially of subsidiary interest to her. His criminality does at one level identify him, largely through the metaphorical force of the motif, with many of the heroes of romantic comedy, but here transgression is not in itself as appealing as it is for the heroine of, say, *Trouble in Paradise* (1932). Whenever in screwball transgression was temporarily absent, it often had to be engendered by the heroine, as in *The Lady Eve* where, in keeping with the film's sinful title, Barbara Stanwyck finally succeeds we assume, right at the end of the film, in turning Henry Fonda's priggish ingenu, even if only for a night, into an unrepentant immoralist. In *French Kiss*, on the other hand, a film made in some respects against the grain of far more permissive times, transgression is almost taken for granted, so what really matters now in suitors to the Meg Ryan character and, by implication, to the audience, are responsibility, reliability and trustworthiness, all qualities related here to the land, nature and, by extension, durability and harmony of character. The union of the lovers here places in sharp relief one of the key features of the Meg Ryan persona in characteristic films like *When Harry Met Sally*, *French Kiss* and *Sleepless in Seattle*: her natural freshness and radiance and the projection of the idea that in her no durable resentments or ill-feelings, no insincerity and devious- ness, could ever be suspected. Billy Crystal, Tom Hanks and Mathew Broderick are all perfect partners for Meg Ryan because her instinctual attachment to them is founded on a perception of their suspicion of modernity and their embrace of tradition. For all his playful swagger and comic one-liners, Billy Crystal wants to settle down, Tom Hanks is a father in search of a mother, and even in *Addicted to Love* the Meg Ryan character, initially portrayed as a creature of the urban ghetto, eventually prefers Matthew Broderick the hick from Nebraska over the suave French sophisticate by whom she was initially captivated. All three stars are characterised both on and offscreen by a comparable almost pubertal, safe and feminised masculinity, the perfect complement to the onscreen Meg Ryan brand of ultimately domesticated femininity.

In *When Harry Met Sally* Meg Ryan remarks 'I don't want to spend the rest of my life in Casablanca married to a man who runs a bar'. The humour of the remark, as of the fake-orgasms and many other comic Meg Ryan scenes, recalls Freud's argument that the purpose of jokes – though here I am stretching the comments on jokes to include the comic in general – is to lift prohibition on the taboo areas of the mind (1983). Jokes release tension; they are a defence mechanism, subverting the repression of aggressive and sexual drives. The technique of the joke must, however, be sufficiently skilful to avoid direct engagement with the serious material on which it relies which, if treated without subtlety, would merely trigger off defence mechanisms to negate the intended effect of humour. Both the verbal wit and the comic situations of the Meg Ryan films conform in this respect to Freudian theory, but with an added social dimension that reaffirms both the narcissistic drives of the character and something of the contradictory ideology which speaks through her. The Meg Ryan character's preference for Paul Henreid over Humphrey Bogart records the triumph of domesticity over heroic male stoicism; the fake-orgasm indirectly prioritises the tender over the priapic.

In both cases the Meg Ryan character is an agent of the comic in strategies designed not to make her look ludicrous but, as Freud puts it *vis-à-vis* the comic in general, to achieve admiration:

Mankind have not been content to enjoy the comic where they have come upon it in their experience; they have also sought to bring it about intentionally, and we can learn more about the nature of the comic if we study the means which serve to *make* things comic. First and foremost, it is possible to produce the comic in relation to oneself in order to amuse other people – for instance, by making oneself out clumsy or stupid. In that way one produces a comic effect exactly as though one really were these things, by fulfilling the condition of the comparison which leads to the difference in expenditure. But one does not in this way make oneself ridiculous or contemptible, but may in some circumstances even achieve admiration. (Freud 1983: 260)

Furthermore, Meg Ryan places others – the enemies of her ideology of romantic love – in comic situations, above all through exposure, one of many resources – including caricature parody and travesty – at the disposal of the comedian. Often the technique follows the Freudian pattern, but in line with the traditions of romantic comedy, and in view of the deliberately constructed persona of softness and sincerity, the degradation of the dignity and the exposure of the shortcomings of her comic targets are always handled with extreme care. Thus revenge on her ex-lover in *Addicted to Love* falls short of serious injury, her termination of the relationship with Walter in *Sleepless in Seattle* executed with touching sympathy.

Films like *When Harry Met Sally* release culturally programmed defence mechanisms that reassure their audiences even while appearing to endorse a post-feminist ideology of female assertiveness: they affirm female equality while reassuring their audiences that assertiveness is not synonymous with aggression. As played by Meg Ryan, the heroine of films like *When Harry Met Sally* is not castrating but 'challenging'. In a conversation with Harry, following abandonment by one of her lovers, Sally remarks: 'I'm too dificult'. Significantly, Harry is made to reply that she is not difficult but 'challenging'. The male here does not flee from the powerful woman; on the contrary, he stays to admire her, to regard her as a positive, welcome challenge. Rather than construct a narrative around the gradual erosion or disavowal of female power, this film, like all the others, encourages acceptance of the new realities, although it does so with rhetoric as steely as a marshmallow.

CODA: THE LABOURS OF LOVE

The defeat of scepticism through affirmations of love and an unthreat-ening, approachable heterosexual femininity is the most significant contribution of the Meg Ryan character in these comedies of love. The assertiveness of her modern/traditional, childish/maternal, healthy/edgy but, above all, bisexuality-and-lesbianism-free persona, encourages the modern male to wriggle out of his commitment-and-castration-fearing cocoon of narcissistic self-containment. Meg Ryan promises that rather than lead to alienation, humiliation or entrapment, heterosexual romance can result instead in the fulfilment of desire. Her contribution to these comic narratives enhances, as Northrop Frye argues *vis-à-vis* the pattern of all romantic comedy, the mode's pursuit of identity, in both its social and individual forms, releasing the former from its irra-tional laws, and the latter from repression (1965). Overwhelmingly, the Meg Ryan persona is nevertheless, almost in spite of itself, surrounded by edginess and disturbance. The commodification of perfection – of healthy, good girl sweetness and light – so appealing to audiences growing up in the climate of changing attitudes towards gender, the ubiquity of squalor, permissiveness and crime, often seems, even though only very gently, to problematise the persona. Audience awareness of negative publicity also plays into reception of her screen roles which sometimes fail, for all their fluffy charm, to be totally convincing in their projection of a Miss Goody Two Shoes fantasy. In this context, scenes like those of the hotel porter's abrupt treatment by Meg Ryan in *French Kiss*, or forthright remarks like 'Take me to bed or lose me forever' in *Top Gun* (1986), though ultimately recuperated by the *soufflé* rhetoric of the persona, offer just enough of a hint of the frustrations, performativity and iron resolve not entirely concealed by the cute-as-candy construction of the 1990s' version of the girl-next-door. Meg Ryan's Oedipalisation – she is, after all Sean Connery's daughter in *The Presidio* (1988), Einstein's *protégée* in *IQ*, and a USAF officer in *Courage under Fire* – suggests at times, very faintly, that the process has its unexpected side-effects. Though belonging to the more affirmative end of the spectrum, not even Meg Ryan romantic comedies remain unconsciously spared the contradictions embedded in the reality principles of modern life.

NOTE

1 Mulvey refined her original formulation in 'Afterthoughts on Visual Pleasure and Narrative Cinema in Relation to *Duel in the Sun*' (1981).

WORKS CITED

Babington, Bruce and Peter William Evans 1989. *Affairs to Remember: The Hollywood Comedy of the Sexes*. Manchester: Manchester UP

Bernal, Maria 1995. 'Meg Ryan', *Fotogramas and Video*, no. 1823, September: 60–6

Butler, Judith 1990. *Gender Trouble: Feminism and the Subversion of Identity*. New York and London: Routledge

Cowie, Elizabeth 1997. *Representing the Woman: Cinema and Psychoanalysis*. London: Macmillan

Creed, Barbara 1993. *The Monstrous-Feminine: Film, Feminism, Psychoanalysis*. London and New York: Routledge

Dyer, Richard 1979. *Stars*. London: British Film Institute

Ehrenreich, Barbara 1983. *The Hearts of Men: American Dreams and the Flight from Commitment*. London: Pluto

Francke, Lizzie 1994. *Scriptgirls: Women Screenwriters in Hollywood*. London: British Film Institute

Freud, Sigmund 1957 (1921). 'Group Psychology and the Analysis of the Ego'. In *The Standard Edition of the Complete Psychological Works of Sigmund Freud*. Trans. James Strachey, Anna Freud, Alix Strachey and Alan Tyson; ed. James Strachey. London: Hogarth Press, vol. XVIII: 107–8

Freud, Sigmund 1983 (1905). *Jokes and Their Relation to the Unconscious*. In The Pelican Freud Library, 6. Trans. James Strachey; ed. Angela Richards. Harmondsworth: Penguin

Frye, Northrop 1965. *A Natural Perspective: The Development of Shakespearean Comedy and Romance*. New York: Harcourt, Brace and World

Gledhill, Christine, ed., 1991. *Stardom: Industry of Desire*. London and New York: Routledge

Haskell, Molly 1987 (1973). *From Reverence to Rape: The Treatment of Women in the Movies*. Chicago and London: University of Chicago Press

Holland, Norman 1968. *The Dynamics of Literary Response*. New York: Oxford University Press

Iley, Chrissy 1993. 'What Makes Meg a Star?', *Sunday Times*, 5 September: 6–7

Irigaray, Luce 1985 (1977). *This Sex which Is not One*. Trans. Catherine Porter. Ithaca, New York: Cornell University Press

Morin, Edgar 1957. *Les Stars*. Paris: Seuil.

Mulvey, Laura 1981. 'Afterthoughts on Visual Pleasure and Narrative Cinema in Relation to *Duel in the Sun*', *Framework*, nos. 15/16/17

Neale, Steve and Frank Krutnik 1990. *Popular Film and Television Comedy*. London: Routledge

Rowe, Kathleen 1995. *The Unruly Woman: Gender and the Genres of Laughter*. Austin: University of Texas Press

Stacey, Jackie 1994. *Star-Gazing: Hollywood Cinema and Female Spectatorship*. London: Routledge

Thompson, Douglas 1989. 'Falling in Like Is Very Hard to Do', *Mail on Sunday*, 24 September: 88 and 90

Wexman, Virginia Wright 1993. *Creating the Couple: Love, Marriage, and Hollywood Performance*. Princeton: Princeton UP

SELECT BIBLIOGRAPHY

Babington, Bruce and Peter William Evans 1989. *Affairs to Remember: The Holly-wood Comedy of the Sexes*. Manchester: Manchester UP

Baker, Houston A., Jr., 1993. 'Spike Lee and the Commerce of Culture'. In Diawara, ed., 154–76

Baraka, Amiri 1993. 'Spike Lee at the Movies'. In Diawara, ed., 145–53

Barthes, Roland 1990 (1977). *A Lover's Discourse: Fragments*. Trans. Richard Howard. Harmondsworth: Penguin

Bartosch, Bob 1987. *Jump Cut*, no. 32: 3–4

Belsey, Catherine 1985. *The Subject of Tragedy: Identity and Difference in Renaissance Drama*. London and New York: Methuen

Benson, Sheila 1989. 'Review of *When Harry Met Sally*', *The Los Angeles Times* 'Calendar', 14 July: 1

Bernal, Maria 1995. 'Meg Ryan', *Fotogramas and Video*, no. 1823, September: 60–6

Blount, Marcellus and George P. Cunningham, eds, 1996. *Representing Black Men*. New York and London: Routledge

Bogle, Donald 1994 (1973). *Toms, Coons, Mulattoes, Mammies, and Bucks: An Interpretive History of Blacks in American Films*. Oxford: Roundhouse

Bordwell, David, Janet Staiger and Kristin Thompson 1985. *The Classical Hollywood Cinema*. New York: Columbia University Press

Britton, Andrew 1983. *Cary Grant: Comedy and Male Desire*. Newcastle upon Tyne: BFI

Brown, Georgia 1989. 'Review of *When Harry Met Sally*', *Village Voice*, 18 October: 68

Brunette, Peter 1991. 'Singleton's Street Noises', *Sight and Sound*, August: 13

Buckley, Michael 1989. 'Review of *When Harry Met Sally*', *Films in Review*, October: 484

Butler, Judith 1990. *Gender Trouble: Feminism and the Subversion of Identity*. New York: Routledge

Butler, Judith 1993. *Bodies that Matter: On the Discursive Limits of 'Sex'*. New York: Routledge

Cavell, Stanley 1981. *Pursuits of Happiness: The Hollywood Comedy of Remarriage*. Cambridge, MA: Harvard UP

Chafe, William H. 1995. *The Unfinished Journey*. Oxford: Oxford University Press

Chauncey, George 1994. *Gay New York: Gender, Urban Culture, and the Making of the Gay Male World 1890–1940*. New York: Basic Books

Chown, Jeffrey 1988. *Hollywood Auteur*. London and New York: Praeger

Comino, Jo 1995. '*Only You*', *Sight and Sound*, 5, 10 (October): 48

Conroy, Marianne 1996. 'No Sin in Lookin' Prosperous'. In James and Berg, eds, 114–37

Cook, Pam 1989. 'Review of *When Harry Met Sally*', *The Monthly Film Bulletin*, 57, 671 (December): 377

Cowie, Elizabeth 1997. *Representing the Woman: Cinema and Psychoanalysis*. London: Macmillan

Creed, Barbara 1993. *The Monstrous-Feminine: Film, Feminism, Psychoanalysis*. London and New York: Routledge

D'Emilio, John and Estelle B. Freedman 1988. *Intimate Matters: A History of Sexuality in America*. New York: Harper & Row

Daly, Mary 1991. *Beyond God the Father*. London: The Women's Press

Dargis, Manohla 1995. 'Method and Madness', *Sight and Sound*, June: 6–9

De Rougemont, Denis 1956. *Passion and Society*. London: Faber

Deleyto, Celestino 1994. 'Parody, Feminism, and the Ending of *Something Wild*'. In *Proceedings of the 16th AEDEAN Conference*, José M. Ruiz, Pilar Abad and José M. Barrio, eds. Valladolid: Universidad de Valladolid, 347–55

Deleyto, Celestino 1994/95. 'The Narrator and the Narrative: The Evolution of Woody Allen's Film Comedies', *Film Criticism*, XIX, 2 (Winter): 40–54

Denzin, Norman K. 1991. *Images of Postmodern Society: Social Theory and Contemporary Cinema*. London: Sage

Diawara, Manthia, ed., 1993. *Black American Cinema*. New York and London: Routledge

Duchen, Claire 1988. *Feminism in France*. London: Routledge & Kegan Paul

Dyer, Richard 1979. *Stars*. London: British Film Institute

Dyer, Richard 1994. 'Action!', *Sight and Sound*, 4, 10 (October): 7–10

Eagleton, Mary 1986. *Feminist Literary Theory*. Oxford: Basil Blackwell

Easthope, Anthony 1986. *What a Man's Gotta Do: The Masculine Myth in Popular Culture*. Boston: Unwin Hyman

Eco, Umberto 1985. 'Postmodernism, Irony, the Enjoyable'. In *Modernism/Postmodernism*, Peter Brooker, ed. London: Longman, 225–8

Ehrenreich, Barbara 1983. *The Hearts of Men: American Dreams and the Flight from Commitment*. London: Pluto

Ehrenreich, Barbara 1990. 'Feminism and Class Consolidation', *Dialogue*, 90, 4: 52–6

Ehrenreich, Barbara 1995. 'The Decline of Patriarchy'. In *Constructing Masculinity*, M. Berger, B. Wallis and S. Watson, eds. New York and London: Routledge, 284–90

Engels, Friedrich 1986 (1884). *The Origin of the Family: Private Property and the State*. Harmondsworth: Penguin

Evans, Jeff 1996. 'Something New: Music as Re-vision in Jonathan Demme's *Something Wild*', *Popular Music and Society*, 19, 3: 1–17

Foucault, Michel 1981 (1976). *The History of Sexuality, Vol. 1: An Introduction*. Trans. Robert Hurley. Harmondsworth: Penguin

Francke, Lizzie 1994. *Scriptgirls: Women Screenwriters in Hollywood*. London: British Film Institute

French, Marilyn 1985. *Beyond Power: On Women, Men and Morals*. New York: Summit Books

Freud, Sigmund 1957 (1921). 'Group Psychology and the Analysis of the Ego'. In *The Standard Edition of the Complete Psychological Works of Sigmund Freud*. Trans. James Strachey, Anna Freud, Alix Strachey and Alan Tyson; ed. James Strachey. London: Hogarth Press, vol. XVIII: 107–8

Freud, Sigmund 1983 (1905). *Jokes and Their Relation to the Unconscious*. In The Pelican Freud Library, 6. Trans. James Strachey; ed. Angela Richards. Harmondsworth: Penguin

Freud, Sigmund 1981 (1910). 'A Special Type of Choice of Object Made by Men (Contributions to the Psychology of Love I)', *On Sexuality*. In The Pelican Freud Library, 7. Trans. James Strachey; ed. Angela Richards. Harmondsworth: Penguin, 227–42

Freud, Sigmund 1981 (1912). 'On the Universal Tendency to Debasement in the Sphere of Love (Contributions to the Psychology of Love II)', *On Sexuality*. In The Pelican Freud Library, 7. Trans. James Strachey; ed. Angela Richards. Harmondsworth: Penguin, 243–60

Freud, Sigmund 1984 (1915). 'Instincts and Their Vicissitudes', *On Metapsychology: The Theory of Psychoanalysis*. In The Pelican Freud Library, 11. Trans. James Strachey; ed. Angela Richards. Harmondsworth: Penguin, 105–38

Frye, Northrop 1957. *Anatomy of Criticism: Four Essays*. Princeton, NJ: Princeton UP

Frye, Northrop 1965. *A Natural Perspective: The Development of Shakespearean Comedy and Romance*. San Diego, New York and London: Harcourt Brace Jovanovich

Garber, Marjorie 1992. *Vested Interests: Cross-Dressing and Cultural Anxiety*. New York: Routledge

Gardner, Helen 1970 (1959). '*As You Like It*'. In *Modern Shakespearean Criticism: Essays on Style, Dramaturgy, and the Major Plays*, Alvin B. Kernan. New York: Harcourt Brace Jovanovich

Gates, Henry Louis, Jr., 1991. '*Jungle Fever*; or, Guess Who's Not Coming to Dinner?' In *Five for Five: The Films of Spike Lee*, Spike Lee and David Lee, eds. New York: Stewart, Tabory & Chang, 162–9

Giddens, Anthony 1992. *The Transformation of Intimacy: Sexuality, Love and Eroticism in Modern Societies*. Cambridge: Polity Press

Gilroy, Paul 1993. 'Spiking the Argument: Spike Lee and the Limits of Racial Community'. In *Small Acts: Thoughts on the Politics of Black Cultures*. London and New York: Serpent's Tail

Girgus, Sam B. 1993. *The Films of Woody Allen*. Cambridge: Cambridge UP

Gledhill, Christine, ed., 1991. *Stardom: Industry of Desire*. London and New York: Routledge

Goodman, Joan 1991. 'Breaking the Last Taboo', *Evening Standard*, 11 April: 21, 24

Hamilton, Kendall 1997. 'Blowing Smoke', *Newsweek*, 80, 3 (21 July): 54–61

Hansen, Miriam 1986. 'Pleasure, Ambivalence, Identification: Valentino and Female Spectatorship', *Cinema Journal*, 25, 4 (Summer): 6–32

Harker, Andrew 1987. 'Women and Work', *Dialogue*, 77, 3: 2–7

Haskell, Molly 1987 (1973). *From Reverence to Rape: The Treatment of Women in the Movies*. Chicago and London: University of Chicago Press

Henderson, Brian 1978. 'Romantic Comedy Today: Semi-Tough or Impossible?', *Film Quarterly*, 31, 4 (Summer): 11–23

Hirsch, Foster 1991 (1981). *Love, Sex, Death and the Meaning of Life: The Films of Woody Allen*. New York: Limelight Editions

Hoberman, J. 1991. 'Tale of Two Cities', *Village Voice*, 11 June: 59, 62

Holland, Norman 1968. *The Dynamics of Literary Response*. New York: Oxford University Press

hooks, bell 1990. *Yearning: Race, Gender and Cultural Politics*. Boston, MA: South End Press

Horton, Andrew S., ed. and intro., 1991. *Comedy/Cinema/Theory*. Berkeley, Los Angeles and Oxford: University of California Press

Iley, Chrissy 1993. 'What Makes Meg a Star?', *Sunday Times*, 5 September: 6–7

Irigaray, Luce 1985 (1977). *This Sex which Is not One*. Trans. Catherine Porter. Ithaca, New York: Cornell University Press

Irons, Glenwood 1992. *Gender Language and Myth*. Toronto and London: University of Toronto Press

James, David E. and Rick Berg, eds, 1996. *The Hidden Foundation: Cinema and the Question of Class*. Minnesota and London: University of Minnesota Press

James, Henry 1966. *The Bostonians*. Harmondsworth: Penguin

Jameson, Fredric 1989. 'Nostalgia for the Present', *The South Atlantic Quarterly*, 88, 2: 517–37

Jeffords, Susan 1993. 'Can Masculinity Be Terminated?' In *Screening the Male: Exploring Masculinities in Hollywood Cinema*, Steven Cohan and Ina Rae Hark, eds. London and New York: Routledge, 245–62

Jeffords, Susan 1994. *Hard Bodies: Hollywood Muscularity in the Reagan Era*. New Brunswick, NJ: Rutgers University Press

Jordan, G. and C. Weedon 1995. *Cultural Politics*. Oxford: Basil Blackwell

Karnick, Kristine Brunovska and Henry Jenkins, eds, 1995. *Classical Hollywood Comedy*. New York and London: Routledge

Kleinhans, Chuck 1996. 'Class in Action'. In James and Berg, eds, 240–63

Kleinhans, Chuck 1997. 'Independent Features: Hopes and Dreams'. In *Independent Features: Hopes and Dreams*, Jon Lewis, ed. Durham: Duke UP

Krutnik, Frank 1990. 'The Faint Aroma of Performing Seals: The "Nervous" Romance and the Comedy of the Sexes', *The Velvet Light Trap*, no. 26 (Fall) 57–72

Krutnik, Frank 1995. 'A Spanner in the Works? Genre, Narrative and the Hollywood Comedian'. In Karnick and Jenkins, eds, 17–38

Laing, Dave 1971. *Buddy Holly*. New York: Studio Vista

Lasch, Christopher 1991 (1979). *The Culture of Narcissism: American Life in an Age of Diminishing Expectations*. New York and London: W. W. Norton

Lee, Spike 1991. *Jungle Fever*. Production Notes

Lent, Tina Olsin 1995. 'Romantic Love and Friendship: The Redefinition of Gender Relations in Screwball Comedy'. In Karnick and Jenkins, eds, 314–31

Leo, John 1984. 'The Revolution Is Over', *Time*, 9 April: 48–53

Lewis, C. S. 1936. *The Allegory of Love*. Oxford: Oxford UP

Lewis, Jon 1995. *Whom God Wishes to Destroy: Francis Coppola and the New Hollywood*. London: Athlone

Lubiano, Wahneema 1996. '"But Compared to What?" Reading Realism, Representation, and Essentialism in *School Daze, Do the Right Thing*, and the Spike Lee Discourse'. In Blount and Cunningham, eds, 173–204

Luhr, William and Peter Lehman 1989. *Returning to the Scene: Blake Edwards, Volume 2*. Athens, Ohio: Ohio UP

McCann, Graham 1990. *Woody Allen: New Yorker*. Cambridge: Polity Press

Marshall, Judi 1984. *Women Managers: Travellers in a Male World*. Chichester: John Wiley & Sons

Marx, Karl and Friedrich Engels 1988 (1888). *The Communist Manifesto*. London: Penguin Books

Maslin, Janet 1979. 'Review of *Starting Over*', *The New York Times*, 5 October: C8

Moi, Toril 1988. *Sexual/Textual Politics*. London: Methuen

Morin, Edgar 1957. *Les Stars*. Paris: Seuil

Mulvey, Laura 1981. 'Afterthoughts on Visual Pleasure and Narrative Cinema in Relation to *Duel in the Sun*', *Framework*, nos. 15/16/17. Reprinted in L. Mulvey, *Visual and Other Pleasures*. London: Macmillan, 1989

Mulvey, Laura 1989 (1977). 'Notes on Sirk and Melodrama'. In *Visual and Other Pleasures*, L. Mulvey. Bloomington and Indianapolis: Indiana UP, 39–44

Musser, Charles 1995. 'Divorce, DeMille and the Comedy of Remarriage'. In Karnick and Jenkins, eds, 282–313

Neale, Steve 1992. 'The Big Romance or Something Wild?: Romantic Comedy Today', *Screen*, 33, 3 (Autumn): 284–99

Neale, Steve and Frank Krutnik 1990. *Popular Film and Television Comedy*. London and New York: Routledge

Nelson, T. G. A. 1990. *Comedy: The Theory of Comedy in Literature, Drama, and Cinema*. Oxford and New York: Oxford UP

Neupert, Richard 1995. *The End: Narration and Closure in the Cinema*. Detroit: Wayne State UP

Patterson, Alex 1992. *Spike Lee*. New York: Avon Books

Penley, Constance and Sharon Willis, eds, 1993. *Male Trouble*. Minneapolis and London: University of Minnesota Press

Purdie, Susan 1993. *Comedy: The Mastery of Discourse*. London: Harvester Wheatsheaf

Rich, B. Ruby 1995. 'Slugging It out for Survival', *Sight and Sound*, 5, 4: 14–17

Rose, Mary Beth 1988. *The Expense of Spirit: Love and Sexuality in English Renaissance Drama*. Ithaca and London: Cornell UP

Rowe, Kathleen 1995. 'Comedy, Melodrama and Gender: Theorizing the Genres of Laughter'. In Karnick and Jenkins, eds, 39–59

Rowe, Kathleen 1995. 'Melodrama and Men in Post-Classical Comedy'. In *Me Jane: Masculinity, Movies and Women*, Pat Kirkham and Janet Thumim, eds. New York: Lawrence & Wishart, 184–93

Rowe, Kathleen 1995. *The Unruly Woman: Gender and the Genres of Laughter*. Austin: University of Texas Press

Ruiz Pardos, Manuela (forthcoming). 'Male Images in the New Romances: Towards the Construction of a New Romantic Hero'. In *Proceedings of the 20th AEDEAN Conference*, ed. Pedro Guardia and John Stone. Barcelona: Universitat Central de Barcelona, 563–7

Rutherford, Jonathan 1992. *Men's Silences: Predicaments in Masculinity*. London and New York: Routledge

Salingar, Leo 1974. *Shakespeare and the Traditions of Comedy*. Cambridge: Cambridge UP

Sargent, Lydia, ed., 1981. *Women and Revolution: A Discussion of the Unhappy Marriage of Marxism and Feminism*. Boston: South End Press

Sedgwick, Eve K. 1985. *Between Men: English Literature and Male Homosocial Desire*. New York: Columbia UP

Seidman, Steve 1981. *Comedian Comedy: A Tradition in Hollywood Film*. Ann Arbor: UMU Research Press

Seidman, Steve 1991. *Romantic Longings: Love in America, 1830–1980*. New York and London: Routledge

Seidman, Steve 1992. *Embattled Eros: Sexual Politics and Ethics in Contemporary America*. New York: Routledge

Shakespeare, William 1975 (1623). *Twelfth Night*. Lothian, J. M. and T. W. Craik, eds. The Arden Shakespeare. London and New York: Methuen

Shaw, Arnold 1970. *Sinatra*. London: Hodder

Shore, Mitchell 1996. 'Multiculturalism and Spike Lee's Mixed Messages'. *Cineaction*, May: 57–65

Silverberg, Cory 1996. 'More than the Violence: A Reading of Intergenerational Relationships in *Do the Right Thing* and *Jungle Fever*', *Cineaction*, May: 66–72

Skin Deep 1991. 'The Current Cinema', *New Yorker*, 17 June: 100–1

Sklar, Robert 1997. 'Taking Hollywood by Storm: Behind the Triumph of Independent Films', *The Chronicle of Higher Education*, 43 (14 March): B7

Smilgis, Martha 1987: 'The Big Chill: Fears of AIDS', *Time*, 16 February: 26–9

Smith, Gavin 1991. 'Identity Check', *Film Comment*, 27, 1: 28–37

Stacey, Jackie 1994. *Star-Gazing: Hollywood Cinema and Female Spectatorship*. London: Routledge

Stephens, Gregory 1995. 'Romancing the Racial Frontier: Mediating Symbols in Cinematic Interracial Representation', *Spectator*, 16, 1 (Fall/Winter): 58–73

Sterritt, David 1989. 'Review of *When Harry Met Sally*', *Christian Science Monitor*, 2 August: 11

Studlar, Gaylyn 1988. *In the Realm of Pleasure: Von Sternberg, Dietrich, and The Masochistic Aesthetic*. Urbana and Chicago: University of Illinois Press

Suárez, Juan A. 1996. *Bike Boys, Drag Queens and Superstars: Avant-Garde, Mass Culture and Gay Identities in the 1960s Underground Cinema*. Bloomington and Indianapolis: Indiana UP

Thompson, Douglas 1989. 'Falling in Like Is Very Hard to Do', *Mail on Sunday*, 24 September: 88 and 90

Viano, Maurizio 1987. 'Something Wild', *Film Quarterly*, 40, 4: 11–16

Walters, Danuta Suzanna 1995. *Material Girls*. Berkeley and London: University of California Press

Wallace, Michele 1992. '*Boyz N the Hood* and *Jungle Fever*'. In *Black Popular Culture*, Gina Dent, ed. Seattle: Bay Press, 123–31

Weeks, Jeffrey 1992. *Sex, Politics and Society*. Harlow: Longman

Wernblad, Annette 1992. *Brooklyn Is Not Expanding: Woody Allen's Comic Universe*. London and Toronto: Associated University Presses

Wexman, Virginia Wright 1993. *Creating the Couple: Love, Marriage, and Hollywood Performance*. Princeton: Princeton UP

Wood, Robin 1986. *Hollywood from Vietnam to Reagan*. New York: Columbia UP

Worsley, Peter 1990. *Marx and Marxism*. London: Routledge

INDEX

Page references in italics refer to film stills. References to notes are to the text page where the superscript indicator occurs.

216